# On the Way
*to*
# Eternity

# On the Way

*to*

# Eternity

Angus Smith

REFORMATION PRESS

2023

© 2023 by Reformation Press
11 Churchill Drive, Stornoway
Isle of Lewis, Scotland HS1 2NP

www.reformationpress.co.uk

Edited by Dr Robert J Dickie and Dr Catherine E Hyde
Cover photograph: Douglas McGilviray
Cover design: A4 Design and Print
Printed by Lulu (www.lulu.com)

**British Library Cataloguing-in-Publication Data**
A catalogue record for this book is available from the British Library

**ISBN numbers**
978-1-872556-59-8 paperback
978-1-872556-60-4 hardback
978-1-4466-9499-2 e-book (EPUB format)

All rights reserved. No part of this publication may be reproduced, stored in a retrieval system, or transmitted, in any form or by any means, without the prior permission in writing of Reformation Press, or as expressly permitted by law, by licence, or under terms agreed with the appropriate reprographic rights organisation.

# Contents

Introduction .................................................................... 7
Biographical sketch ...................................................... 9

## Sermons

1 The Great Supper ................................................. 57
2 Perseverance ......................................................... 75
3 Nicodemus ............................................................ 91
4 Three approaches by the woman of Canaan ..... 109
5 The builder of Zion and his materials ............... 124
6 Three lonely people ............................................ 139
7 Help and guidance for the downcast ................ 157
8 The promise of the Holy Spirit .......................... 170
9 No room in the inn ............................................. 185
10 Remember Lot's wife .......................................... 200
11 The time of Paul's departure .............................. 212
12 Trial, deliverance and preservation ................... 227
13 Paul's experience of the law ............................... 242
14 Comfort to the sorrowing Church ..................... 255
15 The glory of the city of God .............................. 267
16 Scoffers in the last day ....................................... 282
17 God's poor and contrite people ......................... 296
18 Delighting in public worship ............................. 311

# Introduction

ETERNITY stretches out before each one of us. The Rev. Angus Smith regularly referred to this matter in his sermons, faithfully and lovingly reminding his hearers that they—as well as he—were on their way to eternity. In bringing this recurring theme to their attention, he emphasised the person and work of Christ, and God's sovereignty in the salvation of sinners.

*On the Way to Eternity* is therefore a fitting title to this collection of eighteen sermons, which were preached on the Lord's Day to congregations on the Isles of Lewis and Harris. The wording of the title is all the more poignant when the context of these sermons is appreciated. Mr Smith's health was starting to decline, and he himself was nearing eternity. The concluding sermon in this collection was delivered in April 2019, he preached for the last time a mere four weeks later, and he passed to eternity just over three months after that final service in Stornoway.

The publisher gratefully acknowledges the work of Norman and Donella Campbell in recording and meticulously transcribing the sermons, and the help of Dr Catherine Hyde in editing the material for publication. The photograph of Mr Smith was kindly provided his family.

Thanks are also due to Norman Campbell for writing the well-researched biography of Mr Smith, with the invaluable help of Mrs Johan Smith and family. Much background information for the biography was provided by Donald A Morrison of Ness and Alex Morrison of Newvalley.

In publishing this collection of sermons, it is the prayer of the publisher that God would bless these sermons to the eternal benefit of readers.

Stornoway, December 2023

# Biographical sketch

ANGUS SMITH was born on 25<sup>th</sup> December 1928 in Glasgow and was largely brought up in the Govan area of the city. His parents Kenneth and Jessie were both from North Tolsta on the island of Lewis.[1]

The spirituality of that island shaped him. It had become Protestant at the Reformation but largely remained in religious formalism. The beginning of the evangelical revival came in the late eighteenth-century with some converts under the preaching of Rev. Lachlan Mackenzie who served from 1782 to 1784 as assistant minister in the parish of Stornoway.[2]

Bible-focused Gaelic-medium schools staffed by converted teachers began work in 1811 at Bayble, in the Point district. Their expansion and influence was followed by the preaching

---

[1] Kenneth was brought up at 58 Tolsta, and Jessie at 30 Tolsta. The publishers are grateful to Mr Alex Morrison, Newvalley, Lewis (whose father was a second cousin of Mr Smith) for his assistance. The names of the constituent parts of North Tolsta have changed over the centuries.

[2] Mackenzie (1754–1819) went on to be the noted parish minister of Lochcarron until his death in 1819, encouraging the Lord's people and showing discernment of future trends. JR Macintosh in *Dictionary of Scottish Church History and Theology* (ed. NM de S Cameron) (Edinburgh: 1993; henceforth *DSCHT*), p. 522. His sermons were published in two volumes in 1928. More recently some were republished as *The Happy Man: The abiding witness of Lachlan Mackenzie* (Edinburgh: Banner of Truth Trust, 1979) and *Rock of Ages* (Stornoway: Reformation Press, 2017).

of the itinerant evangelist Finlay Munro from 1818.[3] The blessing from these means was consolidated by the commencement of evangelical ministries in the Church of Scotland, the first being that of Rev. Alexander Macleod in 1824 in the parish of Uig on the west side of the island.[4]

It is worthy of note that Angus Smith's great grand-father, John Smith, had been the first man resident in Tolsta to profess faith publicly after the evangelical revival came to the Lewis in the 1820s. He was examined for membership by the Kirk Session in Knock, Point, as there was no separate congregation in Back or Tolsta at that point.

### Childhood in Glasgow

Kenneth Smith moved from Lewis to Govan in Glasgow to work in the shipyards. Angus was fourth of the five boys in the family. The eldest was his half-brother Murdo Kenneth Murray, who later became a Free Church minister.[5] The four

---

[3] Murdo MacAulay, *Aspects of the Religious History of* Lewis (n.p., 1985), pp. 53, 124, 130–131.

[4] *Ibid.*, pp. 62, 108–112. Rev. Alexander Macleod (1786–1869) served in Dundee Gaelic Church (1819–1821), in Cromarty (1821–1824), and in Uig from 1824 until 1844. In 1844 he moved to Lochalsh Free Church and two years later to Rogart in Sutherland. See also *Diary and Sermons of the Rev. Alexander Macleod, Rogart (formerly of Uig, Lewis), with brief memoir by D. Beaton, Wick* (Inverness: Robert Carruthers & Sons, 1925): this has been reprinted with a fuller biographical sketch by a prominent minister of the Disruption Free Church as *Showers of Blessing* (Stornoway: Reformation Press, 2022).

[5] Murdo K Murray was born on 22nd December 1907 and died on 16th August 1984. He was buried in Gress cemetery, Lewis. He served in Strath, Skye from 1942 until 1947, in Carloway from 1947 until 1963, and Knock (Lewis) from 1963 until 1974. He was Moderator of the General Assembly of the Free Church in 1970. GNM Collins, *Annals of the Free Church of Scotland 1900–1986* (Edinburgh: Lindsay & Co., 1987x1994), pp. 35, 64.

brothers born in Glasgow were John, Iain,[6] Angus and Kenneth.[7] Both parents spoke the Gaelic language at home and Kenneth insisted that the children speak the language to him. He helped them as they took their turn at family worship to read a verse from the Gaelic Bible. So many islanders lived in Govan that the language was often heard on the streets.

When Mr Smith was interviewed in retirement about his memories, he recalled that poverty was rife in his childhood and that Kenneth (senior) was unemployed for twenty years. As a schoolboy, Angus Smith wore tweed clothing given by the Glasgow Corporation to children from the poorest families and these experiences gave him abiding compassion for the underdog and the poor.[8]

The family attended the Free Church in Govan. This had its roots in a 'Highland Mission' which held Gaelic services from 1865 onwards. It became a sanctioned charge in 1874 and was known as St Columba's Free Gaelic Church, Govan. A group of 35 people refused to follow the 800 members and adherents into the Free Church union with the United Presbyterians in 1900, which formed the United Free Church. This small group had built a church in 1910 on Church Street (a location which

---

[6] Iain died in 2013, aged 87.
[7] Kenneth Smith (1930–2011) married Catherine M Matheson (1939–2011) in 1968. He was minister of Campbeltown from 1968 to 1971, Lochalsh from 1971 to 1980, Kilmuir and Stenscholl from 1980 to 1984, and Knock (Lewis) from 1984 to 1996. In retirement he lived in Upper Bayble, Point. He associated with the Free Church (Continuing) after the division of 2000, often supplying the pulpit in their Knock & Point congregation.
[8] *Sgeulachd Beatha*, BBC Radio nan Gaidheal. 24/12/2015. 'An t-Urr. Aonghas Mac a' Ghobhainn—a bheatha thràth am Baile Ghobhainn' [The Rev. Angus Smith—early life in Govan]. The five-part radio series, (hereafter *Sgeulachd Beatha* with episode date) was produced and narrated by Maureen Macleod of South Dell, Ness. Translations are by the writer.

later became known as Briton Street) with the congregation continuing the name St Columba Free Gaelic, Govan.[9]

Mr Smith's first minister was a native of Kiltarlity (Inverness-shire), the Rev. William Fraser, who served Govan between 1924 and 1938. Gaelic was heard every day on the streets of Govan; Mr Fraser built up the congregation by inviting to church people he heard speaking the language. He was succeeded in 1939 by Rev. Alexander Macleod, who was translated to Back Free Church on Lewis in 1947. In the 1950s, there was a Gaelic service at 11am, an English service in the afternoon and services in each language at 6pm, alternating between the main church and a downstairs hall.[10]

Both Mr Smith's parents were respected for their godliness and their careful observance of the Sabbath.[11] Angus Smith often spoke of the impact that their witness had on him. Like other homes in the congregation, the Smiths gave hospitality to young and old. This kindness often took practical form. The writer has been told of Mrs Smith's kindness and patience in teaching a new convert how to read Gaelic. One evening Mr Smith's father was talking to young converts on the way into the tenement. A friend just behind him said: 'You'll never see such a lovely sight as the old Christian.' He replied: 'I have: the

---

[9] In the 1860s a similar mission was begun in the same area by the Church of Scotland. In 1929 this congregation united with the St Columba's Govan United Free Church, and following further linkages the congregation was under the ministry of the Gaelic preacher and broadcaster, the Rev. Thomas M Murchison. Ian R MacDonald, *Glasgow's Gaelic Churches: Highland religion in an urban setting 1690–1995* (Edinburgh: Knox Press, 1995), pp. 73–75.

[10] Donald John MacAulay *Memories of My Father, A Biography of Rev. Murdo Macaulay (1907–2001)* (King's Lynn: Biddles Books Ltd., 2018), p. 110.

[11] Jessie Smith died in 1966. Kenneth Smith died in the Cross (Isle of Lewis) manse in 1970.

young Christian.' On another occasion, sitting on the elders' bench, Kenneth saw Jessie come in with their three sons. She put them into the family pew before herself. By this time, all three were showing spiritual interest in following the means of grace. The elder next to him remarked to Kenneth that he had a greater blessing in the family than many others. Kenneth responded with words from 2 Corinthians 10:17: 'But he that glorieth, let him glory in the Lord.' The elders' conversation was in Gaelic, in which the text reads: 'Ach an tì a nì uaill, dèanadh e uaill as an Tighearna.'[12]

Kenneth had a love for reading and singing the *Spiritual Hymns* of Peter Grant in non-worship settings.[13] Angus Smith shared that esteem for them, and other sound spiritual songs in the language. He would have echoed the words of the Free Presbyterian minister who reviewed a volume of Grant's hymns, stating that they had been 'much admired by spiritually-minded Gaelic-speaking Highlanders throughout the world. … We bespeak this book all success.' That reviewer added: 'While we approve of scriptural hymns as literature, in the same way as we approve of scriptural sermons, we are entirely opposed to the use of hymns in the public and private worship of God.'[14]

---

[12] I am grateful to a person involved with the 1950s Govan Free Church for these two anecdotes.

[13] Peter Grant (1783–1867) was first awakened spiritually through hearing the hymns of Dugald Buchanan (1716–1768). He became a Baptist itinerant missionary and then pastor in Grantown on Spey. Donald E Meek in *DSCHT*, pp. 377–378: 'Peter Grant'. In 2000, BorderStone Press published *The Lost Sermons of Scottish Baptist Peter Grant* on Kindle.

[14] N.C. [Rev. Neil Cameron], 'Peter Grant's Spiritual Hymns', in *Free Presbyterian Magazine* (hereafter *FPM*) Vol. 31, (January 1927), p. 351; Vol. 31, (March 1927), p. 436. The Rev. Neil Cameron (1854–1932) was an early leader in the Free Presbyterian

Summer holidays usually took the Smith boys north to their parents' home village of North Tolsta. Here they enjoyed freedom to play and to swim to the grassy island on Loch Tanavat on the moor. However, at the outbreak of World War Two Mr Smith's parents sent him and his brother Kenneth to North Tolsta with a view to longer, war-time residence there. From 13th September 1939 to 5th December of that year, they attended the local school and lived with their widowed paternal aunt, Mrs Kirsty Graham, at 84 School Road.[15] While in Tolsta, the news came that their brother John in Glasgow had died of tuberculosis at the age of 16. Their parents then took Kenneth and Angus back to Govan to maintain the close family bond.[16]

### Early spiritual experience

Angus Smith came under concern of soul as he contemplated John's death. He dated the period of his conversion to the time after his return to Govan during those early war years. Mr Smith spoke of his early spiritual experience:

> I was listening carefully to the minister. He'd speak about Christ and how you needed to believe in him to be saved. I'd be listening but wouldn't get Christ for my soul. 'You're telling about it, but you're not telling it correctly or else I would grasp it,' I'd be saying to myself as I listened to him. I decided to read the entire Bible, from Genesis to the end. I'd be about 12 years old. I'd pray but would not get Christ. I would ask my mother if someone could get to heaven without having Christ. I eventually reached the conclusion that I wouldn't be saved.

---

Church and minister of the Glasgow congregation from 1896–1932.
[15] In Gaelic, Mrs Graham was known locally as *Bean Tiffian*. The writer is grateful to Alex Morrison for this information.
[16] *Sgeulachd Beatha*, 24th December 2015.

I went to church with my mother one evening and wasn't listening. I started speaking to Christ, something I hadn't done before. I don't know how or why, but the Lord must have been in the thing. I said, 'Oh Christ, thou knowest that I am seeking thee but not finding thee. I've done my best to find thee.' I started telling how I was reading and praying, and that he knew all of that. I said to him, 'If thou sendest me to hell, I won't say one word against thee because I'm a sinner and recognise that I deserve hell, but if thou should have mercy on me, I'll be singing thy praises to all eternity. However, it is thine own will that I desire: thy will be done.' I then said to myself, 'It's strange that you came to that place where you said to God, "Thy will be done"—you were never in that position.'

As a minister now, I know for someone to say to the Lord, 'Thy will be done,' means that your will has been changed by the Lord and that you are obeying him and that it's the work of salvation in the soul. I didn't know that. However, I knew that a little spark of hope had come into my soul: could it perhaps be the Lord's work to make you think like that? You never thought like that before. That spark was like a person building the fire in the morning as we saw it at home. A person finding a little ember in the ash and adding others to it and in time you saw a flame growing, and with peats on it the fire caught. That's how it grew in my soul as the weeks passed. The thought, 'Perhaps I have Christ, maybe I have him,' eventually became the thought, 'I am certain that I have Christ.'

In those days I could speak to other children about their soul, but I couldn't say a word to my father or mother: they were too holy for me, that's how I saw it. I'd say to myself, 'If you say a word to your father about this, he'll look through you and say, "I can see into your heart and know you so well and don't believe you."' I was afraid to say anything to him and concluded that when I'd be as holy as my father, I'd go out to the prayer meeting. I'm still not as holy as him and have been in the ministry for many years. I was twenty years old before I went to the prayer meeting. That's what was keeping me back: I didn't have the courage.[17]

Later, as a young man, the preaching of the late Rev. Murdo Macaulay (who preached in Govan from 1949 until 1956, and afterwards in Back, Isle of Lewis) was also a great help to him. Mr Smith would recall how Mr Macaulay used to look at his congregation individually while preaching, rather than quickly scan the people from one side of the church to the other. He recalled Mr Macaulay stating in company that while minister in Govan Free Church, he had recognised new spiritual interest in everybody who later began to show it. The exception was Angus Smith. He had come under concern of soul before Mr Macaulay had come to Govan as minister.[18]

### Call to the ministry

On leaving school, Mr Smith did his National Service in Libya and Palestine.[19] On his return he taught in the Govan Sabbath School and underwent teacher training. This was followed by two years' teaching in Airdrie.[20] He taught English, history and geography, with occasional maths (as there was a shortage of teachers in that subject), as well as Bible teaching.[21] It was at this time that the sense of the Lord's call to the ministry matured.

After the Free Church accepted his application, he studied at the Free Church College for three years. Mr Smith had a par-

---

[17] *Sgeulachd Beatha*, 24th December 2015.
[18] This was reiterated in Donald John MacAulay, *Memories of My Father, A Biography of Rev. Murdo Macaulay (1907–2001)* (King's Lynn: Biddles Books Ltd., 2018), p. 129.
[19] A form of compulsory military service for men aged 17 to 21 years old, and which normally lasted eighteen months.
[20] 'Call at Ness', *Stornoway Gazette*, 11th May 1968, p. 1.
[21] *Sgeulachd Beatha* 7th Jan 2016.

ticular affection for the professor of Systematic Theology, Robert A Finlayson.[22] The divinity students often supplied congregations, travelling there on Friday evenings and returning to Edinburgh on Monday. Professor Finlayson would always ask where they had supplied, and the texts preached on. No matter the topic in his lectures, Finlayson always began each lecture with the word 'God'.

Divinity training was rigorous:

> I felt we had too much to do in the College. Each professor thought that their subject was the one to which we should give most time! We had Greek, Hebrew, Systematic Theology, Church History, and a lot of other topics including sermon preparation techniques and how to conduct weddings and funerals. Systematic Theology was my favourite subject, but I felt we didn't get enough time to do the languages. A knowledge of the Biblical languages is very important. The language professors did make clear that they were not going to give us a full knowledge, but a working knowledge, so that we would have a basis for life-long study of each language. … I've been doing some every day in old age: I've done more Hebrew since retirement than I ever did during my pastoral ministry. The College also had preaching classes where they'd critique your sermon. You met other men and some from other churches. That was good. You got fellowship with them.[23]

Mr Smith completed his studies in summer 1958.[24] On July 3rd of that year he married Johan Maclean, a nurse from Shawbost

---

[22] Lochcarron native Roderick Alexander Finlayson (1895–1989) served as minister in Urray (Ross-shire) and Hope Street in Glasgow before his professorship in the Free Church College. JD Macmillan in *DSCHT*, p. 321: 'Finlayson, Roderick Alexander'.
[23] *Sgeulachd Beatha*, 7th January 2016.
[24] The College teaching staff at this time were: Hebrew and Old Testament (also College Principal)—Peter W Miller; Apologetics, Homiletics and Pastoral Theology—David Mackenzie; Systematic

in Lewis, whom he had met in after-church gatherings at the homes of Glasgow Christians unable to attend the public means of grace.[25] Mrs Smith had been raised in a Christian home and community of warm piety, where she had mixed with many of the godly from all over the island.[26] The wedding—in the Free North Church, Inverness, on a beautiful day—was conducted by Mr Smith's half-brother, the Rev. Murdo K Murray. A talking point at the reception was the telegram from the Rev. Murdo Macaulay: 'Congratulations. May Jacob's fountain water your garden.'[27] A few months afterwards, the couple moved to Skye as Mr Smith was ordained as a minister and inducted to the Uig and Snizort[28] congregation of the Free Church, in November 1958.

### Snizort, the first ministry

The church and manse in Snizort had been built next to the site of a meeting-house erected for services held by the main figure in the nineteenth-century evangelical revival on Skye,

---

Theology—RA Finlayson; Greek and New Testament—William John Cameron; Church History and Church Principles—Alexander M Renwick. John W Keddie, *Preserving a Reformed Heritage* (Kirkhill: Scottish Reformed Heritage Publications, 2017), pp. 355–356.

[25] Johan grew up in 4 New Shawbost. Her father's name was Murdo Maclean; her mother's maiden name was Mary MacAulay. Mary's family home had been in Shawbost Park. Johan's sisters and brothers were Mary, Kirsty-Mary, Christine, Malcolm Donald and Malcolm (the Rev. Calum Maclean, 1931–2020).

[26] For much useful and edifying material on this congregation, see Malcolm Macleod, *Echoes of an Era: Shawbost Free Church of Scotland, its origins and history* (Lewis: Loch na Muilne Publishing, 2014).

[27] Telegrams were read out at wedding receptions. Mr Macaulay's was seen as a reference to the spiritual blessing the Saviour brought to the woman of Samaria at Jacob's well.

[28] The two main villages, almost nine miles apart.

the blind catechist Donald Munro.[29] Converted in 1805 under the preaching of the SPGH missionary[30] John Farquharson, the catechist had seen a time of great blessing in the years 1812 to 1814 in northern areas of the island. The ministry of Rev. Roderick Macleod (1795–1868) in Bracadale, and later in Snizort, had been the instrument of many conversions and the consolidation of the gospel witness in Skye, both in the evangelical wing of the Church of Scotland and then the Free Church from its creation in 1843.[31]

Several Free Church congregations in Skye had experienced long vacancies after 1900 but were exhorted by home missionaries working across large distances and cycling in all weathers.[32] Bracadale had been without a pastor until 1930.[33] The Kilmuir and Stenscholl charge had similarly been without a minister until the translation of Rev. Kenneth MacRae from Lochgilphead in 1919.[34] The Snizort and Uig congregation was vacant for a relatively short period, from 1900 to 1906, but was

---

[29] For Munro and the crop of godly people raised in the following decades, see Roderick MacCowan, *The Men of Skye* (Glasgow, Edinburgh and Portree: J MacLaine, 1902; repr. Edinburgh: Scottish Reformation Society, 2013), pp. 23–46.

[30] SPGH: The Society for the Promotion of the Gospel at Home. For the SPGH and Munro, see Douglas Ansdell, *The People of the Great Faith: The Highland Church 1690–1900* (Stornoway: Acair, 1998), pp. 41–42. See also Donald E Meek, *DSCHT*, p. 316: 'Farquharson, John'.

[31] Roderick Macleod, *DSCHT*, p. 533: 'Macleod, Roderick'.

[32] Salaried lay-preachers, usually serving one particular congregation, although they could be moved on to other stations.

[33] Kenneth J Macleay, *Alexander MacAskill of Drynoch* (Beauly: Free Church Manse, 1968), pp. 1–13.

[34] Iain H Murray (ed.) *Diary of Kenneth A MacRae: A record of fifty years in the Christian ministry* (Edinburgh: Banner of Truth Trust, 1980), pp. 144–148. Mr Macrae (1883–1964) served in Lochgilphead from 1915 to 1919, Kilmuir and Stenscholl from 1919 to 1931, and Stornoway from 1931 to 1964.

again without a minister from 1911 until 1920. The second post-1900 ministry ended when the minister demitted his charge in 1932.[35]

Mr Smith's immediate predecessor in the Uig and Snizort congregation was the Rev. Malcolm Macleod. He had been licensed to preach in 1930, following which he was ordained and inducted to the Bracadale congregation on Skye. He accepted a call to Snizort in 1934, retiring in 1956. However, he continued to preach until 1964 when a stroke took away his speech. He died in March 1968. Mr Smith wrote movingly of Mr Macleod's continued usefulness after the latter's health broke down:

> It may be that the four years spent on his bed without the power of articulate speech were, in the gracious purpose of God, the most precious in the eyes of his Lord. His ministry was then one of prayer, but many yearned to hear his sweet, winsome pulpit appeals once more. Could it be that the Lord had determined, in a dark day of declension, to give this servant wholly to prayer? Many will remember how, when calling to see him, he would point to the floor, asking his guest, in the manner of Zacharias, to kneel and pray. Many too will remember the fragrance of the man, and the amazing freedom usually experienced with him in prayer.[36]

The Presbytery of Skye and Uist met in Portree on 27th August and were informed that the Uig and Snizort congregation wished to call Angus Smith. The Presbytery then met at Snizort on Thursday 16th September to moderate in a 'closed

---

[35] Rev. Murdo AN Macleod, Free Church (Continuing) minister in Snizort, provided this information.
[36] 'In Memoriam Rev. Malcolm Macleod, Snizort', *Free Church Monthly Record* (henceforth *Monthly Record*) (May 1968), p. 91.

call'.[37] Rev. Kenneth Mackay of Bracadale[38] presided at that meeting and preached on Acts 11:13–14.[39] The call was signed by eight elders, two deacons, twenty-two communicant members and eighty adherents, a total of 112. All in all, including children, it is estimated there were around 220 to 230 people in the congregation. That not all signed the call may reflect 'vacancy fatigue' among the adherents, the people having already sent seven unsuccessful calls to ministers in the previous four years.[40]

Mr Smith's induction took place on 4th November. The Rev. Norman Macleod, Portree,[41] preached at from 1 Timothy 4:16. 'Take heed unto thyself and to the doctrine; continue in them; for in doing this thou shalt save thyself, and them that hear thee.' Mr Smith's predecessor, the Rev. Malcolm Macleod, 'feelingly and suitably addressed the congregation', and the Rev. Alexander Macfarlane of Kilmuir addressed the newly-inducted minister.[42]

---

[37] A 'closed call' is when there is only one minister's name for consideration.

[38] Mr Mackay (1916–1993) was a native of Calbost in the Park area of South Lochs in Lewis.

[39] 'And he shewed us how he had seen an angel in his house, which stood and said unto him, Send men to Joppa, and call for Simon, whose surname is Peter; who shall tell thee words, whereby thou and all thy house shall be saved.'

[40] 'Ordination and Induction at Snizort', *Monthly Record*, July–August 1959, p. 154. The writer is grateful to Rev. Murdo AN Macleod of Snizort Free Church (Continuing) for the information about the calls.

[41] Mr Norman Macleod (1912–2002) was pastor of Lochalsh from 1950 to 1958 when he became minister of Portree, moving in 1973 to the Callanish congregation and retiring in 1998.

[42] Born in Marvig, Lochs in Lewis, Mr Macfarlane (1915–1979) had served in Sleat (Skye) and Great Bernera (Lewis), then pastored the combined Skye charge of Kilmuir and Stenscholl from 1954 to 1970, and Shawbost (Lewis) from 1970 to 1979.

The Snizort congregation was scattered, and the extremities were thirty miles apart. Mr Smith was helped by two missionaries in the Uig section: Alasdair Maciver and then Malcolm Macleod.[43] Services were also held in Arnisort, a village between Snizort and Dunvegan. Mr Smith took one Sabbath a month in Uig, with services both ends of the Lord's Day. The missionary based in Uig would cover for him in Snizort that Sabbath. When the Smiths first came to the congregation, they spent a week living in Uig with Mr Maciver, who took Mr Smith to meet the people in that district. For his first five years in Snizort he had no car, so he either walked or cycled, or got lifts from some in the congregation.

Mr Smith preached a series on the Gospels when he took up the Snizort pastorate. He did this consecutively, passage by passage rather than chapter by chapter. At his first communion season in the congregation, Mr Smith was assisted by Rev. Murdo K Murray and by Rev. Norman Macleod, Portree. Mrs Smith was in hospital in Inverness at this time, awaiting the birth of their first child. All the couple's four children—Jessie Mary, Ruth, Murdo and Shona—were born during his Snizort ministry.[44]

Fitting in with the community was eased by speaking their language (Gaelic) and being familiar with the culture, but for the

---

Malcolm Macleod, *op. cit.*, pp. 36–37. See: 'Ordination and Induction at Snizort', *Monthly Record*, July–August 1959, p. 154.
[43] Alasdair Maciver from Aird Tong in Lewis was a missionary in Skye from 1954 to 1964, and then after a short period in Canada he served successively in Staffin, the joint charge of Tobermory and Coll, and then Waternish. He died in 1987. Malcolm Macleod worked in Coll, Glenelg, and Uig (Skye). He died in 1973. Kenneth J Smith, *A Sower and his seed: Air a' Mhisean A Sower and His Seed* (Stornoway: Stornoway Gazette, 1998), pp. 8, 10.
[44] The couple celebrated their diamond wedding anniversary with friends and family in the summer of 2018.

new minister this included learning how to work with animals. Mr Smith explained:

> When in Snizort, my wife wanted us to have a cow. We had a glebe of forty acres.[45] I wasn't so keen: I was a Glasgow boy. We agreed a compromise of a white goat. The person who sold the goat told me to put up a little table on which the goat would stand as you milked her. I learned to milk the goat. A minister asked me on the phone if it was true that we had a goat and that I as a Glasgow boy was doing the milking. I said it was. 'Which end of it are you are you milking?' he teased me. We did get a cow eventually. It came from Lewis and the Skye people were amazed that we hadn't got one from the good stock on that island.[46]

While on Skye, Mr Smith was involved in an event which brought him to international notice. On Sabbath, 4th June 1965, he and some fifty supporters lay down on the Kyleakin pier in Skye. This was to stop cars which were coming off the first scheduled Lord's Day ferry service from Kyle of Lochalsh.[47] Most of the islanders had signed a petition against the Lord's Day ferry when it was first proposed. Members of Parliament, the Skye District Council and the Inverness County Council had been sympathetic to this local opposition. For some the sit-down event was a justifiable action against a commercially motivated tourism operation which threatened the sanctity of the Lord's Day and therefore a key strand of the island culture, while others disapproved of this action. Speaking in 2004, Mr Smith denied the implication in a recent newspaper article that he had 'demonstrated' on the Lord's Day. He stated:

---

[45] The historical term for a piece of land that provided supplementary income for a minister.
[46] *Sgeulachd Beatha,* 7th January 2016.
[47] The mainland port lying less than a mile across the sea. The ferry was replaced by the Skye Bridge in 1996.

I have never demonstrated on the Lord's Day. I went to Kyleakin and took several men with me after holding a public meeting during the week on the issue. It was not a demonstration.

The Superintendent of the Police said to me, 'I will give you twenty minutes,' and I replied that I did not come for that. I came to stop the ferry and the reason for this is the Fourth Commandment. In my house I would have no one dishonour the Lord's Day. None of my children, nor any in my house, would be allowed to go gallivanting on the Lord's Day. I believe the Fourth Commandment covers my son, my daughter and the very beast—it covers all in my household. During the ferry issue we covered three-quarters of the island and had about 70 per cent support and could have had 90 per cent. Everything was on our side, but the Company forced the ferry on us. I was arrested and put in a cell—but I was preaching that night.[48]

Sabbath ferries took more than two decades to spread in the north-west Highlands. A service from Skye (Uig) to North Uist (Lochmaddy) began on 21st May 1989, Skye to Raasay on 2nd May 2004, and the Sound of Harris on 9th April 2006. An air service to Stornoway commenced on 27th October 2002, and this was followed by a ferry service between Ullapool and Stornoway on 19th July 2009.

A lesser-known campaign in which Mr Smith was involved was against the sale of alcohol in the parish of Snizort. It was not uncommon for the churches to oppose expansion of licensing hours, but in this case local ministers triggered the use of a little-used law to call a Veto Poll.[49] Four licensed prem-

---

[48] *Proceedings of Synod together with Reports & Accounts May 2004*, p. 8.

[49] The Temperance (Scotland) Act came into operation in 1920. It provided for a local poll of electors to exercise control over the granting and renewal of licences for the sale of excisable liquor.

ises in the parish faced a ban on the sale of alcohol if the poll had gone against them. However, the vote on Tuesday 21st November 1967 was 239 for 'No Change' and 237 for 'Change'.[50]

His main focus was the spiritual needs of the people in the area. There was a godly lady in the congregation who had many doubts and fears throughout her Christian life as to whether the work in her soul was the genuine work of God. In her final five weeks of life, these clouds seem to lift and she had great assurance. She told Mr Smith that she was now greatly surprised at the doubts and fears which had troubled her.

There were solemn experiences, such as the final visit to another lady. At an evangelistic rally twenty-five years previously—held on Skye but organised by an external agency—she had stood and shouted three times, 'Saved, saved, saved!' However, she had not attended church since the rally. Mr Smith stated:

> I visited her. She was now on her deathbed. I spoke to her for her soul. She started laughing as if she was mocking me. It horrified me, I found it so dreadful. She then turned and said to her husband to remember that there was to be a sheep sale the next day at twelve noon. That's what was on her mind on her deathbed. Before twelve noon the next day she was in eternity. Things like that brought home to me how solemn everything was. I'd laugh with other people and have fun with others and children and laugh, but behind everything, I always remember eternity and that every one of us is going to the great eternity. And if we don't have Christ we will have nothing. I don't judge anyone by saying that. I don't know

---

[50] 'Skye Hoteliers Jubilant at Poll Result', *Press and Journal*, Thursday 23rd November 1967, p. 1. The rules required 35% of the total electorate to vote for no licences to be permitted in the parish.

where that woman's soul went, and leave that in the Lord's hands, but that's what happened.[51]

## Ministry in Lewis

In 1968 Mr Smith accepted a call from the Cross (Ness) congregation of the Free Church of Scotland on the island of Lewis. He had not been told through the normal channels that it was in the offing, but as soon as he was told about the potential by a friend, Mr Smith felt that he would be led to accept it.[52] On 30th April 1968 at a meeting of the Free Church Presbytery of Skye and Uist, held in Portree, a call was tabled from Cross. Commissioners[53] from Lewis were the Rev. Kenneth J Nicolson, Barvas,[54] Interim Moderator of Cross, and Mr Donald Gillies, elder.

The gospel had come to Ness in the second decade of the nineteenth century. The evangelising influence of the Gaelic Schools had reached the district by 1815. It was in Ness that the evangelist Finlay Munro first set foot on the island of Lewis in 1818, immediately speaking to a woman about her soul at the sheiling near the shore where he had been put ashore.[55] The southernmost village in the district, Galson, had been the scene of the labours of teacher and preacher John

---

[51] *Sgeulachd Beatha,* 7th Jan 2016.

[52] *Sgeulachd Beatha,* 21st Jan 2016.

[53] When a call is discussed at the Presbytery of which the recipient is a member, commissioners representing the minister's current and potential congregations respectively, speak about why he should refuse or accept it.

[54] An accomplished preacher and Gaelic spiritual poet, Mr Nicolson (1911–2010) had been minister of Portree Free Church before Barvas. For a brief biography and nineteen poems with English translations, see Coinneach I MacNeacail, *Deatach: Rannan leis an Urr Coinneach I Macneacail* (ed. Peigi F NicDhòmhnaill) (Stornoway: 2011).

[55] Murdo MacAulay, *op. cit.,* pp. 53, 124, 130–131.

Macleod from 1820.⁵⁶ The godliness of Caithness affected Ness through its fishermen joining the large numbers of young men from Lewis at the herring fishery based in Wick from the 1830s onwards.⁵⁷ They heard the gospel preached for the Gaelic fishermen by Rev. Archibald Cook of Bruan,⁵⁸ and from 1837 by the eminent lay preacher Alexander Gair.⁵⁹

The area became a separate congregation from the parish of Barvas with the construction of its own church in Cross in 1828. The following year it gained its first minister, the evangelical Finlay Cook,⁶⁰ an able all-round pastor who sensitively guided the people with warm doctrine and sound spiritual advice. His four-year pastorate was followed by that of John Macrae (known in Gaelic as *Macrath Mòr*—'Big Macrae')⁶¹

---

⁵⁶ *Ibid*, pp. 142–156.

⁵⁷ Rev. George Davidson, *The New Statistical Account of Scotland*, Volume XV (Edinburgh and London, 1845), pp. 95, 101: 'Latheron'.

⁵⁸ Archibald Cook (1788–1865) served in Bruan, Caithness, from 1822 to 1837, the North Church in Inverness from 1837 to 1844, and in Daviot from 1844 to 1865. For his Caithness ministry, see Norman Campbell, *One of Heaven's Jewels: Rev. Archibald Cook of Daviot and the (Free) North Church, Inverness* (Stornoway: n.p., 2009), pp. 56–65.

⁵⁹ John Macleod, *Bypaths of Highland Church History* (Edinburgh: Knox Press, 1965), pp. 115–124; Douglas Somerset, 'Separatism in the North of Scotland: 5. Alexander Gair', *FPM* Vol. 111, May 2006, pp. 143–150.

⁶⁰ A brother of Archibald Cook, Finlay Cook (1778–1858) was an Arran-born preacher who served in the Achreny mission in Caithness from 1827 to 1829, then in Cross from 1829 until 1833 when he became minister of the East Church Inverness. In 1835 he became pastor of Reay parish in Caithness. He and the congregation joined the Free Church in 1843. See Alexander Auld, *Ministers and Men in the Far North* (Wick: 1868 and 1891; repr. Glasgow: Free Presbyterian Publications, 1956), pp. 71–83.

⁶¹ John Macrae (1794–1876) was translated from Cross to Knockbain in the Black Isle in 1839, with further pastorates in

from 1833 to 1839. Most of the congregation joined the Free Church at the Disruption in 1843. Several other ministries followed.[62] That of the Rev. Duncan Macbeath from 1879 to 1891 was perhaps best remembered in the following century in Ness. A man of deep discernment who had spoken to the Question[63] in Ferintosh at the age of sixteen, he had served for thirty years in urban evangelism as town missionary in Inverness before his Lewis labours.[64]

A small Free Presbyterian congregation was formed in Ness in 1894. Most of the Free Church congregation remained until the 1900 union with the United Presbyterian Church. A division ensued, with the vast majority of the people of Ness siding with the post-1900 Free Church, but a small group entered the United Free Church. This was the reverse of the national situation, where the majority of Scottish Free Church ministers entered the newly formed denomination. In 1929, the

---

Greenock Gaelic Church (1849–1857), Lochs (1857–1866) and Carloway (1866–1871). See Roderick Macleod, *DSCHT,* p. 537: 'Macrae, John (1794–1876)'. See also GNM Collins, *Big Macrae: the Rev. John Macrae (1794–1876): Memorials of a Notable Ministry* (Edinburgh: Knox Press, 1976).

[62] Murdo MacAulay, *op. cit.*, pp. 74–81.

[63] This meeting takes place on the Friday of the communion season, a day set apart for self-examination. It involves discussion of evidences of conversion using a suitable text from the Bible known as 'the Question'. An elder proposes the text, a minister then makes introductory remarks ('opening the Question'), several professing men 'speak to the Question' as requested by the presiding minister, and another minister (if available) makes concluding remarks (and corrections if necessary).

[64] John MacMillan, 'Rev. Duncan McBeath, Lewis', *The Free Church of Scotland Monthly* (February, 1892). p.44. For his Inverness missionary work see Norman Campbell, *op. cit.*, pp. 162–179. For Macbeath in Ness, see Murdina D MacDonald, *Blackhouse God's House: A Lewisman recalls the world he left behind* (Meadville, PA: Christian Faith Publishing, 2019), pp. 152–163.

United Free congregation in Ness followed that denomination's union with the Church of Scotland, but they did not merge with the old Ness Church of Scotland group until 1935. At the time of Mr Smith's induction in 1968, the Church of Scotland with its main building in Cross,[65] and the Free Presbyterian congregation based in Lionel with a meeting house in Skigersta,[66] remained the two other Bible-believing congregations in the district. Older Ness people could also recall the Sabbath School and services in the village of Adabrock, which were run on Brethren lines in the early decades of the twentieth century by a Lionel man, John Nicholson, and his wife Nora (née Cushing).[67]

The Ness district had seen increased spiritual fruit from the beginning of 1923. The Rev. Norman Macleod wrote:

> A revival of considerable intensity broke out throughout the district. Cottage meetings were started, special evangelical services were arranged, and visiting ministers were invited to

---

[65] The Church of Scotland ministers in the district during his time were the Revs Duncan Mackinnon (1965–1973), John Ferguson (1973–1980), Alexander Macdonald (1982–1991), and Kenneth John MacPherson (1993–1998). Hamish Taylor, *Church of Scotland, Parish of Cross-Ness, A Historical Outline 1911–2006* (Flodabay: 2006), pp. 9–11.

[66] Two Free Presbyterian pastorates in Ness overlapped with that of Mr Smith. John Nicolson (1919–1977) served in the area from 1964 to 1971. 'Rev. John Nicolson, Tain', *FPM* Vol. 86 (January 1981), pp. 14–18. William Maclean (1907–1985) became the missionary in Ness in 1941 but after divinity training served as its minister from 1948–1962. He then pastored Gisborne in New Zealand from 1962 to 1973, Grafton in New South Wales from 1973 to 1976, and Ness for a second pastorate from 1976 to 1985. 'The late Rev. William MacLean M.A., Ness', *FPM* Vol. 90 (December 1985), pp. 378–385.

[67] Neil TR Dickson, *Brethren in Scotland 1838–2000: A social study of an evangelical movement* (Carlisle: Paternoster, 2002), pp. 123, 186.

preach. At the Communion in 1924 there were 15 new communicants. ... The conversions ceased in 1926 when the Rev. Roderick Macleod accepted a call to the congregation of Dumbarton. There was no outward excitement connected with this movement, but there was much silent weeping and deep contrition of heart. The revival touched persons of all ages. One interesting feature was that the number of men affected was greater than the number of women.[68]

Like other Lewis congregations, Ness experienced the ebb and flow of the Holy Spirit's working, one feature of which was that specific villages could experience renewal. A preaching visit to Tolsta Chaolais, Lewis, in 1902 by the then Free Presbyterian minister of Stornoway, George Mackay, was the initial instrument God used for a number of conversions there.[69] A Ness village which enjoyed blessing in 1939 was Swainbost. Twelve of its residents were among the twenty-six professions of faith the Free Church congregation saw between 1939 and 1942.[70]

It was to a community still aware of these patterns of church life that Mr Smith came in 1968.[71] The family initially moved

---

[68] Mr Macleod adds that at the Communion in 1924 there were 15 professions of faith. 'At each of the following Communions up to 1926 there were 11 to 14 admissions to the Lord's Table. Altogether over 100 new members were added to the Communion Roll of the Free Church'. Norman Macleod, *Lewis Revivals of the 20th Century* (Stornoway: Hebridean Press Service, 1988), pp. 9–10.

[69] *Ibid.*, pp. 6–9.

[70] The writer acknowledges the help of Donald A Morrison, Ness, with the statistics.

[71] Mr Smith's predecessors in the charge in the twentieth century had been: Duncan MacDougall (1909–1918), Roderick J Macleod (1920–1927), Alexander Macleod (1929–1939) and John M Morrison (1940–1966). Mr Morrison was Moderator of the General Assembly in 1955. He remained resident in Ness when

to Shawbost in March, as the Cross manse was being renovated. The daytime induction in Cross on Wednesday 29th May attracted an estimated 2000 worshippers, including a bus-full of friends from Skye. It was remembered as a day of still, hot weather. Some people sat on the church stairs while others stood outside.

The Rev. John MacSween, Point,[72] preached from Ephesians 3:8.[73] The Rev. Kenneth J Nicolson, Barvas, 'exhorted the congregation', and the Rev. Angus Finlayson, North Tolsta,[74] addressed the new Ness pastor.[75] An estimated 500 people sat down to a lunch in the Lionel School canteen afterwards.[76]

The Kirk Session met Mr Smith for the first time at the Cross manse. He told a BBC *Radio nan Gaidheal* interviewer: 'They

---

Mr Smith was inducted. George NM Collins, *Annals of the Free Church* (*op. cit.*), pp. 34, 53.

[72] Mr MacSween (1910–1982) was pastor of Tongue (Sutherland) from 1941–1947, subsequently serving in Canadian congregations, and then in Point from 1966 to 1976. See John MacSween *Sermons by the late Rev. John MacSween M.A.* (Stornoway: Stornoway Gazette Publications, 1999) and *An Inestimable Privilege* (n.p., 2021).

[73] 'Unto me, who am less than the least of all saints, is this grace given, that I should preach among the Gentiles the unsearchable riches of Christ'.

[74] Mr Finlayson (1897–1973) was minister in Struan (Skye) from 1936 to 1938, and in Scalpay from 1938 until 1948 when he was inducted to the newly created Lewis charge of North Tolsta, which had previously been part of Back Free Church. For a selection of his sermons and addresses, see Angus Finlayson *No More Sea* (Stornoway: 1975). Mr Finlayson was commemorated further in a Gaelic elegy. Iain MacRath, *Tuireadh agus Dìoghlum* [Lament and Gleanings] (Stornoway: An t-Ùghdar, 1982), pp. 15–16: 'Marbhrann do'n Urr. Aonghas Fionnlasdan' [Elegy for the Rev. Angus Finlayson].

[75] 'Cross: Induction', *Monthly Record* July 1968 p.144.

[76] 'Induction at Cross', *Stornoway Gazette* June 8th 1968, p. 5.

were so nice; I never got a Session like them. I bonded with them and they with me. There was no trouble or bother. It was as if I had gone to a communion season. The office bearers helped me in every way. Every home greeted me so nicely. These were the best days I ever had—in Ness'. He added that whenever he met a Ness person or heard a Ness Gaelic accent he would 'rejoice'.[77]

The new family in the manse settled in well to the local community, attending the schools there and making lifelong friendships. The new minister visited all the homes in the first fourteen months of his pastorate, accompanied by an elder. A cross-country running champion in his youth,[78] he was now kept fit attending to sheep, cows, hens and a vegetable plot.

Some of the oldest people in the community he now served had lost family members in several drownings in the late 19th century, when fishing boats were wrecked. Many more lost loved ones in armed conflict and the *Iolaire* tragedy of Jan 1st 1919,[79] or had themselves served in two world wars. Mass migration in the 1920s and desperate poverty in the 1930s were fresh in many minds. Even the oldest were familiar with everyday mainland life through summer mainland work in the herring fishing and hotel work, apprenticeships in the Clyde shipyards, or having sailed the seven seas from Vancouver or Montreal to the Mediterranean, Australia and New Zealand.

---

[77] *Sgeulachd Beatha*, 21st Jan 2016.
[78] See *Fios*, Fri 30th Aug 2019 (Ness, 2019), p.8: 'Rev. Angus Smith (1928–2019)'.
[79] In total, 201 people died—174 servicemen returning to Lewis, and 18 to Harris, with the remainder being crew and passengers—after *HMY Iolaire* struck rocks at Holm just outside Stornoway harbour. See John Macleod, *When I Heard the Bell: The loss of the Iolaire* (Edinburgh: Birlinn, 2009); Malcolm Macdonald and Donald J MacLeod, *Darkest Dawn: The story of the Iolaire tragedy* (Stornoway: Acair, 2018).

Many of the older women had been employed as servants in rich city households.[80]

The Ness people had shared in a measure of relative prosperity in the 1950s and 1960s. The main 1960s employment opportunities in the district were Harris Tweed weaving, fishing, the Merchant Navy, and crofting. The Scottish Cooperative Wholesale Society shop in Habost employed local people from the late 1950s. This shut around 1970. Subsequently the textile/knitwear manufacturer, Heather Valley, operated a factory on the site until around 1990, where around 30 people worked.[81] A number of Ness women worked as home helps. From the 1970s onwards, traditional occupations declined but other industries partly made up for this. These included building construction and oil rig manufacturing (at Arnish on Lewis and at mainland sites such as Kishorn and Nigg Bay, Ross-shire). These opportunities were accompanied by new jobs from the creation in 1975 of a single-tier local authority for the islands, the Western Isles Council, (later renamed in Gaelic as *Comhairle nan Eilean Siar* in 1997), as well as increasing health board employment.[82]

---

[80] For an overview of the island culture and its interface with church life in the 20th century, see John Macleod, *Banner in the West: A Spiritual History of Lewis and Harris* (Edinburgh: Birlinn, 2008), pp. 231–278.

[81] After the closure of the factory, the building was used by the Ness Historical Society. Following the Society's move to Cross School in November 2011, the site was redeveloped for housing. I am grateful to Donald A Morrison for this information.

[82] A historian noted of the impact of the new local authority: 'Life in the island has acquired a new vitality. ... Schools seem to have gained a new lease of life, especially those in which Gaelic has become a medium of education'. Donald Macdonald *Lewis A History of the Island* (Edinburgh: 1978; republished 1983, 1990, 2004), p. 196.

Ness caught the rising tide of cultural confidence in the West Highlands and Islands during the 1970s. Members of the congregation were involved in the local authority's innovative bilingual education project, as well as grass-roots initiatives such as the creation of the Ness Historical Society in 1977.[83] A community cooperative set up in 1978 operated a shop, a mobile shop, agricultural machinery hire and other facilities. A vigorous civic life including a community council and district news magazine developed.[84]

Lewis saw cultural and lifestyle changes too. By the late 1970s, traditional practices such as manse-based and home-based weddings were gone. Urbanisation, centralisation of jobs, growing car ownership, as well as the slow abandonment of peat cutting for fuel and planting crops on the crofts, were in progress. Family worship morning and evening were in decline. Walks or driving for leisure on the Lord's Day were carried out by 'many people'.[85]

A great sadness for the community was the decline in population. Between 1979 and 1999, the area covered by the Cross Free Church congregation (Eoropie to South Galson) saw a 27.6% drop, from 1790 to 1296 inhabitants. This trend continues to the present day.[86]

---

[83] The organisation is more generally known by its Gaelic title, Comunn Eachdraidh Nis.
[84] Not all the initiatives lasted but the legacy was a community buy-out of the land in Galson Estate in 2007.
[85] Donald Macdonald, *Lewis: A history of the island* (Edinburgh: Gordon Wright, 1978, repub. 1983, 1990, 2004), pp. 194–197.
[86] The decline from 1979 to 2019 was 34%. The figures have been tracked every five years by a Ness teacher Donald Macritchie. *Fios*, Friday 13th January 2009, pp. 1, 9: 'First increase in population in 30 years'; *Fios*, Friday 1st February 2019, pp. 1, 3: 'Survey confirms continuing population decline.'

One irritation for Lewis residents was the frequent portrayal of the islands as remote, primitive and clergy-dominated, with inhabitants incapable of independent action or thought. This was inaccurate, as the area was fully exposed to the winds of change whether economic, social or ecclesiastical. The streetwise Govan Gael in the Cross Manse knew that the island people were often socially conservative but radical and independent-minded in outlook.

Mr Smith preached five times a week—twice on the Lord's Day and during the week at three of the district prayer meetings. A Lord's Day morning service took place in the main church building in Cross. Sabbath evening services took place there and in the congregation's three smaller district meeting houses—in Galson, South Dell and Lionel. A total of five hundred people attended public worship on Lord's Day evenings in the four Free Church buildings associated with the congregation. Around 40% of the community attended public worship every week with perhaps a further 10% attending at least once a month.[87] Weekday prayer meetings took place in all four buildings. So embedded was the Gaelic language in the community in 1968 that although there were fifty professing

---

[87] The writer's estimate of weekly attendance for the early 1970s is based on Mr Smith's frequent recollection of five hundred people on Sabbath evenings across the four Free Church services. The writer heard Mr Smith state this in company in January 2018. In addition, 150 attended frequently at the Church of Scotland (a figure kindly provided by Rev. John Murdo Nicolson in consultation with his congregation) and 60–70 at the Free Presbyterian Church (statistic from a worshipper of the time). This total of around 700 weekly worshippers was from a total population of around 1800. Community surveys in the early 1990s from Barvas and Point showed around 10% in these areas attending church at least once a month, but not quite weekly. The estimate chimes with that for the Shawbost area of Lewis in the same decade, cited in John Macleod, *Banner in the West*, p. 327.

men in the congregation who could be asked to lead in prayer in public, none were used to doing so regularly in English.

Twice a year, the monthly prayer meeting in Cross on Monday evenings turned into a 'Fellowship meeting', the alternative name for a 'Question meeting'. This allowed young Christians the opportunity to gain experience in 'speaking to the Question', as older, mature believers from other congregations were normally given priority at the communion season Fellowship meetings. Mr Smith's first such in-house fellowship meeting at Cross Free Church remained memorable. One speaker recalled how his colleagues in a Glasgow shipyard would try to get him to swear. On one occasion his task had been to hold a tool, for another man to hit with a hammer. The other man hit his hand. He was holding and rubbing the hand but did not swear. The man admitted afterwards that he had deliberately hit him to see if he would swear with the pain.

Mr Smith's Ness ministry was blessed by the Holy Spirit and the large congregation continued to see conversions. The period 1970 to 1976 was a time of blessing in Cross, with fifty-four people professing faith.[88] Like other ministers on the island experiencing spiritual growth in their congregations at that time, Mr Smith was quietly thankful to the Most High, rather than given to making public pronouncements on the matter. Decades later, in a very rare reference to numbers, he recalled that in one seven-year period, attendance across the four district prayer meetings associated with the congregation had grown by a total of 120 people.[89] In one year in the late 1980s twenty new attenders were to be seen at the prayer meetings.[90]

---

[88] Donald A Morrison provided this statistic.
[89] *Sgeulachd Beatha*, 21ˢᵗ Jan 2016.
[90] A person connected to the congregation provided this figure to the writer was told this in the late 1980s.

Mr Smith was appointed Moderator[91] of the Free Church General Assembly in 1986.[92] His many duties included visiting Reformed denominations in Northern Ireland and Holland. He recalled particularly the Dutch fishing village of Urk, where the monument to drowned fishermen touched him, given the similar experience of many Lewis communities including Ness.

Mr Smith articulated a vision for the maintenance of the Reformed witness in Scotland which highlighted the need for holy living, impartial church discipline, informed and faithful commitment to ordination vows by church office bearers, exclusive Psalmody unaccompanied by instrumental music for public worship, the use of reliable manuscripts and appropriate methods in translating the Bible. He campaigned for these emphases in the church and in public life. Like a number of ministerial contemporaries, he found himself in challenging situations at various levels of the Church's decision-making, through principled convictions and very occasionally over strong personal disagreement.

### The move to the Free Presbyterian Church

In 1997, Mr Smith retired from the pastoral ministry and moved to Marybank, a suburb of Stornoway.[93] He subsequently applied to join the Free Presbyterian Church of Scot-

---

[91] A Moderator in Presbyterian churches acts as chairman of a church court. Being chosen as Moderator of the General Assembly in the Free Church of Scotland is an honour usually reserved for senior ministers.

[92] The Free Church General Assembly normally meets in the St Columba congregation building on Johnstone Terrace, Edinburgh.

[93] His successors in Cross were the Revs Kenneth M Ferguson (2000–2012) and Ewen Matheson (2014–present).

land as a retired minister. He was formally accepted on that basis at the Church's annual Synod in May 1999.[94]

He explained his move to the Free Presbyterian Church many years later in a BBC Gaelic radio programme. 'My wife and I discussed it and decided that we should go to the Free Presbyterian Church which had the same foundations as we had ourselves: they had the Word of God and the *Westminster Confession of Faith*. Also, they had walked out many years ago when the Declaratory Act came in. That Act allowed a minister to accept the *Confession of Faith* as it was, or accept it with small changes, and therefore not accept it in its entirety. This meant that there could be two groups of ministers in the one church. We left and came to the Free Presbyterian Church. We found nothing but tenderness and love since we came into it.'[95]

He went on to preach almost every Sabbath and at weekly prayer meetings, and also assisted at around twelve communion seasons a year.[96] He was deeply appreciated in the Free Presbyterian Church for his preaching at communions and supply, and for his warm gentleness among people, with the welfare of people's souls as his primary concern.

He frequently preached in the Stornoway Free Presbyterian congregation. His ability to put people at ease and encourage conversation on the Scriptures and the Lord Jesus Christ made him a welcome guest in many homes. He believed that Chris-

---

[94] 'Matters arising from private meetings of Synod'. *Proceedings of Synod together with Reports & Accounts.* (May 1999), p. 19.
[95] *Sgeulachd Beatha* 21st Jan 2016.
[96] The season is made up of preparatory services running from Thursday to Saturday, followed by the sacrament dispensed on Sabbath morning, a service with a gospel message in the evening, and concluding with the thanksgiving service(s) on the Monday.

tians speaking to each other about the Saviour and his work would help spiritual growth.[97]

The year after joining the Free Presbyterian Church, he was asked to take services in North America. He and his wife travelled via New York and Toronto to the province of Ontario. There he preached at Chesley, Mount Elgin and Troy. After a month in Canada he went on to spend a further month in Texas, where he assisted at the first-ever communion season in the congregation at Santa Fe. He wrote of the fellowship and great kindness shown at both centres.[98] Mr Smith gave an address to the FP Church's Theological Conference held in December 2000. His paper was on 'Purgatory in the Light of Scripture'.[99]

Mr Smith faithfully attended the Church's annual Synod from 1999 until 2015, missing only two meetings. He served as a member of the Church's Religion and Morals, Sabbath Observance, and Outreach committees until 2008.[100] In a wide-ranging speech to the 2004 Synod Mr Smith raised concerns about social and moral change. He exhorted the members: 'We need a lot of prayer; we need to love one another in the Lord and to support each other—we are not perfect creatures; we need to be fighting against these things at a Throne of Grace. We need the spirit of prayer in our Church and to be broken

---

[97] For example, on the Lord's Day, 5th April 2015, preaching on Acts 12:5, Mr Smith said the Lord's people should not bottle up and hide their experiences from fellow believers. They should speak of what the Lord has done.
[98] Rev. A Smith, 'Report of Deputy to Canada and USA', *Reports of Standing Committees of Synod* (Glasgow 2001), pp. 69–70.
[99] *Proceedings of Synod together with Reports & Accounts May 2001*, p. 76.
[100] See *Proceedings of Synod together with Reports & Accounts* for the years 1999–2018.

before God, and we also need the blessing of the Holy Spirit. May God bless us.'[101]

The work to promote and protect the Lord's Day was close to his heart. A report to the 2004 Synod spoke of the Sabbath Observance Committee's protest to a businessman in the Western Isles who had opened his shop on the Sabbath. A courteous reply had been received in which he expressed his willingness to discuss the matter with a member of the Committee. Mr Smith had been chosen to have the discussion with the businessman. The Synod report stated: 'In the end there was no meeting of minds on the matter and we understand the shop continues to open on the Sabbath.'[102]

During the 2005 Synod discussion of the Sabbath Observance Committee report, Mr Smith expressed concern about the spiritual climate of the country. He added, 'Another matter is that of religious hatred which has to do with the Sabbath Day. I do not know how soon that is going to be at our door, friends. I think we should study it and pray every day as to what we are going to do. We cannot change what we preach. How then are [we] going to react as a Church? Take it to the Throne of Grace.'[103]

In 2008 Mr Smith was appointed as the committee's 'Speaker on Sabbath Observance'. At the 2009 Synod it was reported that in this capacity Mr Smith had given a public talk in

---

[101] *Proceedings of Synod together with Reports & Accounts May 2004*, pp. 6–7.
[102] 'Sabbath Observance Committee's Report', *Proceedings of Synod together with Reports & Accounts May 2004*, pp. 21–22.
[103] *Proceedings of Synod together with Reports & Accounts May 2005*, p. 6.

Dingwall Academy. This had been advertised in local newspapers. Sixty people had attended.[104]

Mr Smith had a heart for young people. He attended the Church's Youth Conference in April 2000,[105] where he gave a talk on 'The Angel of the Covenant'. This was subsequently published in the *Young People's Magazine*.[106] Mr Smith spoke on 'The Fall, its effect and extent' at the 2003 Youth Conference held in Inverness. Talks were given by other ministers on Creation, and on the 'Apostle of the North', Dr John Macdonald of Ferintosh. There were also Church history tours to Cromarty and the historical site of open-air communion gatherings at the 'Burn' at Ferintosh on the Black Isle.[107] He also provided an account of the three-day conference for the Church's youth publication.[108]

Two interests—the spiritual good of young people and the godly of past days—were combined in another article published in the *Young People's Magazine* in 2006. This told the story of Marion Macleod of Elphin, Assynt. Mr Smith underlined the encouragement that a young believer had received from

---

[104] 'Sabbath Observance Committee's Report', *Proceedings of Synod together with Reports & Accounts May 2009*, pp. 20–21.
[105] 'Welfare of Youth Committee's Report', *Proceedings of Synod together with Reports & Accounts May 2000*, pp.71–72.
[106] Published as a five-part series entitled 'The Angel of the Covenant' in *The Young People's Magazine* (henceforth *YPM*). '1. The First appearances', *YPM* Vol. 70 (November 2005), pp. 211–213; '2. Appearing to Abraham', *YPM* Vol. 70 (December 2005), pp. 229–231; '3. Appearances to Isaac and Jacob', *YPM* Vol. 71 (January 2006), pp. 6–7; '4. Appearances in the Wilderness', *YPM* Vol. 71 (February 2006), pp. 30–32; '5. Appearances to Joshua and Afterwards', *YPM* Vol. 71 (March 2006), pp. 46–48.
[107] The 'Burn' was a natural amphitheatre with good acoustics.
[108] 'Youth Conference Report 2003', *YPM* Vol. 68 (June 2003), pp. 115–116.

overhearing the aged Marion's prayer. The young girl was growing in painful awareness of indwelling sin. Marion had said, 'Lord, save me from the hell within my own heart.'[109]

To mark his 60th anniversary as a minister in November 2018, the Stornoway Free Presbyterian congregation organised a presentation following the weekly prayer meeting on Thursday 24th January 2019. In his speech of thanks, he said that he had 'met with nothing but love and kindness' in the denomination. He spoke of getting cards the month before, when he had turned 90. He had been amazed how many people knew he was 90 years old and 60 in the ministry. When he started as a minister at the age of 29, he thought he would do well if he served for 30 years. He spoke of the privilege of preaching, which was more precious to him than anything else except the salvation of his own soul. On Mr Smith's 90th birthday, the Stornoway minister Dr James R Tallach had preached on Psalm 90:1—'Lord, thou hast been our dwelling place in all generations'—which Mr Smith regarded as 'a card from the Lord'. Then on the following Lord's Day morning, a divinity student, John Campbell,[110] preached on the same text—'a second card from the Lord'. And in the evening Mr Campbell had preached on another verse in Psalm 90—'a third card from the Lord'.[111]

## Aspects of Mr Smith's ministry

Throughout his long ministry, Mr Smith embodied the words of Paul: 'Now then we are ambassadors for Christ, as though God did beseech you by us: we pray you in Christ's stead, be ye reconciled to God' (2 Corinthians 5:20). He addressed his

---

[109] '*Meran Mhòr*', *YPM* Vol. 71 (May 2006), pp. 87–89.
[110] Mr Campbell went on to serve as the minister of the Staffin FP congregation from August 2022 until his death in May 2023.
[111] The writer acknowledges the assistance of a friend present at the event, who took a note of what was said.

hearers very directly, and lovingly pleaded with them to seek Christ as their own personal Saviour from sin. His hearers often heard the expression: 'Friends, we are all on the way to eternity.' He also encouraged believers to pray earnestly. He emphasised the person and work of Christ, and God's sovereignty in the salvation of the sinner.

The words of Mr Smith in his obituary for Mr Macleod, his predecessor in Snizort, seem appropriate to himself: 'Malcolm Macleod aimed primarily at the heart in his preaching, never seeking to teach theology in a dry academic manner. His personal piety enhanced all that he said and did. His was not a spirit of levity, as the things of Christ and the welfare of souls were constantly before him. He was kindness itself to the children, and the picture one has of him in the mind's eye is that of a man with a gentle smile and kindly eyes who yearned for the good of Jerusalem.'[112]

Mr Smith believed strongly that an important part of the ministry was that a pastor should often engage with the people at a personal level. A number of people who had not previously attended church regularly began to do so after talking to Mr Smith; some traced the beginning of soul concern to these conversations. His view of the Lord's preparing and equipping for the ministry was that the person called was to be humbled. 'Paul was terrified of himself. He felt that he was the chief of sinners and that it was amazing that he ever got mercy. The Lord was keeping him down, bringing home to him how he really was. He was showing him how weak he was in himself. That's the man the Lord sent to Corinth.'[113]

---

[112] 'In Memoriam Rev. Malcolm Macleod, Snizort', *Monthly Record*, May 1968, p. 91.

[113] Cross Free Church Cassette Ministry MG 556. Rev. Angus Smith, MA. 1 Cor 2:1–5, '*Bunaite an t-Soisgeul*', [The Foundation of the Gospel], no date. Translation by the writer.

An important part of Mr Smith's own spirituality was a love for the Psalms. Among his favourites were Psalms 72 and 89. The words of Psalm 78:52–55 were particularly precious to him:[114] 'But made his own people to go forth like sheep, and guided them in the wilderness like a flock. And he led them on safely, so that they feared not: but the sea overwhelmed their enemies. And he brought them to the border of his sanctuary, even to this mountain, which his right hand had purchased. He cast out the heathen also before them, and divided them an inheritance by line, and made the tribes of Israel to dwell in their tents.'

He was a student of Scripture and of books to help in his studies. When he began teaching, he bought most of his Christian books in second-hand shops, as this period preceded the upsurge in Christian publishing from the late 1950s.[115] Mr Smith was an avid reader, carefully cataloguing in a card index system where he had read useful comments on various Scripture verses and chapters. The reality for a minister studying to preach five times a week—twice on the Lord's Day and at three prayer meetings—was that multiple-volume sets of books were not read from cover to cover. Completing every page of John Owen's six volumes on the Epistle to the Hebrews was not a feasible option but he found that Arthur W Pink's book on the epistle reflected much of Owen's work.

---

[114] The writer owes this information to a member of the Smith family.

[115] The Sovereign Grace Union had been the main UK publishers of Puritan and Reformed material in the early twentieth century. See Matthew J Hyde, *Unity in Diversity: The Sovereign Grace Union 1914–1939* (Southampton: Huntingtonian Press, 2015), pp. 12–14, 26, 31. A resurgence of large-scale Reformed book publishing resulted from the establishment of the Banner of Truth Trust in 1957. John J Murray, *Catch the Vision: Roots of the Reformed recovery* (Darlington: Evangelical Press, 2007), pp. 109–125.

Mr Smith liked to contrast two commentaries on the Epistle to the Romans: Hodge was 'sound but bare', whereas Haldane was 'full of the spirit of the gospel'. A key tool to which he turned throughout his ministry was Fairbairn's Bible dictionary.[116]

Three Free Church colleagues for whose godliness in precept and example he had great respect were Kenneth A Macrae of Stornoway,[117] James Morrison of North Uist,[118] and Angus Finlayson, North Tolsta. Their strong support of the Reformed witness in Scotland and internationally, as well as their concern to encourage Christians to act as salt and light in the public sphere, also created a bond.

The decline of biblical Christianity in Scotland since the time of the Reformation, but particularly in the late nineteenth and twentieth centuries, was a great burden to Mr Smith. He told a BBC Gaelic radio programme: 'Satan is out to break up churches. That's one way to defeat your enemy—break it up. Make them fall out. Satan works like that. The Lord has his children in each group. Groups can go down so quickly. A

---

[116] Patrick Fairbairn, *Imperial Bible-Dictionary* (London, Glasgow and Edinburgh: Blackie & Son, 1866).

[117] Iain H Murray (ed.), *Diary of Kenneth A MacRae* (*op. cit.*). For MacRae's public statements on economic and social concerns, see pp. 471–474.

[118] Scalpay-born Mr Morrison (1910–1982) served as pastor of North Uist Free Church from 1942 to 1982. Concern for the economic and cultural wellbeing of the largely crofting and fishing population, as well as a desire to help preserve the Lord's Day, saw him successfully stand for election as a District and later County Councillor. His biographer refers to his being vigorously outspoken in Church courts and adds that his administrative abilities should have been harnessed by church committees. George NM Collins, *Gleanings from the Diary and Ministry of James Morrison* (Edinburgh: n.p., 1984), pp. viii, 4, 30–42, 96, 136.

church can go so low that she is no longer a church. No one should be ruling in a church except converted people but I'm afraid that many have come in and have the upper hand, who have not been converted.'[119]

Writing in 1992, he gave his views on differences between believers. 'The three congregations in Ness today are evangelical, and the Bible is accepted as the infallible word of God by all three. Christians from all three can, and do, have fellowship with each other. This is the world where the warring enemy of souls manages to break up churches. He can also manage to put wedges between true Christian brethren, even in the same denomination. He hates Christian unity. Unfortunately in an imperfect world there are times when groups can see no other way of preserving their heritage intact other than by breaking away.

'We think of the wonderful mystic Church of Christ which must appear one day in its glory, as the Bride of Christ in gold of Ophir, on the right side of the Groom, the Lord Jesus Christ. The true Large Church will then be displayed with a host which no man can number. Those whom the Father has given the Son in the eternal covenant will all be there. They will be the mystic building, the mystic temple, and also the spiritual priests.'[120]

Mr Smith spoke of the sovereignty of God in conversion. Ministers sometimes found that it was not the sermons they thought would be blessed which turned out to be used by the

---

[119] *Sgeulachd Beatha*, 21st Jan 2016.
[120] Angus Smith, *An Eaglais Mhòr* [*The Large Church*] (Cross: n.p., 1992), pp. 38–39. A further denomination emerged after Mr Smith's retirement. A group separated from Cross Free Church in the spring of 1999. In 2000 it joined the Free Church (Continuing). The congregation built a church in North Dell and gained their current pastor, Rev. Greg MacDonald, in 2004.

Lord. He knew of two people who traced their conversion to a prayer he offered in public. A colleague had once preached in a congregation other than his own and felt he had completely failed in the task. Two years later he returned there for a communion season: a woman professed faith, telling the Kirk Session how that very sermon had been blessed to her conversion.

As a result of the Holy Spirit working in his own soul as a boy, Mr Smith felt strongly that he should communicate with the children as well as the adults from the pulpit. He once spoke of hearing sermons as a young person, of which he could hardly understand a word. He aimed to explain theology and feed the adult Christians, but at the same time remember the young.[121]

Mr Smith made a point of not contradicting the interpretation of texts given by ministers if he was preaching in their pulpits. He did so to avoid hurting the feelings or undermining the work of these brother ministers in any way. These differences could, for example, be about Bible characters, on the timing of whose conversions Mr Smith differed from other preachers. One exception was at a Lewis communion season before retirement, when he preached about Jacob. He believed that Jacob had been a convert from his childhood in the home, under the example of his mother Rebekah; and that neither of his meetings with the Lord in Penuel and Hebron had been Jacob's call by grace.[122]

---

[121] *Sgeulachd Beatha*, 21st Jan 2016.

[122] The writer is grateful to a hearer for this anecdote. On the Lord's Day morning of 1st Nov 2015, while preaching on Isaiah 43:1–2, he as an aside gave as his view that Jacob was a believer from early childhood, adding that he was not definite about it. He based it on the words in Genesis 25:27 that state that Jacob was 'a plain man'. The Hebrew word rendered 'plain' seems to mean

Gospel-preaching Highland churches and the distinct culture of the communities they serve were sometimes the subject of mockery in literature and the media.[123] However, while not agreeing to every approach from journalists and writers, Mr Smith saw the media as an opportunity to witness for Christ. His views on the decline in the observance of the Lord's Day were the usual topic, but opportunities to address the need for personal conversion and a wider range of subjects also presented themselves. One notable contribution was in the Everyman documentary, *The Last Stronghold of the Pure Gospel*.[124] Two more sustained instances were the five-part BBC *Radio nan Gaidheal* series quoted in this biographical article, and an episode of the television series, *Sin Thu Fhèin*, in which he was courteously challenged by Ness-born writer and educationalist Finlay Macleod.[125]

Mr Smith believed in learning from others, particularly through conversation about the Bible and spiritual experience. As a divinity student he had benefitted from fellowship with Johan's uncle Angus Maclean. Familiarly known as *Gobha Shiaboist* (the Shawbost blacksmith), he loved talking of the

---

'perfect' or 'complete' and Mr Smith said it was only used of the righteous in the Old Testament.
[123] Reporters based in the area were among the honourable exceptions, such as the *Herald* Highland correspondent, David Ross.
[124] This was directed by Michael Rafford. Discontent at the title tended to overshadow recognition of the film-maker's achievement. It was first broadcast on the BBC in England on the Lord's Day, 21st January 1979. In Scotland it was first shown on Monday 30th April at 3.15pm, and was repeated on the Lord's Day, 6th May that year. 'BBC Free Church film date switched to Monday', *Press and Journal* (Thursday April 26th 1979), p. 3. An assessment and reflection by Lewis Christians appeared with material from the original programme on BBC Alba in June 2011.
[125] This was first broadcast on the BBC Alba channel on Wednesday 7th March 2012 and has been repeated.

things of God.[126] Questions he posed to the divinity student included: 'Was Christ's human nature in the grave, and was his Person there?' Mr Smith found these questions to be helpful in clarifying his theological thought.

A friend who regularly spoke to the Question at the communion season Fellowship Meeting in Ness was Angus Macleod from Shawbost, a man described in his obituary as 'one who walked with God' and from whom 'the love which the Lord had shed abroad in his heart diffused its fragrance in prosperity and adversity'.[127] Mr Smith often looked back fondly in retirement to the many spiritually-minded people in Ness and further afield who frequently asked his views on passages of Scripture. He also recalled benefitting from the friendly cut-and-thrust of theological debate in the privacy of manse studies when assisting and neighbouring ministers would be together at communion seasons. In company with non-ministerial friends, he encouraged Biblical discussion through simple questions.

Reflecting in old age on the ministry, Mr Smith said that he 'pitied a young minister in this day. ... The minister should look to two vineyards—firstly, that of his own spiritual walk before God (not, in the main, seen of men), and that of his congregation in the labours of the ministry.' The second 'depended on the first'. He urged that a preacher 'be a man of prayer' and that in going to the Word, 'he should look first for food for his own soul, and beware the formality of looking at

---

[126] Mr Maclean lived at 50 North Shawbost. He died in 1967, aged 89.
[127] Mr Macleod was known locally as *An Coileach* and lived at 40 South Shawbost. Rev. J Morrison, 'Angus Macleod, Elder, Shawbost', *Monthly Record*, March 1998. The writer thanks the Rev. Malcolm Macleod, Shawbost for his assistance. See also Malcolm Macleod, *Echoes of an Era: Shawbost Free Church of Scotland, its origins and history* (*op. cit.*), p. 55.

once for pulpit texts'.[128] After fifty years as a minister, said Mr Smith, 'it was yet a great mystery to him how one was given a text for a sermon. The Lord did it. The Spirit did it.' A new minister 'must be most aware of the danger of pride. He would be in situations, at times, of great frustration, when the temptation to speak in anger would be strong. He must look to the Lord to keep him.' He added that a new minister 'should be much in the homes of his people, meeting them in their own situation and in their own need. He should love all men and women; love especially the lost. He should seek to turn every conversation to the things of the Gospel, and strive—amidst inevitable difficulties and disappointment—to be kept from bitterness.'[129]

Mr Smith was prepared to change traditional practice where scriptural and appropriate. By the 1970s, English-language services had already been slowly introduced on one Lord's Day evening per month in the main church building. However, Cross began English services on a Lord's Day morning, while retaining the time-honoured Gaelic mid-day service, from around October 1988. The trigger had been the arrival of a large non-Gaelic-speaking family in the area.[130] He told a writer that one benefit had been that 'a few English and Lowland Scots' had begun to attend as a result.[131] Cross was only the second Free Church congregation in rural Lewis to introduce Lord's Day morning English services.[132]

---

[128] *Stornoway Gazette*, 27th November 2008, p. 8. Contributed article.
[129] *Ibid.*
[130] I am grateful to Donald A Morrison for furnishing the date.
[131] Fiona MacDonald *Island Voices* (Irvine: Carrick Press, 1992), pp. 63–69 'Rev. Angus Smith Cross, Lewis'.
[132] The Back congregation had begun Lord's Day morning English services in March 1988, while retaining the mid-day Gaelic one. The writer is grateful to the recent Interim Moderator, the Rev.

## Biographical sketch

As social media and technology developed in the first decades of the twenty-first century, he shared concerns about the negative aspects of the internet. However, he occasionally mentioned in preaching the opportunity afforded by new technology for people to have in-vision real-time contact with others overseas: a development in providence which illustrated the Lord's power to arrange in some future time for preaching the gospel throughout the world.

He rarely raised the specific topic of the millennium, but was known to take the 'amillennial' view of the end of the world, *i.e.*, that the 'last days' are the period from Christ's first coming to his second coming.[133] He did not agree with the post-millennial expectation of a long period (sometimes envisaged as a literal thousand years) of mass conversions and righteous living. However, he looked forward to the time when the gospel would spread through all nations, and he prayed for the conversion of those in other religions.

---

Ewen Matheson, and Session clerk, Iain Mackinnon, for this information. See also Neil Murray *Chum Fios Bhi aig an Àl ri Teachd: Back Free Church 1891–1991* (Stornoway: n.p., 1991), p. 69. From late 1989 until late 1990, Crossbost rotated languages at 12 noon and 6pm, but did not introduce an extra Lord's Day morning service. It then reverted to Gaelic at 12 and English at 6pm. Following Presbytery encouragement in 1993 for congregations to examine the language issue, and a written request by some members, Crossbost from April 1994 held an English service at the same time as the Gaelic at 12. The writer acknowledges the painstaking assistance of Murdo Macleod, Leurbost, Session clerk of Crossbost, in gleaning these details. See also John Macleod, *Banner in the West* (*op. cit.*), pp. 327–328. There is now (2023) no weekly Lord's Day Gaelic preaching in any Free Church congregation in rural Lewis.

[133] Mr Smith did occasionally preach in the book of Revelation, however, recommending that it be studied prayerfully through the prism of the Psalms, the Song of Solomon, Ezekiel and Daniel.

## The final years

Mr Smith often spoke of his increasing sense of his own sin. In Stornoway on the Lord's Day, 29th April 2018, he used a striking expression in prayer. He asked the Lord to show seeking souls that the Lord could raise them from the dunghill, and that 'they might see that he can save them *from* the uttermost as well as *to* the uttermost'. He continued to study the Scriptures every day, even on the very rare occasions that a preaching engagement was not on the immediate horizon. He also enjoyed the opportunity to catch up with reading Christian literature denied him by the pressure of pastoral work.[134]

More than a decade before his death, his health began to decline slowly. This did not restrict his preaching activities, although medical intervention became more necessary in the final years of his life. His last sermon was preached on the morning of Sabbath 12th May 2019 in Stornoway Free Presbyterian Church. His text was 1 John 3:1–3.[135] The theme was the children of God and the hope of heaven. He was taken to hospital that night. After then being lovingly cared for at home, he was transferred to the Bethesda Hospice in Stornoway. He passed away there just before 11 pm on Tuesday 27th August 2019.

---

[134] One example was reading Patrick Fairbairn on *Prophecy* during his last few months of life.

[135] 'Behold, what manner of love the Father hath bestowed upon us, that we should be called the sons of God: therefore the world knoweth us not, because it knew him not. Beloved, now are we the sons of God, and it doth not yet appear what we shall be: but we know that, when he shall appear, we shall be like him; for we shall see him as he is. And every man that hath this hope in him purifieth himself, even as he is pure.' A recording of the sermon is available on the FP Church website (www.fpchurch.org.uk).

# Biographical sketch

The funeral worship on Friday 30th August in the packed Stornoway Free Presbyterian building was conducted by the pastor, Rev. Dr James R Tallach. He was assisted in prayer by the Revs Kenneth D Macleod (Inverness) and Neil M Ross (retired, latterly of Dingwall and Beauly). The first singing was in Gaelic from the first three stanzas of Psalm 23.[136] The rest of the worship was in English and the main reading in Psalm 122. The concluding praise was in Psalm 103:1–7.[137] Mr Smith's remains were buried in the Habost cemetery in Ness.

Mr Smith often preached about heaven. One striking example was in Uig (Lewis) Free Presbyterian Church on the evening of Sabbath 31st July 2017, when his text was Psalm 27:4.[138] Mr Smith had commented: 'Heaven is a place of study, enquiry, questioning, and admiring the beauty of the Lord which is his holiness.' The words of his obituary for his predecessor in Snizort also appear appropriate to Mr Smith: 'The voice … rings out … in praise of his Redeemer as his soul revels with delight in the fellowship of the One he sought so earnestly to proclaim to fellow sinners. … The stones from the bed of Jordan have been made a cairn[139] on the bank of Canaan, and glory dwells forever in Immanuel's land.'[140]

NORMAN CAMPBELL
Stornoway, November 2023

---

[136] Ness FP elder John Alex Murray was the Gaelic precentor.
[137] The praise was led by Stornoway FP elder Dr Robert J Dickie.
[138] 'One thing have I desired of the Lord, that will I seek after; that I may dwell in the house of the Lord all the days of my life, to behold the beauty of the Lord, and to enquire in his temple.'
[139] A cairn is the Scottish word for a built pile of stones. See Joshua 4:1–20.
[140] 'In Memoriam Rev. Malcolm Macleod, Snizort', *Monthly Record* (May 1968), p. 91. The words 'Immanuel's land' are from a poem *The Sands of Time are Sinking*, composed by Ann Ross Cousin (1824–1906) and based on the last sayings of the Scottish minister Samuel Rutherford (*c.* 1600–1661).

# Sermons

# 1

# The Great Supper

19th November 2017, Lord's Day morning, Uig

*Then said he unto him, A certain man made a great supper, and bade many: and sent his servant at supper time to say to them that were bidden, Come; for all things are now ready.*
Luke 14:16–17

THE Lord Jesus was very often asked to go to homes to eat and drink with people, and very often at the homes of Pharisees. You would think perhaps that he wouldn't be invited to such homes, but he was. Maybe they thought at one time that he would be friendly to them and not expose them, but just be like themselves, and conform to their ways. But of course, he was God in the flesh. He was totally pure and holy, and he did expose them when he was among them. Even when he was at food with them he would expose them.

At the beginning of the chapter we read, 'And it came to pass, as he went into the house of one of the chief Pharisees to eat bread on the Sabbath day, that they watched him.' It's as if they were going out of their way to watch him, seeking to find fault in some way or other so that they could accuse him.

'And, behold, there was a certain man before him which had the dropsy.' It may be that they were responsible for this man being there—the situation may have been set up.

'And Jesus answering spake unto the lawyers and Pharisees, saying, Is it lawful to heal on the sabbath day? And they held their peace. And he took him, and healed him.' When he asked the question, 'Is it lawful to heal on the sabbath day?' they should have said, 'It is lawful.' The Pharisees used to write commentaries. Those who wrote commentaries should surely say, 'Yes, it is lawful.' They were the scribes of Scripture—the same word as we have in Gaelic, *sgriobh*—they used to write copies of Scripture. All of these people would know fine well that it was lawful to heal on the sabbath day.

So Jesus rebukes them. He asks them, 'If you have an ass or a sheep, or any other animal, that falls down a pit on the Sabbath day, will you not take it out? Will you not take your cow out to water on the Sabbath day, if it's tied in a stall?' These were things that were works of necessity and works of mercy, and they were commanded by the Lord. Works of mercy and works of necessity were not just permitted but commanded to be done on the Sabbath day. But they set this up to trap Jesus, that they might be able to accuse him of breaking the Sabbath day.

That shows us the kind of people he was among. It shows us that the priestly class and those who were associated with them, on the whole, were against him and they were seeking to destroy him, even early on in his ministry.

Among the things Jesus said at this meal, in verse 12 we find him speaking and telling those who had feasts to bring the poor and the maimed and the blind to these feasts. The Pharisees had no intention of bringing the poor, the maimed, the blind. They wouldn't have taken the man whose body was

## 1  The great supper

swollen up with the dropsy, except that they sought to catch Christ by seeing whether he would heal that man on the Sabbath day. Oh the evil that is in the heart of man! It was evident that the one who could heal a disease that nobody could heal, was working by the power of God.

Coming to verse 15, it says: 'And when one of them that sat at meat with him heard these things, he said unto him, Blessed is he that shall eat bread in the kingdom of God.' The man that said that seemed to be thinking of the future, that the time would come when God's people would be gathered together and they would eat bread in the kingdom of God. 'Bread' just means 'food' in this context. What he said was true. 'Blessed are they!' But the Lord took it up and gave a parable to that man. 'Then said he unto him (to that very man), A certain man made a great supper, and bade many. And sent his servant at supper time to say to them that were bidden, Come; for all things are now ready.'

We should like to take up a few things.

First of all we have the gospel supper. Then we see men making excuses: 'And they all with one consent began to make excuse.' Then we see, thirdly, the invitation given to outsiders. And the Lord said: 'Go out quickly into the streets and lanes of the city, and bring in hither the poor and the maimed, and the halt, and the blind'—the very kind of people the Pharisees would never dream of taking in. You see, to them if a man was blind, he must have sinned, or his parents must have sinned. Even the very disciples of Christ were caught up in that teaching—it had been given to them before they were disciples. When they saw a man who was blind they asked Christ, 'Who sinned, that man or his parents, that he was born blind?' And Christ dismissed all that. It wasn't that reason at all, but his blindness was for the glory of God, because he gave the man sight and he gave the man grace. But anyway, that was how they reasoned. If a man was maimed, if he lacked a limb, did he sin? And they even spoke of the child sinning in the womb and other things like that, or they spoke of the parents sinning before and the Lord bringing judgment upon them. The lepers were the same, the blind, the deaf, and so on. The Pharisees said, 'We don't want these people at our feasts. No, none of these.'

So we'll consider just these three things—the gospel supper, the excuses, and the invitation. And we pray that the Lord would be with us and help us when we think of these things because you and I have a soul, a precious soul, going into eternity. And unless the Word of God is blessed to you and myself, we'll be lost, we won't be at that great feast.

## 1. The gospel feast

The great feast here is the gospel feast, the feast we're all invited to by the Lord Jesus.

'A certain man made a great supper, and bade many.' There are two words here speaking of greatness. One is that it was 'a great supper'.

The gospel is a great supper. It's a wonderful supper. It's the greatest meal that this world knows. People will laugh at us saying that, but it doesn't matter. It's a meal for the soul. Most men and most women have nothing for their soul. They are seeking to feed their souls on dust and things that can never satisfy, chasing the fancies of their own minds, their own imaginations, their pleasures in this world. They think these things will satisfy a soul! No, friends. Only this feast, only the gospel, only believing in Christ as our Saviour, is going to satisfy the soul. Christ is the food and drink for the soul. Nothing else, nothing else.

# 1 The great supper

This great feast is called a great supper. This tells you the night is coming. You can see the very approach of night at the supper. And the night is approaching for our lives. Our lives are short. The darkness of the night is touching us, every one of us, as soon as we come into the world. Life is short.

The other word that shows the greatness of this supper is that it says, 'He bade many.' To begin with, the gospel supper was among the Jews. Christ came into the world, and he was the meaning of the gospel. He *was* the gospel! He was the good news. He came to save sinners. He preached himself as the Saviour of sinners.

He came as a Jew. He was born a Jew and was brought up among the Jews. He was spoken about in the Old Testament—where he would be born: Bethlehem—and when he would be born: Daniel spoke of that. He came. 'He came to his brethren,' it says, but his brethren rejected him.

So his brethren, the Jews, were the 'many' to whom he came to begin with. You would expect them to crowd around him, to flock around him, to exalt him! But the human heart is so twisted, the human heart is so corrupt, the human heart is so evil and so jealous! These Pharisees wanted a great place. If Christ would praise them, that would be good as far as they were concerned. But instead, he exposed them. He told them the truth. It's only the truth that can set you free, but you've got to believe the truth!

People don't want to believe the truth about themselves. But the Word of God tells us the truth. It's a mirror: it shows us what is in the soul, not what is on the body. Clothes are on the body but the Word of God is telling you what is in your soul. People don't like the soul being made naked before God, the sin being exposed, the corruption of the heart being exposed, the jealousy that is in the heart being exposed, the hatred for holiness that is in the heart being exposed. But you and I have to believe Scripture. We have to believe the Word of God, or else, friends, we cannot be saved.

Some will say, 'Well, the mirror is true in parts but not true in other parts. It's a flawed mirror. It's not all inspired. We don't accept the whole of Scripture.' That doesn't work! When you read the apostles, when you read Christ, they are all saying that the whole of Scripture is the Word of God. We must accept the whole or we accept nothing. The Word of God tells us the truth.

'He bade many.' Many! The Pharisees, the priests, the scribes, the lawyers, the publicans, the sinners, all who were there, who attended the worship of God, who were given the worship of God.

This was the climax of it all. This was the meaning of it all—the meaning of the sacrifices, the meaning of the temple—here it was before them. Christ had come, the great Saviour, the great sacrifice to take away sin, to save sinners. Yes, the great feast, he was there. Christ was the great, great feast, and he was living among them.

So he 'sent his servant at supper time to say to them that were bidden, "Come; for all things are now ready."'

'He sent his servant.' It doesn't say that he sent his servants, plural. It says that he sent *one* servant, to say to these people, 'Come; for all things are now ready.' You see, when the Jews made a feast, perhaps a marriage, or some other great feast, they would kill the animals on the very day that they were feasting. We wouldn't do that. If we killed a sheep we would leave it a few days before we would use the meat, but because of the hot climate, the Jews would kill the animal immediately before the feast. So all things are then ready.

# 1   The great supper

God sent his servant, the Lord Jesus Christ. Christ was there telling them, 'Come to the feast! All things are now ready!' Christ was about to die. The majority of what you have in the Gospels has to do with the last few weeks of the life of Christ. That may seem strange if we want to know about all the other years of his life, but he says, 'Come; for all things are now ready.' 'I'm about to die, I'm about to suffer, I'm about to offer myself up to finish it all: come; for all things are now ready! Believe in me, the Lord Jesus, the one who came, the Messiah, the son of David, the promised One!'

His life was made up of that cry. He cried during his life and he cried on the cross. He called out at last, 'It is finished!' 'Come! Come; for all things are now ready!' God sent out his servant. Yes, the best servant that God ever had. 'Behold my servant, whom I uphold.' Yes, 'mine elect, in whom is my great delight, my servant.' 'Behold my servant.' You don't see great men saying, 'Look at my servant!' They usually tell their servants, 'Do your work and stay out of sight.' But not this servant. God says, 'Look at my servant, listen to my servant, behold my servant!'

Here is a great supper and a wonderful, wonderful message. All was ready! Many did believe in him, but compared to those who did *not* believe in him, they were only a remnant. The people as a whole rejected him. 'I labour for nought,' he said in the Old Testament. Yes, he came to his own, and his own received him not. But to such as did receive him, he gave them power, or authority, to become the sons of God.

That's the wonderful thing to those who believe, to those who accept this gospel. These people in their very acceptance are transformed into the very sons of God. They are adopted, the Holy Spirit indwells them and the Lord himself calls them not only guests but sons, children of God.

## 2. The excuses

'And they all with one consent began to make excuse.' This is speaking mainly of the Jews. The Pharisees, the priests, the scribes, the lawyers were all together, planning together, plotting together, with 'one consent'. They would reject Christ with different words but still a rejection was there among them all, with one consent.

Now at these feasts, especially the marriage feast, you would be called, invited, a while before the marriage. And then at the time of the marriage you would be told again that the marriage is today. As a people, the Jews had been given invitations in the Old Testament, so they knew it was coming. But now the very time of the feast had come, and they all with one consent began to make their excuses.

'The first said unto him, I have bought a piece of ground, and I must needs go and see it: I pray thee have me excused.' Oh, how good-mannered it seems to be: 'I pray thee have me excused.' How polite that is! But behind that politeness is something else. There's nothing wrong with buying a piece of ground, but he says, 'I must go.' 'It's my duty, my first duty, I've got to go to see it.' Why does he want to go to see it? To see if it's good enough, if it's a good piece of ground. But surely you would go to see the ground *before* you would buy it. You don't buy a piece of ground and *then* go to see if it's any good. You wouldn't buy a croft without seeing it first of all—you'd want to see what you're going to buy.

In any case, even if he had bought a piece of ground and had to go and see it, why go to see it at that very time? Surely, if he had bought it, he could go tomorrow or the next day or the next day again. Why did he have to go at that particular time? Why was that going to keep him back from going to the feast, the great feast, the great supper?

## 1  The great supper

It's not only just an excuse, friends. It's a love of sin in the heart that keeps sinners from coming to Christ. Love of the glory of this world, the tinsel glory of this world, keeps people back from coming to Christ. They can put it in many different ways. They can make many, many excuses. It's easy to make excuses. The heart of man is deceitful and desperately wicked, as we read in the Scriptures. The heart of man can go this way or that way. We are sinners when we come into the world, and we learn to sin. We learn to sin more and more, we become more and more subtle, and we become harder. We become greater sinners. And of course, it's easy enough under the gospel to make excuses.

But God does not accept any excuse when we're under the gospel. 'I pray thee have me excused,' the man said, putting it in a polite and nice manner. But, my friends, it wasn't a polite and nice thing before God Almighty. He knows our hearts.

Then there was the second man. 'Another said, I have bought five yoke of oxen, and I go to prove them: I pray thee have me excused.' If he needed five yoke of oxen he must have had a good bit of ground. He would use the oxen to plough and to draw carts or such like, and he could yoke them all together for various purposes, although ploughing was the great thing.

He had bought them, but did he know if they were good oxen or not? Were they young oxen or old oxen? The old ones are used to ploughing, the young ones have to be broken in. Did he know about that? 'Well,' he said, 'I have bought them.' He just bought them. You don't buy an animal without going to see it first of all. You wouldn't buy a horse or a cow without going to see it first of all. But this man said, 'I have bought five yoke of oxen.' Ten of them. 'I never saw them and now I go to see them.' He never saw them before, and now he needs to go to see them. And now he needs to prove them.

But again, why didn't he see them yesterday, or the day before? Or if he had bought them already, why not just leave it for then? There's no great haste for things like that. He could see them tomorrow, or the next day. No, it's the same kind of mind as the other man had. The scribes, the Pharisees, the lawyers, the priests, were all so similar in their hearts. 'I pray thee have me excused.' Another lie in the heart, another lie in the right hand.

And then the third one. 'I have married a wife, and therefore I cannot come.' Why can he not come if he has married a wife? Well, at the Jewish feasts the men would be together, and the women would be together. In the synagogue that's how it was too—the men sat together in one place, and the women sat together in another place. They were used to that, they knew that system. But why couldn't he come? He doesn't explain. We know that among the Jews, when a man married a wife, he was excused from warfare for a year. That always happened, that was the law. But this wasn't warfare, this was a feast! This was a supper, this was a great supper, this was the greatest supper of all!

What a tragedy it is if one marries a wife and because one marries a wife, one ceases to come to the means of grace! Isn't that a tragedy? And she could always follow the heart, or she could follow the head. It's a momentous thing to marry, especially if there are going to be children in that marriage, because it's going to have an impact on the following generations. But it's a beautiful thing to have a man and woman come together in marriage and begin to attend the house of the Lord together, and especially if they both believe in the Lord. That is what cements everything. That is a great blessing, if the Lord will give it to us in marriage—to believe in the Lord together, to have him as our own God.

But this man said, 'I cannot come.' Why couldn't he come? Why couldn't he say why? All he could say was, 'I have married a wife, and *therefore* I cannot come.' He didn't say, 'I'm going to marry her today, at the same time as the feast.' No, it was over and done with. He had already married her.

You see, friends, it was only an excuse. It only means that they all with one consent began to make excuse. This is the human heart and this was the Jewish heart, with one consent rejecting the Lord Jesus.

There were exceptions here and there. The exceptions were mainly from the lower class. Later on, many of the priests believed, but not till later on. They saw what had taken place in the temple when Christ died, when the curtain tore from the top to the bottom. The curtain was beyond human reach, but it tore from the top to the bottom, telling them that it was God's work. This happened at the same time as Christ died, as he cried out, and the same time as the earthquake that exposed the saints of God who were to rise at the same time as Christ. These things affected many. But at this time—yes, and even later on—it was still just a remnant who believed.

Now, how do we compare? We have the gospel. We know that the preaching is that if we trust ourselves entirely to Christ, he is a Saviour who can save us from our sins. Do we come with an excuse?

### 3. The invitation to outsiders

We're coming now to the invitation that was given to outsiders. 'So that servant came, and shewed his lord these things. Then the master of the house being angry, said to his servant, God out quickly into the streets and lanes of the city, and bring in hither the poor, and the maimed, and the halt, and the blind.'

It says he was angry. After all, he had made the supper for them. He had given them their invitations, both the prior invitation, and the later invitation to confirm it. He had sent his servant out to tell them. He had done all that, and they all made excuse. So he was angry. God was angry with the Jews who crucified Christ. So, forty years later, they were destroyed as a nation by God, using the Romans as God's instrument. Then shortly after, the whole nation of the Jews was destroyed. The people were driven out, scattered, sold as slaves. They lost the land of Canaan until 1948. They never came back for about two thousand years because the Lord was angry.

But the lord said to his servant, 'Go out quickly into the streets and lanes of the city, and bring in hither the poor, and the maimed, and the halt, and the blind.' He was not to go out to the country, but to the city. 'Go to those who are rejects, those who are hated by the priests and the scribes and the Pharisees, those who they look down on, because they must be such sinners.' These were the very kind of people the Pharisees would never dream of taking in to a feast.

You see, to the Pharisees, if a man was blind, he must have sinned, or his parents must have sinned. Even the very disciples of Christ were caught up in that false teaching. When the disciples saw a man who was blind they asked Christ, 'Who sinned, this man or his parents, that he was born blind?' Christ dismissed all that: it wasn't that at all. The man's blindness was for the glory of God. He gave the man sight, and he gave the man grace.

The Jews reasoned this way. If a man is maimed, he lacks a limb, so did he sin? They even spoke of the child sinning in the womb, or the parents sinning before, and the Lord bringing judgment upon them. The Jews reasoned the same way about the lepers, the blind, the deaf, and so on. 'We don't want these people at our feasts. No, none of these.' That's what they

## 1  The great supper

said to the man born blind, who explained to them his circumstances and what Christ had done for him. They said to him, 'Thou was altogether born in sin,' and they cast him out.

'Go out quickly into the streets and lanes of the city, and bring in hither the poor, and the maimed, and the halt, and the blind.' The gospel was sent to the poor, those who had nothing, the rejects of society. It's the lower part of society that is mainly blessed by the gospel. The gospel tends to elevate people. You see, when the gospel is blessed, it makes people change the way they talk, and the bad habits, and they live better. The gospel tends to elevate them in the towns and great cities where you have drugs and drink and foul language and immorality. In the days of Christ—and yes, in the days of our fathers, the crofters, who had nothing in the world but their croft and fishing, and next to nothing in their black houses—in some strange way these people seemed to be more receptive of the gospel.

So the servant was sent to the poor and the maimed and the halt—those who lacked limbs, those who were crippled—and the blind, and those who had things wrong with them, those who were in trouble and trial. The Lord very often brings trouble into a person's life, to make him turn to the gospel, to make him turn to Christ. The person doesn't know it, but the love of Christ is behind it. He might say, 'I'm in trouble. I'm in dire straits.' There might even be a death in the home, but the person doesn't know that the Lord is going to bless that death to his soul.

Yes, friends, many things can come upon us. We can lose our homes, we can lose our health, we can lose many things, and yet it can be the Lord who loves our souls who's talking to us in these things, calling us to turn to himself, inviting us to come to the great feast.

These poor people say, 'But we are not fit to come to the great feast! We don't have proper clothing.' The lame man says, 'I can't even walk properly, how can I go?' And the blind says, 'How can I manage to go to any feast?'

'How can I manage?' Ah, but you see, the message was, 'Bring them.' The servant will bring them. They say to Christ, 'I want to believe, but I can't believe. I want to trust and I find I cannot.' But the Lord works in their souls and then in a strange way they find themselves trusting in Christ. The person who says, 'I can't trust in Christ in that way, but I desire with all my heart to trust in Christ,' that person already has trust in Christ. It's the will, you see. If it's the desire of his heart above everything else, the will has been won. And although he may not know it, he's already trusting in Christ, and the time will come when he will see it. The Lord will give him light, the Lord will open his eyes, and give him understanding in his soul to see that he is trusting in Christ to bring him.

So we see the publicans coming to Christ—the tax-gatherers, who were despised by the Jews, whose word wasn't taken at law, whose name meant liar and cheat in the eyes of the Jews—that class seemed to be blessed, strangely enough. The poor and the deprived came to John the Baptist, and they came to Christ. More of them seemed to believe than any other class. 'Bring in hither the poor, and the maimed, and the halt, and the blind.'

Then the servant said, 'Lord, it is done as thou hast commanded, and yet there is room.' The Lord is saying, 'The gospel has been preached to the Jews, now let it be preached to the Gentiles.' 'I brought those in the city, but now let us go outside the city.' 'Preach the gospel', said Christ, 'to every creature.' Yes, to every creature: not just Jews, but Gentiles.

# 1  The great supper

Philip went to Samaria, a mixed people, hated by the Jews, and to his amazement there was a revival in Samaria. When the disciples heard of it they could hardly believe that such a thing was possible, and they sent to Samaria to make sure. Then the Gentiles began to believe here and there. Paul was sent specifically to Europe to preach the gospel.

Yes, the gospel is for Gentiles! Somehow it reached this island. Teachers were sent to teach people to read and to write in Gaelic, and the Bible was the exercise book that they had. And the Bible was like a lion let loose; it began to work its own work among the people.

The servant said, 'Lord, it is done as thou hast commanded, and yet there is room.' There is room for more than the Jews who believed during the days of Christ. So the apostles went out, here and there. They left their families, because it was more important to preach the gospel in a dying world than to stay at home, to stay at the fishing and to stay with the family—important as the families were. One after another the apostles were put to death, here and there, as they preached the gospel.

'And the Lord said unto the servant, Go out into the highways and hedges,' the Gentile world. Go out into the highways, the various lanes, as the word seems to denote—the lanes that are not trodden too often. Go out into the hedges. Why the hedges? Because those who had no homes and wanted shelter would be found sitting under the hedges.

Go out! Don't stay in the cities, go outside, go into the world. Go to the place where they worship their idols, the sun, moon and stars. Go to where they pour their milk into the ground to satisfy their gods, and where they pour their ale into the sea to promote the fishing. Go to these people, these poor dark people sitting under hedges, seeking a false shelter and taking false roads. They are the very tiny lanes, the footpaths where you won't find many people. Go into the darkness of the world outside Jewry. The world was dark outside Jewry. The whole of Europe was dark, and Africa and Asia—all dark. Take the gospel into these places!

And the Lord says, 'Compel *them* to come in, that my house may be filled.' The word 'compel' doesn't mean 'make them' as in, 'take hold of them and force them'. To compel them means to lovingly persuade them. Talk to them about Jesus, talk to them about salvation, tell them about the gospel. 'Tell them about myself,' says Christ. 'Let them know about me! Speak to them, loving their souls. Tell them, persuade them, because I work through the mind as well as through the heart. Let my Word touch their mind and touch their hearts, that they might be made willing by power of the Holy Spirit, that they might come!'

Outsiders, non-Jews, are told to come to the feast, to come to Christ. Come to feed upon the broken body and the shed blood, Christ and his finished work. 'Believe on the Lord Jesus Christ and thou shalt be saved.'

Christ says, 'That my house may be filled.' The house where the feast is will be filled. Yes, it will be filled: there will be no empty places there. The point is, will I be there? Will you be there, in that house, to feast for evermore? 'For I say unto you, that none of those men which were bidden shall taste of my supper.' 'Those who were full of excuses, those who refused, those who did not come: these will never, never taste of my supper.'

Many years ago, I remember as a young man hearing a doctrine that was being preached in Scotland, that was that there was a second opportunity to be saved, even after death. They were saying that God would give people another opportunity in eternity itself. They were saying that God was so merciful, so loving, so kind, that he would give those in hell an opportunity to turn to Christ. But that's *not* what the Lord says. That's not what is taught in Scripture. People will add to Scripture. They will of course say that everyone will be saved. But the Lord Jesus Christ does not say that. The Lord Jesus spoke of men being cast into hell fire forever. Let us believe Scripture. Those who reject the Scripture invitation will never, never, never taste of the gospel feast.

'O taste and see that God is good.' What does that mean? Well, the second part of the text explains it: 'O taste and see that God is good: who trusts in him is bless'd.' Trusting in him—trusting, believing, committing ourselves to the Lord in trust—that is the same as tasting. When we come into that state we have begun to taste the sweetest thing of all—the eternal love of God in Christ Jesus, the blessedness of God in the Saviour. 'O taste and see!' Oh, that we might all know that taste!

May God bless his Word. Let us pray.

## Concluding prayer

Gracious and glorious Lord, we beseech thee to help us, to guide us as we go through this Sabbath day. Give us to think of our own situation personally before thee, because if our soul is to receive any good, we must consider how we are before thee. We pray thee, gracious Lord Jesus, thou who didst walk the streets of Jerusalem and Galilee, bless thine own precious Word to us this day.

Bless our souls. Oh, give us to see that our souls have a great need of thee. We live in a nation in which many do not even know they have a soul. O Lord God, have mercy on our nation. Have mercy on our pulpits in the nation. Raise up true men of God, raise up men who love souls, raise up men who will preach the Word of God, whether it will be received or not, who will preach the true Word of God, even if men will reject it, because thou art blessing those who are faithful. Thou dost not say that thy blessing is upon those who are successful but upon those who are faithful.

Bless thy Word to us and cleanse us. For Jesus' sake. Amen.

# 2

# Perseverance

19th November 2017, Lord's Day evening, Uig

*Or what king, going to make war against another king, sitteth not down first, and consulteth whether he be able with ten thousand to meet him that cometh against him with twenty thousand? Or else, while the other is yet a great way off, he sendeth an ambassage, and desireth conditions of peace. So likewise, whosoever he be of you that forsaketh not all that he hath, he cannot be my disciple.*
Luke 14:31–33

THE theme of this passage is that true godliness, the work of God in the soul, will carry on. It has perseverance, it will not just die out. Whatever dies out is not the work of God. We should like to keep that in mind as we meditate on what we have here.

## Following Christ

In verse 25 it says, 'And there went great multitudes with him.' A very great crowd came after Christ. What does a great crowd mean? Often it means nothing. There are ways and means of drawing great crowds and there are many who employ worldly methods, turning worship into concerts and other things that please the flesh, just for the sake of building up great crowds. But the gospel is meant to aim at the souls of men and women, that they might be brought alive and that God's people might be built up in the holy faith. It would be good if we had crowds who were like that, but alas, that is something that is rare indeed.

Great crowds followed Christ. They wanted to see the miracles. Yes, many were drawn by the teaching—the words that came out of his mouth—and yet many only wanted to be fed by him. Many were willing to make a king of him if he would keep them in food from day to day after they saw his miracle of blessing bread and fishes, and satisfying hunger. These things draw people. If we could take a few loaves and fishes, and whatever else it is that we eat and drink, and bless them and make them multiply, then of course people would follow us. If we could carry out miracles of healing the blind, the maimed, the deaf and so on, then many would follow us. But Christ was not aiming at these things as an end in themselves. These things were only to prove that he was God in the flesh, that he was sent, that he was the Messiah. The real thing he aimed at was that they would listen to what he said and believe in him as their own personal Saviour.

When the great multitude followed Christ, he turned, and spoke to them (verse 25). This is how he combs people out. The gospel does that. It combs them out. Some will give it up, some will stay away, some will turn their backs and never come back. That always happens under the gospel. So he said, in verse 26, 'If any man come to me, and hate not his father, and mother, and wife, and children, and brethren, and sisters, yea, and his own life also, he cannot be my disciple.' We know that the Lord commands us not to hate our enemies, but to love our enemies. We are to love all men, desiring their salvation. But here the Lord uses the word 'hate'. But notice, he says, 'And hate their own life also.' He doesn't mean absolute hate, as we tend to think of the word. Instead, it's a matter of priority. We must love Christ, and so when we come to him we must desire him above our father, above our mother, above our husband and wife, above our son, above our daughter. We must desire him above our own life. That's what he means. There you have the combing out.

You and I can ask ourselves, 'Do I desire Christ above my own life? That is to say, above my own way of living, living my own life? Do I desire Christ, to follow him, to be his, above that kind of life?' People pursue everything that appeals to their lusts and desires. Do I desire Christ above that? When it comes to relationships, do I desire Christ? Do I desire to have my chief relationship with the Lord?' Yes, above father, mother, husband, wife, son, daughter, and so on. That's how it must be. He must have the first place, that's what he's saying. How can he be your God unless he has the first place? He will not take the second place. No, he won't have that. That's not good enough for the Lord. That's not the true work of God. He must have the first place.

### Bearing the cross of Christ

Christ then says, 'And whosoever doth not bear his cross, and come after me, cannot be my disciple.' You might ask, 'What is that? What does that really mean—bearing a cross, carrying a cross?' I remember being in Jerusalem and people were carrying crosses there at the time of year they call Easter. They stopped at the 'seven stations of the cross', as they called them—seven places where they imagined that Christ stopped on the way to Calvary, so as to imitate all that Christ did. But to carry your cross has nothing at all to do with that.

When a man carried a cross, as Christ carried his cross, it meant he was condemned. The apostle speaks of that: when he takes up his cross, he's condemned as far as the world is concerned. But there's another side to it. He says, 'The world is condemned to me. I no longer live for the world: I live for

Christ.' It's a death sentence, as it were. The world says about the Christian, 'I've lost him. I've lost her. He's gone—she's gone—they've turned their backs on what we used to have together in the world.' The way of living, the way of pleasure, the illicit desires and lusts and all these things: they've turned their backs on all that. 'We can only condemn them. We've put a cross on them. They belong to the condemned, as far as we're concerned.' Of course, you also crucify self. 'I no longer live for myself, for my own worldly self. That is crucified on the cross. The "old man" is on the cross: my worldly heart, my fleshly heart is on the cross. That principle is on the cross. I wish to crucify it, I wish to follow Christ.' If we're not in that position, Christ says, 'You cannot be my disciple.'

There's no compromise when it comes to Christ. You see so much compromise in this world. Churches are compromising because the world has come in like a flood and has begun taking over. It's not a question of grace any longer, it's the world taking over the reins of control. You see people who say they are the children of God and they've changed from how you remember the people of God in the past. You see them and you look at them and you say, 'Well, he professes. He sits at the Lord's Table, but I can't see anything different at all about him. He still has the same kind of lifestyle he used to have. He still spends his time looking at television. I never see him looking at the Bible. I never see him talking about the things of the Lord. I never see him in a prayer meeting. I don't see anything about him that tells me that a good work has begun in his soul. I cannot tell that that man has taken up his cross to follow Christ. What denial is there in his life? What has changed? Nothing, only that he says he's a Christian. That's all. There's a stamp, there's a kind of name attached to him now: that's all there is—a label. But he's just what he was.' So that's what Christ means when he says, 'Whosoever doth not bear his cross, and come after me, cannot be my disciple.' We have to follow Christ fully, not half-way, not part-way.

## 2  Perseverance

### Counting the cost of following Christ

Then in verse 28 Christ continues on the same theme. He asks, 'Which of you, intending to build a tower, sitteth not down first, and counteth the cost, whether he have sufficient to finish it?'

Someone might say, 'Yes, I intend to build a tower. I'm going to build a tower. I'm positive that I'm going to build a tower.' But that's easy to say. It's easy to say to yourself, 'Yes, I'm going to be a Christian. I'm really going to be a Christian, there's no dubiety about it, I'm going to be a child of God, that's what I'm going to be.' But Christ says, 'Sit down first. Count the cost.' Are you going to finish? Is the tower going to be finished? What kind of godliness am I going to have?

I have seen various people making a profession during my life, and some of them give me food for thought. I've seen a man coming out on the side of God's people and mixing with God's people, talking, it would seem, with the kind of language that God's people have. But then, after a while, he went back to his old company in the *bothans*—the drinking dens—telling stories and running down Christians among his companions. That man never recovered the place he had. The world itself condemned him, never mind those who knew the Lord.

Oh, friends, we cannot pretend to have faith. We cannot have half a work. We cannot have a half-finished building. What is a half-finished house? You don't build a house for yourself, and leave it as a half-finished house. Are you going to furnish a half-finished house? Are you going to have shelter in a half-finished house? Are you going to sleep in a half-finished house? What is a half-finished house? It's only something to be mocked by people who call you a fool. That is how Christ speaks here: 'Lest haply, after he hath laid the foundation, and is not able to finish it, all that behold it begin to mock him, saying, This man began to build, and was not able to finish.' What advice does Christ give? 'Well,' he says, 'when you begin to build a tower, you've got to sit down and reckon the cost.' Will you manage to finish the house?

Now, what is my trust in Christ going to be? We must know if it is a trust in Christ, if it is true conversion. Do I believe that he can take me through this life, that he can sanctify me, that he can bring me to heaven, that he can do everything for me, or do I not? What kind of life will I have if I follow him? 'Well, I'm going to suffer something. I'm going to lose certain things. But I'm going to gain Christ. I'm going to gain God. I'm going to gain holiness. I'm going to gain all the gifts that he has laid up for me in the eternal covenant, if I have true faith in him.'

When Christ begins to work in your soul then the devil, of course, seeks to oppose all that. The devil says, 'What about this? You love this too much to give it up. Surely you don't really need to give that up?' But it's a matter of the heart. Do I love the Lord Jesus? Will I place him above all? Will I follow him above all? It doesn't mean that you give up everything in this life to follow Christ. It means that you give up all the things that oppose Christ, that are against Christ. You have to sit down and count the cost.

### Christian warfare

Then Christ comes to the same thing again with a different story, a different parable, and that is the one we have here. He says, 'Or what king, going to make war against another king, sitteth not down first, and consulteth whether he be able with ten thousand to meet him that cometh against him with twenty thousand?' It's a matter of war. 'Oh,' you might say, 'surely conversion—surely believing on Christ as my Saviour—cannot be compared to war!' Yes, it's compared to war. What war is that? The Word of God speaks of 'putting on the whole armour of God'. That is, living the life of grace, not relying on your own strength but his strength. Using his strength—against whom, against what?

Well, first of all, using his strength against the devil. You see, in every diet of worship there are devils. Devils come in to war, to keep your soul from hearing properly and meditating properly, to distract you and take your mind away from the things of the Lord. The devils are warring; Satan at their head is warring. And when you begin following Christ, you begin this war. It means you're on Christ's side and not the other side, and it means you're against Satan, against the devil. It means that you're going to face the devil and he's going to seek to afflict you. Of course he is! And the devil is no weakling. The prince of the power of the air is in control in this world, among people, and to a large extent controlling even our parliament. Mankind lies in sin, people lie in the evil one. He's called the prince of the power of the air. He's called the god of this world. He has men and women in shackles, and they do not know it. They are called the slaves of the devil, the slaves of the evil one, and they don't know it. But when the Holy Spirit works in a soul then that person begins to war: he's free, and he begins to fight, and the devil is the first adversary.

Then there is war against the world. The world is made up of so-called pleasures—activities that are against the Lord. The devil showed Christ these immoral things when he tempted him. These things are called the glory of this world, but they are a false glory. People are ambitious. They want a lot of money, they want power, they want place, they want position. As we are by nature, there are many things in this world that we want, and these fill our heart and soul. But when they oppose Christ, they are 'the world'. It's a principle, and we must fight against it.

And then there is what we call 'the flesh'. That is the principle that is within us. The old nature principle that we took with us into the world—indwelling sin. It's within us.

We've got to war within and without: that's the kind of warfare that we will have. The Lord Jesus says, 'You have to consult.' It's no use just rushing into this war and thinking, 'I don't have to give it any thought.' You just rush in, and some would try and bring you into it through an emotional impulse. That's not good enough. Religion just as a matter of feelings is not good enough. When we come to believe in the Lord Jesus Christ it has to be a matter of principle. The will has to be won. We have to believe. That is the proper way: we have to believe in Christ and entrust ourselves entirely and wholly to him—that's what's demanded.

### False professions

In Bunyan's *Pilgrim's Progress*, when Christian left the City of Destruction, another man, called Pliable, came after him to be with him. And we all know what 'pliable' means. It denotes someone who can be easily influenced—can go this way or that way. Pliable was in a hurry to get to heaven and he was asking Christian about heaven. But Christian had a burden of sin. It was a heavy burden, and it was hanging over him. He had to carry it, but Pliable had no worries about sin. Then Christian and Pliable came to a difficulty—a bog, a mire—and they began to sink there. It was difficult to walk and to make their way. At that very first difficulty, Pliable turned back. He said to Christian, 'You can have heaven for yourself.' Pliable went back to the City of Destruction.

Ah, there are many muddy footsteps of those who came back from that miry place to the city called Destruction. Pliable's journey began, but it never really began—it was only an emotional impulse. People like Pliable *thought* they began, but they never *truly* began, and so they went back. That's why we have to sit down, we have to think this whole thing through. The mind has to be in it.

We have to think it through. It's more than church-going. Church-going is good, friends. To listen to the gospel is good. 'Faith cometh by hearing,' that is, by hearing the gospel. When a congregation listens to the gospel, some of them are going to be converted. We would like to say all of them will be converted, but we cannot say that. Whether it's most of them or a smaller portion, we do not know—that's in God's hands—but some of them are going to be converted. 'Faith cometh by hearing.' So it's good to have people listening to the gospel. But church-going is not salvation. Knowing your Bible, even if you could quote the Bible from end to end, that is not salvation.

People put many, many things in the place of true salvation. If you are a Roman Catholic you just have to put yourself in the hands of the priest, and go to confession. Even though you won't know one millionth part of your sins, you're supposed to confess them all to the priest. Then he's supposed to take away your sins in some way or other. But what is he? He's only a sinful man. You tell him about your sins, your improprieties and your lusts, your immorality—and you're only destroying the man who's listening to you. You're harming the very man who's supposed to take your sins away. These things are not of God: these things are of the devil.

Oh friends, let us not have half a work! King Herod heard John the Baptist gladly and did many things for John's sake. Many people might say, 'Well, there's a change in Herod. This cruel man was living in sin. He's taken his brother's wife and she's now called his wife and that's how he lived. But now he does a lot of things for the sake of John.' But then John said to him that he was living in sin, that the wife he had was not his wife but his brother's wife. Then Herod couldn't take any more of it. John was put into prison and Herod nearly slew him right there and then. His wife made sure later on that John would be beheaded. Herod 'heard John gladly', but it wasn't the true work of God.

Take Felix the governor. He wasn't a king, but he was a governor, a man of great authority. He was a judge. A judge dispenses the law, he speaks of right and wrong. When Paul was brought before him and began speaking of the things of God, the things of the soul, Felix began to tremble. 'Oh,' you might say, 'it's good to tremble under the gospel. That's a good sign!' But friends, many have trembled under the gospel and finished in a lost eternity. But Felix went further than that. Felix said, 'Paul, when I have a convenient season, I will send for you again.' Wasn't that a better sign? But what happened? He left Paul in prison for two years. His interest all disappeared like the morning frost: the sun rises, and it's gone, finished. There was nothing there. Nothing in the soul, just an impulse. Fear does things, emotion does things. But when you believe, the whole person is affected: it's not just feeling. It's true that feeling is in it, but the mind is also in it, the soul is in it, the will is there, the whole person is concerned in it.

What about Demas? We're not too sure about Demas. Demas was a preacher. As far as professing the Lord, he was a preacher, and he was helping Paul. But then Demas went back, 'having loved this present world'. There are some who say, 'Well, it's only that he was afraid of suffering.' Well, yes, the Christian can be afraid of suffering but many Christians who have been afraid of suffering have gone through suffering. The grace of God helped them when they were made martyrs. You understand that they might be afraid, but being afraid doesn't destroy grace. The apostle Paul was afraid—he says that—but he preached, he kept going. But Demas turned back, he left Paul. He forsook the gospel. He 'loved this present world'.

## 2 Perseverance

### Consulting with the Lord

'What king, going to make war against another king, sitteth not down first?' He doesn't just rush into the war: he sits down. What is the problem here? 'Can I with ten thousand soldiers go to meet the enemy who has twenty thousand? He's stronger, far stronger, than I am.' Well, you and I are only weak creatures, weak sinners. Of course the devil is far stronger than we are, of course the world is strong, of course the flesh is strong: this consortium of three armies fighting against us is strong.

David's army once fought three armies at the one time and it was agreed if one side of his army was losing, the other side would help them. A million soldiers came to fight David's army, made up mainly of Syrians, and yet he defeated them. In the Christian warfare, the flesh is strong, lust is strong. The things I see and the things I feel in my mind, in my heart—they're strong, they're fearfully strong. And the world, the things in which I lived and delighted—these are strong. I'm fighting against strong enemies, far too strong for me. That's why Paul says, 'Put ye on the whole armour of God. Live by grace, trust in Christ. Believe in the Lord Jesus Christ, and thou shalt be saved.' We are saved right now, saved immediately, when we believe in Christ with our whole soul. We're saved at that point and saved as we go on. Paul speaks of the One who saved him and was still saving him and would save him, in three tenses—past and present and future. Christ was keeping him, saving him as he went through this world, to bring him into glory. Paul knew that he was weak of himself, but said that he was strong in the Lord. 'When I am weak, then am I strong,' he said. And the Lord said to him, 'My grace is sufficient for thee.' Yes! 'My strength is made perfect in weakness.'

So you need to consult. Are you going to fight? When David went to war he always consulted, if you notice David's history.

He always consulted, and he consulted with God, not just with himself. If you just consult with yourself it's going to get you nowhere. But he would consult with God. The high priest had a breastplate, and in that breastplate were two things. We don't know what their shape was, we can only speculate. They were called the Urim and the Thummim. And Urim and Thummim in Hebrew just mean 'lights and perfections', these two things, in the plural. David would come to the high priest with his problems. He would command the high priest to bring his garment with him, with the breastplate, and he would ask the Lord, 'Will I go to fight against this people, or will I not?' Sometimes the Lord would say, 'Go,' and sometimes the Lord would give him a different kind of advice, like, 'Wait until you hear the sound of the wind in the top of the willow trees, then go.' David always consulted the Lord, and he never lost a battle. In some way or other the Lord always gave him a message using the Urim and the Thummim; somehow the high priest was able to indicate what the Lord was saying by the Urim and the Thummim. We have our Urim and Thummim and we can go to it any day we like: the Word of God. We have the whole Bible. We don't need the high priest with the Urim and the Thummim. We have the Word of God, and it will guide us. The Holy Spirit and the Word of God will guide us in this warfare. We must consult with the Lord.

We can think of another man in Scripture who did exactly the same thing: Joshua. Joshua always consulted with the Urim and Thummim that the high priest had. There was just one time when he didn't. That was when the Israelites said, 'Let us attack Ai. Ai is only a tiny city. We don't need many soldiers.' Joshua didn't go to fight that day; he left it to the others. Nobody consulted the Lord, and so the Israelites went to battle, and they lost. The people of Ai came out and defeated them, and the Israelites felt that defeat so greatly that they were afraid that they wouldn't conquer Canaan. Joshua had to go back to the Lord with repentance and fear because of that. But he would normally consult the Lord.

That's how you've got to do it, friend, if you want to live, if you want to persevere, if you want to live the Christian life: you've got to consult with the Lord. You go to the Word of God, you pray that you would be helped to understand what God is saying to you in the Word. You don't rush through it. You take your time, you look at a verse that seems to apply to your situation, you examine it, you read it carefully, you think over it, you ask the Lord to help you, you consult with the Lord. That's how you have to live.

We read in Scripture of those who seemed to believe and yet they were compared to dogs that had vomited. Dogs vomit to bring up the poison they have taken in. We are told that the dogs then returned to their vomit to eat it up again. That happens in the experience of certain people. They are also compared to the swine that delighted in the mire. A pig might be taken out of the mire and made clean, but the nature of the pig is to go back to the mire. The old nature was still there.

The true Christian—the one who perseveres—wars. He sat down, he consulted. 'Can I do it?' He trusted in Christ. 'Yes, by the grace of God I can do it, and only by the grace of God can I do it.' He goes on. There's no other way. He had to change. He had to be born again. Can the leopard change his spots or the Ethiopian his skin? No, it has to be a change in the heart—a change in the man himself, a radical change. He has to be able to say, 'Christ above all. Christ becomes first in my life. Christ is my head, my God, my Saviour.' That is how it must be.

Then we read: 'Or else, while the other is yet a great way off, he sendeth an ambassage, and desireth conditions of peace.' You see, it's the devil, the world, the flesh. The unconverted person says, 'Oh no, no, I can't engage in that war. I want peace. I want to live in peace with the world, I want to live in peace with the lusts of my heart, I want to live in peace with the devil—even if it is the devil, I just want to live in peace. I don't want to go with God's people. No, I'm sending an ambassage. I don't want this warfare. I'm afraid to engage in it.' He can't manage, he can't win, because the work of God is not in his soul. He didn't begin properly, so he cannot finish properly. That's how the unconverted person is.

## Forsaking everything to follow Christ

The Lord goes on to say, 'So likewise, whosoever he be of you that forsaketh not all that he hath, he cannot be my disciple.' It's reckoned up in that way: forsaking, giving up, giving up everything, being willing to give up everything for Christ. Christ is all. Now, the Lord doesn't mean that you give up your wife and your husband and your daughter and all your other relations. But it means Christ is first in your life. That's how it has to be.

Notice how the Lord ends this passage. He says, 'Salt is good: but if the salt have lost his savour, wherewith shall it be seasoned? It is neither fit for the land, nor yet for the dunghill; but men cast it out.' The salt they had was rock salt: it was mixed with grit and sand, not the pure salt that we have. If it was left out and exposed, it could be leached by the sun and by the rain. Through time the salt would be leached out and all you would have left would be the soil or sand, or whatever it was that was mixed with the salt. It wasn't true soil, so it was unfit for the land. It was unfit even for the dunghill. The dunghill was used to manure the land, but the grit wasn't fit even for the dunghill. It was only fit to be cast out, to be thrown away.

That's how the Lord speaks of those who say they are Christians, who say they have begun, who say they are saved, who say that Christ is their Saviour, but yet nothing has changed. It is all just as it was before. There's a label of Christian profession on them. Nobody knows they are Christians until they see them sitting at the Lord's Table. But you don't know them as Christians by their conduct, you don't know them by their speech, you can't tell in any way. Their wives don't see any change in them, their husbands don't see any change, their families don't see any change. Nobody sees any change. They're just as they were. They're just like the salt that lost its savour: not true salt at all. Only a pretend salt. There's no saltness in them. They're not even fit for the land or the dunghill. They're just to be cast out.

People say, 'Well, what a sermon Christ preached!' Friends, if Christ preached a sermon along these lines in our land today, the people in most of our churches would reject him. They wouldn't accept that kind of talk because it doesn't accord with their ideas. But what matters is the truth, and you and I are faced with the truth. You and I have precious souls and we are on the way to eternity. Never mind what people think: it's what Christ says that matters. If Christ says these things, let us believe Christ. He left this writing for you and me. It's for you and me to read and to understand, and to make use of it, and to believe in him for the true salvation of our souls.

May he bless it to us. Let us pray.

## Concluding prayer

O gracious Lord and Saviour, we beseech thee to be with us, to give us to trust in thyself, that we may have our hope and confidence in thee. There is no one else, there is no other way. People seek other ways. People seek a thousand other ways, but they do not seek for Christ who says, 'I am the way, the truth, the life,' and if any man enter in by Christ, that he would in no wise be cast out. Give us to be among those, we pray thee.

Grant to bless us as we part one from another. Do not part from us, we beseech thee. Do not let the devil take our thoughts upon thy Word from us, but grant that thy Holy Spirit would bless these things to our souls. Give us to think of eternity, give us to think of our great need, give us to think of why we were created. Take away our sins, even the sins of worship. For Christ's sake. Amen.

# 3

# Nicodemus

7th January 2018, Lord's Day morning, Leverburgh

*There was a man of the Pharisees, named Nicodemus, a ruler of the Jews: the same came to Jesus by night, and said unto him, Rabbi, we know that thou art a teacher come from God: for no man can do these miracles that thou doest, except God be with him.*
John 3:1–2

THIS is the Gospel according to John. We have four accounts of the Gospel. The Lord could have given it all to us with one account but in his wisdom he saw it appropriate to give us four accounts of the Gospel. It is as if you had four people standing around the cross and in different places. Though they all see it a little differently, yet their accounts all dovetail together. John was the last of the four, he wrote well after the rest, and he completed many things left unsaid by the other three. In the infinite wisdom of God, we have this Gospel placed before us in that manner.

We have here the Word of God, the infallible Word of God which cannot lie. Many, many people have sought to show that the Word of God was wrong here and wrong there. Well, that's what the devil will seek to do. The devil brought lies into the world, deceiving Eve by making her distrust the Word of

God. The devil will seek to make us mistrust the Word of God too. You see, if this not the Word of God, if it is not the truth, how can we rest our souls upon it? The devil sees that, so he sets out to try and make people to believe that it is not trustworthy, so that no soul will rest upon it.

The devil uses many methods. In olden days some zealots collected Bibles and burnt them, and burnt those who would dare to translate the Bible into different languages. Now in modern days we have perhaps two hundred different versions of God's Word in English. Men change things in God's Word to suit themselves. They change things to suit their theology. They change things to make them suit the world. They miss out some things and add in other things. But it is the Word of God that we have.

Christ said to the apostles before he left them, that he was giving them the Holy Spirit to teach them and to show them the truth. He said that the Holy Spirit would bring to their remembrance all that ever he taught them. So, after Christ went to heaven, they were enabled to teach infallibly, to teach without mistakes. They had made mistakes before that, but now, after he rose, the Holy Spirit was with them and in them, and enabled them to teach the gospel infallibly, with no mistakes. And so we have the gospel set before us.

It doesn't matter what the devil does, God will use his Word to bring in his own people wherever they are. Every one of them will believe that this is the true, infallible Word of God. 'He that cometh unto God must believe that he is.' Yes, so we must believe. The devil believes that. The Bible is true, the devil believes it. He trembles, because it is true, and he knows it. He knows that he will finish up in hell. But the gospel is given so that we might believe that this is the Word of God, leading us to Christ—that by believing in Christ we might be saved.

# 3  Nicodemus

It says here that this was a man of the Pharisees, named Nicodemus, and that he came to Jesus by night. We should like to take up two things as the Lord will enable us. First of all, the fact that Nicodemus came by night. Then secondly, a word about the man who was named Nicodemus.

It is John alone of the four writers of the Gospels who speaks of Nicodemus. Nobody else speaks about him, just John: the rest missed him out. But the Holy Spirit gave it to John many, many years later, to speak about Nicodemus, the man who was with Joseph of Arimathaea, taking the body of Christ to the grave. Every time John mentions Nicodemus in this Gospel he mentions that he came by night. As if to say, 'Well, there is something special about this man. This was Nicodemus, who came by night. That was when he came: by night.' So we should like to say a little about that, and then about the man, Nicodemus himself.

## 1. Nicodemus came by night

The name Nicodemus means 'victory of the people' or 'innocent blood'. We do not know anything special we should attach to that. We do not know, but we do wonder that anybody should be called 'innocent blood'. It's such an unusual name. The man named Nicodemus came by night.

God made the world, and when God spoke of the days of creation, he spoke of the evening and of the morning making up one day. It all began with the darkness. God said on the first day, 'Let there be light.' So, because light was created on the first day, he could speak of night and day on that first day and on every day. He spoke of what was made up of an evening and a morning. Not a morning and an evening, but an evening and a morning.

Nicodemus came by night. We don't know why he came by night. He was a ruler, he was among the highest of the land, he was a member of the Sanhedrin, the body that ruled spiritual matters of the land. He was a Pharisee. He was the master in Israel, the one who was in charge, as it were, of Bible teaching in the land. But he came by night. Was it because of his reputation? We know that the apostle Paul, at times, spoke to some of the great people privately because of their reputation. We know Paul did that, but was that why Nicodemus came by night? Or was it because Christ had more time at night? Whatever, Nicodemus had more time than Christ. Was it just an opportunity of talking in private without others being there?

Some of God's people have come to know Christ by night. I knew a man in my own congregation who went to bed, afraid that he was going to a lost eternity. But when he woke up in the morning he had the liberty of God in his soul. Many a precious soul has come to Christ by night. Many, many! It is good to have a night like that in your experience, if you have it. The tragedy is if we have neither night nor day in which we came to know Christ as our Saviour. That is the tragedy, if that is how we are. And it is a tragedy if that is how we are going to enter eternity, without having minutes, without having hours, without having a portion of time in which we came to know Christ in this world. It would be better never to have known the world—better never to have opened our eyes—better never to have seen the light of the sun—if that is how things are going to be. But friends, seek the Lord by day or by night. Seek him above everything else.

Then there was another night. It was at night that Judas Iscariot betrayed the Lord Jesus. Judas came to him when he was in the garden of Gethsemane. He came with torches, and Judas kissed him and he betrayed him. He pointed him out to those who were with him. He did that at night. Yes, it was at night, and Judas went to the eternal night, to the blackness of darkness forever.

It was evening time when Peter denied his Lord. He went out and he wept. Peter wouldn't forget that: never, never, never! It would leave a mark upon him. He would be feeling it all the time, as long as he lived, that he had denied his Lord three times after saying that he would never forsake the Lord, even though all men should forsake him. He said that he would follow Jesus even unto death.

There is time for everything, and the Lord points that out to us in his own Word. We have it in the book of Ecclesiastes, chapter 3, where we read, 'To every thing there is a season, and a time to every purpose under the heaven: a time to be born, and a time to die; a time to plant, and a time to pluck up that which is planted; a time to kill, and a time to heal; a time to break down, and a time to build up; a time to weep, and a time to laugh; a time to mourn, and a time to dance; a time to cast away stones, and a time to gather stones together; a time to embrace, and a time to refrain from embracing; a time to get, and a time to lose; a time to keep, and a time to cast away; a time to rend, and a time to sew; a time to keep silence, and a time to speak; a time to love, and a time to hate; a time of war, and a time of peace.'

There is a season, a time for everything, for all of these different things that come into our experience. It's wonderful if a time comes into our experience when we go to meet Christ, when we are on the road with Christ, when we spend the night just ourselves with the Lord. You see, friends, we have to meet Christ. Every one of us has to meet Christ. Christ will be the judge at the great white throne. Christ is the One who glorified the justice of God in his sufferings, as it was never glorified anywhere else. Christ has therefore been exalted. He's made the judge of the living and of the dead. So Christ will meet me.

I will have to give account for my ministry and my life, and you will have to give account of your own life at the great white throne.

We have the gospel here, the 'good news' as it means, so that we would seek Christ as Saviour to save us from our sins, while he may be found. He can only be found on mercy's ground. Oh, to find Christ in this world! The Word of God shows us Christ, points us to Christ, tells us of him. And he's there, as it were, using the Word to draw sinners to himself, to his feet, so that they may speak to him and to listen to him. What do you say when you speak to him? To speak together with Christ is such a great privilege. And, you know, to meet Christ as your Saviour is the most blessed experience that we can ever have. No angel can have that blessed experience. It's not for angels: it's only for sinners who come to Christ and trust in him and have their sins forgiven and taken away. So Christ becomes our Lord and Saviour and friend and lover for ever and for ever. Oh friends, make use of the Word of God. Make use of it!

## 2. Nicodemus

Secondly, we have something about the man himself. This man was named Nicodemus, and he was a ruler of the Jews. He was a Pharisee. He was in the Sanhedrin, and he is called a master. And when he began to argue, Jesus said to him, 'Art thou a master of Israel, and knowest not these things?' He was a master. That is, he was over the teaching of Scripture in the land. He was the teacher.

This was the man who came to Christ Jesus. He wasn't a believer. He wasn't born again when he came. He didn't know salvation when he came, even though he was, as it were, the professor over all the other teachers in the land. He didn't know the Saviour. He didn't have salvation in his soul. That shows how low things were in the land.

Christ called him a master. Nicodemus knew that Christ was called 'Master'. The word 'Rabbi' or 'Rabboni' is used for 'Master'. When Nicodemus came to Christ he said unto him, 'Rabbi.' Now, Christ had never been to college or university— he had no special education or training. But before Nicodemus could become the master in Israel he must have studied under great teachers. This was a man who was highly educated, and highly taught in the things of Scripture. And yet when he comes to Christ, he calls Christ 'Master'. That needed a lot of humility in a ruler, a Pharisee, a member of the Sanhedrin, one of the élite of the land, one at the very highest, one of the most respected. I wonder if we have humility to come to Christ.

Nicodemus was something like the other ruler, the young man who was rich, who came running to Christ and knelt before him, and asked him what he needed do to be saved. Nicodemus came likewise in great humility. Wonderful, wonderful humility! Yet Christ never calls him 'Rabbi' or 'Rabboni' or 'master'. Everybody else would call him that. He called Christ that; others called Christ that, but Christ never gave Nicodemus that title, although he was the master of masters in the land. Christ was going to take the position that belonged to himself in dealing with this man. No matter how high the man was as a teacher in Israel, he was now meeting the supreme teacher, the supreme Rabbi.

When Nicodemus came, this was what struck him, 'Thou art a teacher come from God.' It did not only strike himself, for he says, '*We* know.' There were others as well. '*We* know that thou art a teacher come from God.' Not a teacher that came from the school of Hillel, or any of the other great teachers in Israel, but a teacher who came from God. That was your college, that was your master. The reason was, 'For no man can do these miracles that thou doest, except God be with him.'

The miracles. We read in the book of Isaiah of the signs that God would give when Christ would come, so that people would know that he came from God. He would give the blind their sight. That may mean little to you today, but think of the man born blind in John 9. That man said that since the world began, it was never heard that a man born blind had his sight restored or given to him. Christ healed the man born blind. He healed the man born deaf. He restored those who were lame and those who were maimed, those who lacked limbs. He took the dead and brought them back alive.

Another sign given by Isaiah was, 'And the gospel was preached unto the poor.' It was preached to those who were made poor by the Holy Spirit. That was one of the marks of the Messiah: preaching to the poor.

Nicodemus said, 'We know that thou art a teacher come from God: for no man can do these miracles that thou doest, except God be with him. So we know God is with you.' He didn't yet know that not only was God *with* Christ but God was *in* Christ—that Christ was God—when he came to Christ. The Holy Spirit did that: he brought him to Christ. Did he bring *you* to Christ? Will he ever bring you to Christ? Will you ever come to believe in him and trust in him, as this man did?

Then we read about the teaching that Christ gave to Nicodemus, the master. Christ as the great Master was now going to teach him. We think, 'Well, what can Christ teach him? Nicodemus is a master in Israel. He'll know a great deal of the Bible.' The Old Testament was what they had. He would know a great deal of it of off by heart, and he would know about the law. This man had been trained so much that he was set above every other teacher. What was Christ going to teach him? Well, he was going to teach him about the new birth: being born again. 'Jesus answered and said unto him: Verily, verily, I say unto thee, Except a man be born again, he cannot see the kingdom of God.'

'Verily, verily.' Now, when you and I pray, we normally finish the prayer with 'Amen'. 'Amen' doesn't mean 'the end'. 'Amen' doesn't mean your prayer is finished. The man of God doesn't finish his prayer when he gets on his feet after praying. He should have a prayerful spirit. He can pray with ejaculations, firing arrows to heaven as he goes through the day, his thoughts going to God continually. 'Amen' doesn't mean the end or 'it's finished'. Amen is another way of saying, 'It is true.' What you have just said in your prayer, you are now witnessing at the very end that it was true.

What kind of prayer do we offer up to God? At the end will we say 'Amen'? Are we saying to God, 'Everything I asked was true. The part that I asked for, to glorify thee, was true.' Leave your 'Amen' out of it, if it's not true.

Now, when Christ says, 'Verily, verily,' it is as much as to say, 'Amen, amen.' When we say 'Amen' it's at the end of a prayer. But here is someone—Jesus—and he's unique. He's the great Master, the great teacher. And when he speaks he very often says, 'Amen, amen,' even before he speaks, before he says anything else. 'Verily, verily': 'it is the truth, it is the truth'. 'Amen, amen.' That is to certify everything he is going to say to Nicodemus, or to anyone else to whom he is speaking, 'This is the absolute truth of God; there's nothing but truth there.' It is so solemn. 'Amen, amen,' or, 'Verily, verily,' as it is translated into the English.

'I say unto thee, Except a man be born again, he cannot see the kingdom of God.' That must have stunned Nicodemus. He said to Christ, 'How can a man be born again when he is old? Can he enter the second time into his mother's womb and be born?' We might say, 'Surely a man like Nicodemus would understand what Christ was talking about: a new birth. A child coming into the world out of the womb, comes out of darkness and into the world. Surely when Christ said, "Ye must be born again," Nicodemus should understand.' The very books that Nicodemus was used to—the Talmud, the commentary that the Jews had—actually spoke of a new birth.

But here is the thing. The Jews believe in a new birth, but in the Jewish mind, Christ was going to come for their sakes. Jews were already going to heaven, except for really bad Jews—sinners and tax-gatherers. They all thought they were going to heaven, except for exceptional sinners (they used the word 'sinners' for them) and tax gatherers. The tax gatherer, who gathered money for Rome, was thought of as a very, very evil man—a liar, a cheat. And they very often were actually so. They added money to the tax for themselves and cheated people, and so their word was never accepted at court. No Jewish court would have a tax gatherer as a witness. They were reckoned to be rogues. In Jewish eyes, sinners and publicans were not going to heaven. But they believed that Jews in general were going to heaven. They were the children of Abraham. They had the prophecies. God had been their God. When you have a Pharisee, he was a super-Jew. When you have one who belonged to the Sanhedrin, the court that rules spiritual matters, he too was a super-Jew. And when you had a man who was the supreme teacher of Scripture in the land, who would dare to say that he was not going to the kingdom of heaven?

The Jews speak of being born again, but for the Jews, being born again meant a Gentile, a non-Jew, coming to be a Jew. When a Gentile came to be a Jew he had to be baptised. He had water sprinkled on him by the priest. He was washed— that's how they put it—washed from his Gentile past, from his Gentile being, and brought into Jewry and then he became a

Jew. He was born again. That's the only way which Nicodemus could understand it. To speak of a Jew being born again—to speak of a ruler being born again, a member of the Sanhedrin being born again, the master teacher in Israel being born again—that didn't make sense to Nicodemus. Ah, well, you could say to many in our own land, maybe to the Archbishop of Canterbury, 'Ye must be born again.' He wouldn't believe you either. He thinks he has it all, the head of the Church of England, and yet his manner and his speech, they betray him and show what he is. And there are others too, of the same kind.

Christ says, 'Except a man be born again, he cannot see the kingdom of God.' Now, how can you see the kingdom of God? How can you see the kingdom over which Christ rules, to become a citizen of it? He doesn't mean seeing it from the outside. He means experiencing it, seeing it from the inside. Unless you are born again into the kingdom, you cannot see it. You won't understand the things of the kingdom until you're in it. You won't understand what it means to love God. You might speak of him, but you won't know him. You won't understand the fellowship of Christ. You won't understand sanctification. You won't understand the meaning of the praise and the worship that belongs to heaven. You won't understand. Your eyes won't be open. No, they won't be open, but you'll be like one of these small animals—cats or dogs—which are born with their eyes closed for a while. You won't understand because you won't see.

You won't see unless you are born again. It's no use people thinking that they're on the way to heaven just because they go to the Lord's Table. They think they're not sinners any longer; they're on the way to glory. But they're not on the way to glory. It's no use thinking you're in the kingdom just because you become a member in a church. No, friends. 'Ye *must* be born again.' Three times Jesus raises it, speaking to this man. Three times! 'Ye must be born again.' And the 'must' is so important. It is a 'must'. There is no side-tracking, it's a 'must'. And except you and I be born again, we shall not see—we will not experience—what it is to be in the kingdom of God.

Again, when Christ spoke to Nicodemus about it, he said, 'Except a man be born again, he cannot *enter* the kingdom of God'. He's now making it more evident. This seeing is really entering. Nicodemus cannot enter. The master is an outsider. Oh, what humiliating teaching! The teaching of Christ is telling him that he's outside the kingdom. That he—Nicodemus—with all his profession, is outside.

There are people who cannot tolerate it if you say to them that they are sinners, that they are going to hell, that they are totally unworthy. They cannot stand it. They cannot endure it, because they are not humble enough to accept the truth before God. Amen, amen; verily, verily. They are not humble enough before God to accept that.

Oh friends, accept all that God says, all that Christ says. It's for the good of your own soul and my soul. I knew somebody who told me of a police sergeant who used to attend the Church of Scotland. The man knew this sergeant very well and he often asked him, 'How did the Sabbath go?' And the sergeant would say something about the sermon. Then one day the sergeant said that the minister was leaving. The old minister went, and after a while a new minister came along—a young man. And the sergeant was asked on the Monday, 'How was the sermon yesterday?' 'Oh,' he said, 'the new minister's a young man and he had the cheek to tell people older than himself that they were all sinners.' The cheek to tell them that they were all sinners? You see, the sergeant needed humility, but he didn't have it. Later on, that policeman came to appreciate the minister, but not then.

## 3  Nicodemus

Nicodemus says, 'How can a man be born when he is old? Can he enter the second time into his mother's womb and be born?' Jesus answered, 'Verily, verily, I say unto thee, Except a man be born of water and of the Spirit, he cannot enter into the kingdom of God.' You notice that Jesus says again, 'Amen, amen.' Now he's adding to his teaching. He's teaching this man, because this man is but a child. Jesus is emphasising again, the second time and again a third time, 'Except a man be born again.'

Now Jesus speaks of water and of the Spirit. Nicodemus would recognise the part about water. He knew that a Gentile was washed when he became a Jew. They called it washing. The priest sprinkled the Gentile with water—that was part of the initiation—and the Gentile then became a Jew. He was washed from his old heathen life.

Christ adds to that. He said, 'Except a man be born again of water *and of the Holy Spirit.*' He's going to honour the Holy Spirit. He teaches that what is born of the flesh—in the natural way—is flesh. Our children are of the flesh. They're born in a natural way. But that which is born of the Spirit is spirit. They must be born of the Spirit in order to enter the kingdom of God. That is what Jesus is teaching—that being born again is the same as being born of the Spirit, of the Holy Ghost. That was seen to be something new.

Just think of what Jesus is saying. 'Marvel not that I said unto thee.' Nicodemus would marvel but Jesus said, 'Marvel not that I said unto thee, Ye must be born again.' Now, Nicodemus was a Pharisee. The Pharisees were seeking to combat the Greeks and the Romans, who were bringing in idolatry and idolatrous customs. The Pharisees' aim was to separate themselves from them. They wanted pure worship. They believed they were going to heaven, and when they became Pharisees, they became super-Jews. They had no problem about going to heaven. They believed they were better than other people—they were the super-Jews, the separate ones.

What did the Pharisees seek to do? They made themselves better and better. How could they do that? They didn't have the Holy Spirit living in their hearts, they weren't really true believers. They made themselves better, but it was only a matter of outward show—by good works, by standing in the porch of the temple, and also, as Christ said, by making long prayers. Everyone heard them making long prayers, full of quotations for everyone to hear. People would say, 'These godly, godly men!' When the Pharisees went into the temple, they gave a gift, making sure there were lots of spectators to see them handing over their gifts. They were out seeking to have more praise from people. The only way they knew was to do things. For example, they wore phylacteries, boxes containing texts that they bound to their foreheads and arms when they prayed, but they made the phylacteries 'broad', broader than what other people wore, so that they would be seen. Then people would say, 'He's a Pharisee. He's a super-Jew. He's a godly, godly man.'

But it was all outward. Christ said the Pharisees were like whited sepulchres, and they went to worship as whited sepulchres, so that nobody would touch them inadvertently and make them be defiled. They're like sepulchres, Christ said, and inside there's only the bones of dead men. That's all. They're walking tombs, walking sepulchres. They didn't know it, but that's what they were.

So what was Christ doing to this tree, with its branches and its outward fruit? He was cutting the tree down, bringing the tree down to the ground, destroying it. Pharisaism had to be destroyed in the heart of Nicodemus. 'Ye must be born again.' Christ was using the language which described the Gentile becoming a Jew. So he was saying to Nicodemus, 'You are a great sinner. You must become a believer in me—a believer in me as your Saviour. Ye must be born again. The teaching—the new teaching, the deep teaching—the Spirit will teach you.' Nicodemus was like a tiny child who knew nothing before the great Master. Ah, that the great Master would teach us, for we too must be born again!

Christ says here: 'Except a man be born of water and of the Spirit. … That which is born of the flesh is flesh; and that which is born of the Spirit is spirit.' He speaks of the Spirit teaching this man about the Holy Spirit. Nicodemus had heard very, very little about the Holy Spirit among the Pharisees.

Christ says, 'The wind bloweth.' The word for 'wind' and the word for 'spirit' are exactly the same word. So you can say 'the spirit' or 'the wind'. 'The wind bloweth where it listeth.' It blows where it wills.

'Thou hearest the sound thereof, but canst not tell whence it cometh, and whither it goeth: so is everyone that is born of the Spirit.' The wind, the Spirit, are silent, or they *can* be silent. The wind can be so silent that you don't even hear it. The wind can also be like a hurricane so that you *do* hear. You hear the sound thereof. But 'the wind bloweth where it listeth'. We don't know what direction: today it may have changed to the west, yesterday it may have been to the east. We don't know. It changes, it circles around us, it may come from there and go to here. We can't control it though, either the wind or the Holy Spirit.

The Holy Spirit blows as he desires. He can come into our congregations. Maybe he comes very quietly, just enough that a soul there begins to listen for eternity. It is so quiet, and the only thing he knows is that the Word of God is drawing him. He wants to hear more about Christ. He wants to hear more about salvation. He wants to hear more about being born again. He wants to hear more about what it is to believe, what it is to have faith.

Another soul might be there and when the wind blows, it's like a hurricane. The effect is so great, he cries, 'I'm going to a lost eternity. A lost eternity! Where is Christ? Where can I find him? What will I do?' There is a great noise in the soul. It is the sound of the voice of the Holy Spirit, the voice of God speaking to the soul. When the children of Israel heard the voice of God from the mount when Moses was there, they couldn't endure it. They couldn't endure the voice of God when he spoke the Ten Commandments from the mount. And Moses said, 'I exceedingly fear and quake.' The sinner says, 'Where is the Saviour? Where is the priest? Where is the blood, that I might be saved? Oh, show me, tell me anything at all!'

What must we do then? You must do as Nicodemus did. We must go just to Christ. 'Thou art the teacher sent from God. Be my teacher. Lead me, O Lord, in thy path. Show me thyself. Show me thyself as the way of life, as Saviour, as God, as my Redeemer, as the One who can take away my sins. Shew me thyself. Let the Holy Spirit show thee to me, that I might know thee as my God and be with thee for evermore, for this life passes.'

Yes, the wind is invisible, and the Holy Spirit works invisibly. Who sees the Holy Spirit? Who knows what is taking place in your heart? He's invisible because he's the Holy Spirit. And he's not predictable: you cannot tell him what to do. The Holy Spirit is God, and he's the one who shows Christ to your soul. When he comes to your soul, you see Christ. He shows you Christ. You see Christ, you believe Christ, and Christ will become your Redeemer. It's beautiful, mysterious.

How can these things be? How? That was the great question. Did Nicodemus come to know the answer? Yes, he came to know the answer. He came to trust in Christ as his Saviour. He was a secret disciple. Just think of it: a ruler of the Jews, a Pharisee, a member of the Sanhedrin, the ruling council in spiritual matters—a disciple of Jesus!

Nicodemus was a disciple in secret to start with. But then when Christ died and the disciples fell back and were afraid to come out, Nicodemus came out into the open. He and Joseph of Arimathaea took the body of Christ from the cross. They took him from the cross, they took away the spikes, the nails, and they covered the body with ointments—pounds of precious ointments. And they wound him round and round with the winding sheet, and they carried him and laid him in a new tomb, in which never man had yet been laid.

Nicodemus did that. He's in glory today and he'll never, never forget that he met Christ during the night. And he'll never forget the night when he took the body of Christ down from the cross. That had to be done before six in the evening. He'll never forget that evening when he and Joseph carried the body of the Redeemer and laid him in the sepulchre. He'll never forget that. That was part of his experience.

Do you have any experience regarding Christ? Any experience at all? What matters is not having the body of Christ but believing in Christ, because that is what comes of being born again. May that be your portion and may that be my portion.

May God bless his Word.

## Concluding prayer

Gracious and glorious Lord we beseech thee to bless us. Give us to glorify thy great name in our hearts. Lead and guide us on this Sabbath day and grant the Holy Spirit to be among us. Grant the Holy Spirit to show Christ to our soul, our precious, precious soul, lest we perish without Jesus, without salvation. Bless our children, bless our families, bless our near and dear ones, we beseech thee. Oh, grant to plough the earth out of the furrows, plough the soil and plant and put thy seed there, in a prepared soil. Glorify thy great name. Go before us this Sabbath day. Cleanse us. For Jesus' sake. Amen.

# 4

# Three approaches by the woman of Canaan

7ᵗʰ January 2018, Lord's Day evening, Leverburgh

*And, behold, a woman of Canaan came out of the same coasts, and cried unto him, saying, Have mercy on me, O Lord, thou son of David; my daughter is grievously vexed with a devil. But he answered her not a word. And his disciples came and besought him, saying, Send her away; for she crieth after us. But he answered and said, I am not sent but unto the lost sheep of the house of Israel. Then came she and worshipped him, saying, Lord, help me. But he answered and said, It is not meet to take the children's bread, and to cast it to dogs. And she said, Truth, Lord: yet the dogs eat of the crumbs which fall from their masters' table. Then Jesus answered and said unto her, O woman, great is thy faith: be it unto thee even as thou wilt. And her daughter was made whole from that very hour.*
Matthew 15:22–28

WE should like to look at these words, seeking help from the Most High, the only one who can bless the Word to our souls. We should seek to look at them prayerfully, looking to himself. First of all, the background regarding this woman. And secondly, this woman coming to Christ seeking his help, and how she came to him with three approaches.

## 1. The woman and her background

We read in verse 21, 'Jesus went thence, and departed into the coasts of Tyre and Sidon.' Here is something very, very unusual. The Lord's ministry was within Judaea—the tiny country of Judaea. He spent his whole life there except at one stage when he was a babe in Egypt. But now in his three-year ministry he is confined to the land except for this one time, when he went to the very boundary of Tyre and Sidon. He went there, as the Bible speaks of it in another place, 'not desiring that any should know about it'. He went there in a private, secret manner, as it were. But God had a purpose there and it wasn't going to remain private and secret. It was the purpose of God that Christ and this woman would meet. This woman did not belong to the Jews in any way whatsoever. That reminds us that the gospel is not just for Jews but for non-Jews, for Gentiles as well as Jews—for such as we are, as well as for the descendants of Abraham.

So here we see Christ in the coasts, on the border of Tyre and Sidon. 'Behold, a woman of Canaan came out of the same coasts.' She was there at the very border with Tyre and Sidon. Elsewhere we are told that she was a Syrophoenician—that just tells us the nations from which she came. We are also told that she was a Canaanite. She belonged to the land of Canaan. She was descended from the Canaanites, who were conquered by Joshua, and many of them were destroyed and cast out. She was a descendant of these people. She's also called a Gentile. She was just an outsider, one who didn't belong to the Jews. See the wonder of it! The Canaanites were descendants of Ham, the son of Noah, and they were cursed away back in the days of Noah. But that judgment wouldn't take place until many, many years later. Hundreds and hundreds of years later,

## 4  Three approaches by the woman of Canaan

in fact, when they were so full of iniquity, so full of idolatry, so full of the sins of Sodom and Gomorrah. When the time came that God meant to wipe out the Canaanites, he used Joshua to do that, and he gave the Israelites the land. However, there were some Canaanites who weren't wiped out. There were some who persisted, and this woman belonged to them. You see, she had to be saved. She was in the eternal covenant. She was in the Book of Life.

God looks after providence—who we come from, who our parents are, where we are born, how we are born. He looks after all these things in his own wonderful way. We should seek to find out about his hand in our own experience and history. We can trace that if we go back just a little in the history of our own Long Island. Just over two or three hundred years ago, our ancestors here worshipped idols. They used to pour milk down into fissures and cracks in the rocks, worshipping the gods underground, the fairies and such like. They used to pour their ale into the water so that the god of the seas would bless the fishing. They were a darkened people, without God, without hope. And God in his mercy sent the gospel into the island. We tend to forget that. Many are celebrating at the end of the year, and they have forgotten all about the past. They are celebrating they do not know what. Being joyful wasn't because of the end of a year; it wasn't because of the beginning of a year. Why were they joyful? Why not be joyful during the year, during the summer? Why be joyful in winter? It all goes back to the worship of certain gods at that time of the year. However, you see, salvation can reach the darkest of the dark. It reached this Canaanite woman. It can reach the greatest sinner. Ah, that's how the apostle Paul thought of it, who called himself 'the chief of sinners'. But he could say, 'I obtained mercy.'

This woman happened to have a daughter who was possessed by a devil. People wonder about devil possession. The devil moves many people. The devils come and go. They drew the hearts of men and women. They have access, you see. But God doesn't usually give a person over to the devil in this way to the point that it can be said that 'he's devil possessed'. That is when the devil says, 'He's mine. I'll stay here. I won't move. I'll use his whole mind. I'll use his mouth. I'll use everything he does. He's mine completely and he's so taken over, so possessed, so enslaved, that he's always as if hell was there already.' People wonder about that, when it's obvious that in the days of Christ the devil was given special permission to possess men and women. Christ had to be tested. He came into the world to conquer the devil, and the devil was given great permission to take people over, to possess them. And it may be that it wasn't just in Judaea. In a certain measure it may have been all over. But the gospel tends to drive the devil back. The gospel tends to change the morality of a people, to change nations. Even if people are unconverted, the gospel has power among them. But in the days of Christ, it is undoubted that many in Judaea were given over to possession, and Christ was there to fight the devil and to overcome the devil in that way, as well as in every other way.

This lady had a daughter who was devil-possessed. She lived there on the very edge of Judaea, where Tyre and Sidon were. And somehow she heard that Christ was in that house. We don't know how she heard that, because he intended, as far as we can see, that no one would know it. But why did he go there? What was his purpose? She found out. She came. That's how the gospel works. You might come to church, and you might have no thought in the world about the salvation of your soul. Not one single thought! You might be entirely taken up by the things of the world and your pride in your person and your pride in your thoughts. Nobody knows. You're on your own and you think what you think, and you have your own imagination, and you can go around the whole world in your imagination. But then you hear something. It fastens on you,

# 4  Three approaches by the woman of Canaan

it goes home to your heart, and from that moment you cannot get away from the gospel until it takes you over. Chains are broken, bands are broken, prison doors are opened.

## 2. The woman's first approach

The woman made three approaches to Christ. In verse 22 we read about the first of these. 'And, behold, a woman of Canaan came out of the same coasts, and cried unto him, saying, Have mercy on me, O Lord, thou son of David; my daughter is grievously vexed with a devil.'

The term 'son of David' was a Messianic term. The Jews used it when they spoke about the coming of the Messiah. They knew he was a descendant of David. The Jews would call a descendant a son, even if he was a grandson or a great-grandson. It didn't matter how far you went: a descendant of David could be called a son of David. But here was the special Son of David—the Messiah.

'Have mercy upon me, thou son of David.' The Canaanite woman, the woman who belonged to those who were to have been wiped out, is crying to the Jewish Messiah. Ah, you think, surely she has no right to pray, 'Have mercy on me, thou son of David.' Just imagine, a Canaanite, a woman who belonged to these dark, dark people! Imagine her coming shouting after Christ! Ah friends, think of this before you realise how dark we are and how black we are.

'Have mercy on me, O Lord, thou son of David; my daughter is grievously vexed with a devil'. That's it! That was her prayer. No more, just that. It was short. When the Holy Spirit begins working in your heart, it doesn't mean that you start to say long prayers. Oh, no, it's usually short prayers. And they are usually prayers that have no proper order. You don't know big, long texts to string together. You don't have that when the

Holy Spirit begins to work. You're in an agony of soul, you just come with what you have—your bits and pieces of thought, and your words. You don't worry about how you frame them together. The agony of soul is what takes over. You come in that way.

See how Christ answers. 'He answered her not a word.' Not a single word! He didn't say 'yes' or 'no'. He didn't heal, he didn't cast out the devil, he didn't answer at all. Now, there are some who seek the Lord and they say, 'The Lord is not answering. The Lord is not having mercy on me. The Lord means me to cease crying.' But are you going to cease? It is the Holy Spirit working in the soul. So you cannot cease, you cannot stop. If you're able to stop, you are just going to forget it all and go back. But that is not the work of the Holy Spirit. You may feel, 'He'll never listen to me, he won't have mercy upon me.' But when the Holy Spirit works, you'll say, 'I will cry for mercy up to the very grave. Up to the very end. It's what I need, what I desperately desire.'

'But he answered her not a word.' Did you ever have that kind of prayer? Did you ever seem to come up against a wall, as if there was nobody there to hear you? God didn't answer. Was he listening? Did he hear? He didn't answer.

Then we read that his disciples spoke to Christ. And they came with *their* kind of desire. What they said was, 'Send her away; for she crieth after us.' They didn't say, 'She crieth after thee, after thyself.' No, they could hear her crying to Christ, and it wearied them. But her crying didn't weary the Lord. No, friends, prayer doesn't weary the Lord when it is meant, when it is in truth. It may seem that he does not answer, but prayer never wearies him. He's the One who hears, and he is the One who answers as he sees fit. How he answered at this time was by being silent. Yet when he is silent, it's a silence that is not going to make her stop. The Holy Spirit makes her go on.

# 4 Three approaches by the woman of Canaan

Christ spoke to the disciples, who said that she wearied them. And he said to them, 'I am not sent but unto the lost sheep of the house of Israel.' She would hear it and they would hear it. It could be for the benefit of both. He said, 'I am not sent,' and yet he was the sent One. 'I am sent to the lost sheep of the house of Israel.' You would think when he said that, that that would finish her. He said he was sent only to the house of Israel. She was a Canaanite—what had she to do with Israel? What had she to do with the lost sheep of the house of Israel?

You would say, 'Well, that's it. That's the very end. There's no possibility. He's telling her that she's lost, entirely lost.' But no! No, there was something about it that didn't entirely close the door. You see, Christ has lost sheep of the spiritual house of Israel. Israel is not only a people—a literal people—but Israel at times betokens a spiritual people. She took hold of something. You would think she was losing everything, but she took hold of something, whatever it was.

Well, the Lord was driving her back and the Lord was also bringing her forward. Do you remember when Christ wrestled with Jacob? Jacob had his thigh touched by the finger of the Lord and the muscle shrank, and the bone came out of joint. Now, that was the greatest wrestling muscle in the body. So Jacob then became one who was merely holding on. He couldn't fight in that sense, but he was weeping at the same time. He was praying. It was really an exercise of prayer all night with Jesus. But Jacob prevailed with God. Christ said that. He prevailed. God gave him a new name which indicated that he was a prevailer. Yet he was weakened. That's how the Lord works. He seems to weaken in order to strengthen. He seems to make it more hopeless for you when you pray, but then behind it all the Holy Spirit is causing you to carry on.

### 3. The woman's second approach

There was a second approach. 'Then came she and worshipped him, saying, Lord, help me.' Now she came and went on her knees before him. 'She worshipped him.' She took up the attitude of worship. She knelt before him. And the prayer was even shorter this time. It was just, 'Lord, help me.'

When you're desperate, the prayer is short. When Peter was sinking in the waves, when he was trying to walk, that's what he said: 'Lord, help me.' He had no time to say anything else—he was sinking. This woman said the same: 'Lord, help me.' She never said, 'I'm better than anybody else.' She never praised herself. She never in any way made herself to be a lesser sinner than other people. She never pretended she wasn't a Canaanite: everybody around knew that she was that. But still she had the prayer, 'Lord, help me.'

The term 'Lord' itself is a wonderful term. It means an owner, the one to whom you belong. He is called the Lord of heaven and earth: heaven and earth belong to him. He is called 'the Lord of the vineyard': the vineyard belonged to him.

'Lord, help me.' She wanted him to be her Lord and her helper. Did you ever pray that way? Will you ever pray that way? Did you really ever come on your knees to the Lord, desperate, as one who feels that the Lord wasn't listening? But now you come again, and you cry out in desperation, 'Lord, help me.' You honour him. You give him his title: 'Lord.' But you also say, 'Help me.' Me! He is the only one who can help you. There's no other name, no other Saviour.

This time Christ answers her. He said, 'It is not meet to take the children's bread, and to cast it to dogs.' It is not meet—not fit, not proper—to take children's bread, the food that the

## 4 Three approaches by the woman of Canaan

children of the kingdom—God's children—are eating, and to cast it to dogs!

Now you say, 'Well, that surely will finish her. She'll never come back again. That's a total rejection, when he called it the children's bread.' The bread she was seeking is the bread that believers are feeding on. That bread belongs to the children. Christ as Saviour, the blessing of God, forgiveness of sin, all that is wrapped up in his mercy—that's their bread, that's what they feed on.

Under the Jewish law in the Old Testament, it was said that if you had a city with walls, the dogs were to be kept outside the city wall. They were never allowed in; they were unclean. If a dog died, nobody would bury it. They would just drag it out to Gehennah, the Valley of the Son of Hinnom, where all the rubbish was. All the unclean animals were dragged out there. The asses were dragged out there. Sometimes men died and God said about them that they would have the burial of an ass. That was a reference to an unclean animal being dragged out into the Valley of Gehennah, the Valley of the Son of Hinnom. They were just left there to decompose, with nobody bothering about them.

Dogs weren't clean, so they were outside. They were not fit to take the food of those who were inside. It was not meet to take the food of the children and to give it to these creatures. The term 'dog' was also used for non-Jews—the Gentiles. They were called the unclean, they were called the dogs. But a Canaanite was a dog of dogs, something beyond an ordinary Gentile. A Canaanite was one of the accursed people. You might say, 'Well, surely now that is the end of it all.' But the Canaanite woman came again.

## 4. The woman's third approach

The woman approached Christ again. This time she said, 'Truth, Lord.' 'What you are saying is the truth.' Everyone who approaches Christ, whatever the Word of God may say against them, they will always say, 'It is the truth.' What the Lord said is right, correct, the truth. The person who comes to Christ will not contradict the Word of God. He will say, 'It is the Word, the infallible Word, the holy Word of God. It is the truth.' This woman agreed with Christ. 'Truth, Lord.' 'What you are saying, Lord, is the absolute truth.'

But then the woman says, 'Yet the dogs eat of the crumbs which fall from their masters' table.' Now here is a strange thing. How can she speak of anything falling from the masters' table or from the table of the children, and the dogs picking, if the dogs are kept outside? For that was the Jewish law. But when the Romans took over, they kept dogs as pets. So the word she uses is a word that means one of *these* dogs, not the fierce large dogs that roamed outside, that fed on the rubbish and the dead things. She used a term that denoted a small dog, a pet dog, a household dog, one that a Roman or a Greek might have, but not a Jew. So what she was saying was, 'Yes, master, what you say is true, but these small dogs eat of the crumbs that fall from the table.' You see, that kind of dog had come closest to the master at the head of the table, closer even than anybody else at the table. They could come to the very feet of the master and eat the crumbs at the feet of the master.

And, spiritually speaking, the crumbs that those small dogs ate were the crumbs of the children, the food of those who love Christ. That is, spiritually they could feed upon Christ. Here is the boldness of faith, and yet the humility that accompanies faith. We are told to come boldly to the throne of grace, that we might obtain mercy. We are told to come boldly—not with the boldness of the flesh, not with our heads high and

## 4 Three approaches by the woman of Canaan

defiantly. Not with that kind of boldness, but with the boldness that takes hold of you, and believes what God says in his Word. On the basis of what God says, telling us to come and inviting and commanding us to come—with *that* boldness—we come humbly, yet boldly to the throne of grace, to Christ, to obtain mercy. Mercy! The Canaanite woman came that way. 'These small dogs', she said, 'eat of the crumbs, the very food that belongs to the children.' These small dogs identify with the children. They are feeding upon the same Christ as the children. They are believers, just like the children. You see, the Holy Spirit worked faith in her heart—true saving faith that glorified God and glorified Christ. That was the way in which she came.

That was the way in which *she* came. So we have to ask, 'Did *you* ever come to Christ?' Oh, you might say, 'There was a time when I was very, very worried about my soul and I did pray, but I'm not like that now. I've lost that.' Oh friends, it may never come back again!

There are some among us too who have heard the gospel over all these years and yet who have never, ever earnestly, sincerely, with their whole heart, sought God's face and favour. That's the whole purpose of preaching the gospel, that sinners—and we all are sinners—might seek the Lord and come to the Lord, and face the Lord. We are all taught prayer as children, and a lot of prayer is coming to the bedside but not facing the Lord, eye to eye. We have to come face to face with him, and you have to realise that you're coming as a poor, black Canaanite, a poor, black sinner. But you have to come that way. There's no other way in which you can come, but as a sinner. Some people think of improving themselves before they come to Christ. That's madness! You're not going to improve yourself. If you could even begin to improve yourself, why would you then seek Christ? If you can bring about any improvement, you don't need a Saviour: you just want to finish the work that you began. No, friend, you cannot even begin! You only plunge deeper and deeper into the morass, into sin. Oh, we need to come as we are, sinful as we are. Canaanite, Syrophenicians, people of Harris, people of Lewis, people of Scotland, wherever we are, whoever we are, whatever we are.

The woman came. And what faith! What a grasp she took! 'The dogs eat of the crumbs.' What she really said is, 'I am eating of the crumbs. I am eating. It may be the crumbs I'm being given, when the rest are given bread, but I am taking hold and I am feeding, I am eating.'

### 5. The Saviour's commendation

And what was the reply? How did Christ answer this third approach? 'Then Jesus answered and said unto her, O woman, great is thy faith.' There it is: she had come in faith. Faith had driven her, trust in the Saviour had driven her. She believed that he was able, and she believed that he was really willing. You'd almost think he wasn't willing, but she believed that he was able and willing.

Jesus said, 'O woman, great is thy faith.' The woman of Canaan was not an Israelite, but he said, 'Great is thy faith.' You don't need to be of the flesh of Israel to have great faith. We don't know if she had great schooling, great education. We very much doubt it. How could it be, then, that she was a woman of great faith? 'Be it unto thee even as thou wilt.' That is, your desire is granted. 'And her daughter was made whole from that very hour.' Freed from the manacles of the devil, and perhaps freed in a higher sense, set free in Christ. Her daughter was made whole; her prayer was granted.

You can imagine how that woman would be afterward, when Christ had gone back into Judaea and never again came to these borders. When he turned away, how that woman would

## 4 Three approaches by the woman of Canaan

tell her daughter about the Messiah, about her prayer, how she approached him! How that woman would tell her daughter about the glory of Christ, how precious it would be to know Christ! If any parent ever told her or his child, surely this woman would tell her child how things were.

There was a woman once whose daughter's schoolmates began to mock her mother to her, the reason being that her mother's two hands were deformed. The young girl was so upset, but the time came when she spoke to her mother about it.

She said to her mother, 'They make fun of me at school. They mock me at school. They tell me about my mother's deformed hands, and they tried to shame me because I have such a mother.'

'Well,' said her mother, 'I'll tell you about that. When you were a baby, our house went on fire, and I ran into the house to save you out of the fire and my hands were badly burnt in saving you. That's how I received these hands.' And then to her daughter those deformed hands were the most precious hands in the world.

People might despise Christ—and they *do* despise Christ and Christianity and the gospel—but for those who know Christ who showed mercy to them, it doesn't matter what people say. They love Christ, they desire to love him, they desire others to love him. You see, friends, unless we know Christ we will never enter heaven. Never! We have despised the food, we have despised the Saviour, we have despised all that he did. He came into the world to suffer and to die, to satisfy the justice of God, and so to glorify God in satisfying his justice. And that is meant for sinners. The worth of all that he did is laid to the account of sinners who believe. We're justified by faith, we believe, we have faith, and therefore what Christ has done is laid to our account, as if we had done it. What a wonderful salvation that is!

Just a few generations ago there were many poor people on our island who had no money. They had little in the way of food, so they often prayed for food, and they were often anxious because they had no food for their children. But they had godliness among them. And would they have exchanged that godliness and their state of poverty for the riches of the godless? No, because they had it all in Christ. 'O woman, great is thy faith.'

## Application

The great question then is, how are *we* going to spend eternity? Where are *we* going to spend eternity? Time is so short! It's a new year. It's begun, it's running, it's roaring, it's moving. The whole of time from beginning to end is very, very short. Never mind your own age—from Adam until the last man it's going to be very, very short compared to eternity. Think of the endless aeons of eternity to which we are going. Oh, the folly of people who refuse even to think of eternity, to think of what is beyond the grave! The folly of it all! The madness of it all! The devil is putting a blindfold on the eyes of our soul. He doesn't want us to think about these things. He doesn't want us to see, to realise. He doesn't want us to be saved. He wants to destroy souls. He hates your soul, and he would destroy you if he could. And if he destroys you, you will be with himself in a lost eternity—in hell for evermore. But Christ is here in the gospel, friends. The food is there: feed on Christ, he is the food. You speak to Christ. You pray to Christ. You approach Christ. He is the friend of sinners, the Saviour of sinners. He has more pleasure in saving a soul than that soul can ever have of pleasure in being saved.

# 4 Three approaches by the woman of Canaan

May the Lord add his blessing on the preaching of his own Word.

## Concluding prayer

Gracious and holy Lord, we beseech thee to be with us and to help us and to guide us. Give us to be thankful for that woman who died two thousand years ago and went to be with thyself, and who is no longer called a Canaanite in heaven. She's a child of God. She belongs to the people of Christ. She's singing thy praises in heaven, worshipping thee with a perfect worship, higher than the worship of the angels. Lord God, help us to make use of what we read, and make use of what is revealed to us in the gospel, the example that we have of how thy grace works. Grant to bless our precious souls, young and old and middle-aged on this Sabbath evening. O Lord, be with us, we beseech thee. Cleanse us and help us. All for thine own name's sake. Amen.

# 5

# The builder of Zion and his materials

25th January 2018, Lord's Day morning, Uig

*When the LORD shall build up Zion, he shall appear in his glory. He will regard the prayer of the destitute, and not despise their prayer. This shall be written for the generation to come: and the people which shall be created shall praise the LORD. For he hath looked down from the height of his sanctuary; from heaven did the LORD behold the earth.*
Psalm 102:16–19

THIS is a Messianic Psalm—that is, the Messiah is in the Psalm, Christ is in the Psalm. At the very end of the Psalm, we read in verse 23, 'He weakened my strength in the way; he shortened my days.' That is, death was meeting with Christ. 'I said, O my God, take me not away in the midst of my days.' But then the reply he was given from God the Father was, 'Thy years are throughout all generations.' It's not just a matter of being cut off in the middle of your days, at the age of thirty-three, but 'Thy years are throughout all generations. Of old has thou laid the foundation of the earth: and the heavens are the work of thy hands. They shall perish, but thou shalt endure: yea, all of them shall wax old like a garment; as a vesture shalt thou change them, and they shall be changed: but thou art the same, and thy years shall have no end.'

## 5  The builder of Zion and his materials

That passage is taken up again in the New Testament. This Psalm is quoted in Hebrews just to show that it is a Messianic Psalm, and that it is Christ who is speaking. That was the way in which the Father gave him strength and comfort in his human nature, by telling him that he was God the Creator, who changes not. What a strange thing that is! Who would imagine that that would ever happen in the history of this world?—that God the second person would be calling upon the Father in his agony, and the Father would give Christ's human nature strength by reminding him who he really was, that he was the Creator.

The beginning of the Psalm, from verse 2 right down to verse 9, speaks of the suffering of Christ. In verse 2 Christ says, 'Hide not thy face from me in the day when I am in trouble,' and in verse 3 he says, 'For my days are consumed like smoke, and my bones are burned as an hearth.' Christ speaks of his suffering in verse 4. 'My heart is smitten, and withered like grass; so that I forget to eat my bread.' In verse 5, he speaks of his groaning and his bones cleaving to his skin. In verses 6 and 7 he speaks of being alone. 'I am like a pelican in the wilderness,' and 'as a sparrow alone'—yes, alone—'upon the house top.' There was no one among men to uphold him. He never had anybody to pray for him. Nobody among his disciples could understand until he rose from the dead. They did not have proper light, they were misunderstanding his ministry and misunderstanding his kingdom. They misunderstood his suffering and his loneliness. He was 'as a sparrow upon the house top. Mine enemies reproach me all the day; and they that are mad against me are sworn against me.' Then he goes on to say, 'For I have eaten ashes like bread, and mingled my drink with weeping.' Then in verse 10 he says, 'Because of thy indignation and thy wrath, for thou hast lifted me up and cast me down.' And in the next verse, 'My days are like a shadow.' Christ was speaking of his suffering, what he was going through.

Then we come to verse 13 and he says, 'Thou shalt arise, and have mercy upon Zion.' Zion is the Church, and he speaks of the time when the gospel would be blessed, when the Spirit would be poured out upon the Church. 'For the time to favour her, yea, the set time, is come.'

We come now to verse 16, the text we are taking up. 'When the LORD shall build up Zion, he shall appear in his glory. He will regard the prayer of the destitute, and not despise their prayer.' And, 'This shall be written for the generation to come'. And so on.

We have here two things we should like to say a little about, as the Lord would be pleased to help us. The first thing is about the builder of Zion. 'When the LORD shall build up Zion, he shall appear in his glory.' Zion is figuratively the Church. Zion was used to refer to Jerusalem, and both Zion and Jerusalem were used to denote the Church of God. So the Psalmist is speaking here of the builder of the Church, the builder of Zion. And then secondly, he speaks of the materials of the building. 'He will regard the prayer of the destitute, and not despise their prayer.' He's going to build using the destitute 'For he hath looked down from the height of his sanctuary; from heaven did the LORD behold the earth; to hear the groaning of the prisoner; to loose those that are appointed to death; to declare the name of the LORD in Zion, and his praise in Jerusalem.' So the material he's going to use will be made up of poor, perishing sinners. You might think this is useless material, but that is how God will build up his Church.

## 1. The builder of Zion

Christ is addressed in verse 13. The Psalmist says, 'Thou shalt arise, and have mercy upon Zion: for the time to favour her, yea, the set time, is come.' He says, 'Thou shalt arise,' as if someone had been inactive, lying down or sitting down, and

## 5   The builder of Zion and his materials

then this person who had been inactive is now rising to do a great work. For many generations it may have seemed that the work of the Lord was so small, so few seemed to know about the Saviour in this world. But the day was going to come when the gospel would be known world-wide. The day would come, the day of Pentecost, when the Holy Spirit would be poured down, with men from many parts of the world hearing the gospel in their own language. They would go home with that gospel to their own nations. 'Thou shalt arise, and have mercy upon Zion: for the time to favour her, yea, the set time, is come.'

The Lord has his set time for building. He had that set time in our own island, when he came and revealed himself and he began to build. There are many in glory today who were born in Uig and various parts of our island. They are in glory because the Lord came at a set time and began to build. He still builds, he hasn't ceased to build.

The Psalmist goes on to say, 'Thy servants take pleasure in her stones.' God's people have a delight in seeing Zion—the Church—being built up. A delight in seeing people being born again and coming out as witnesses in the world. A delight in the stones—people who were dead in trespasses and sins—made into living stones. And of course, the people of God delight in these stones. They delight in the corner stone—Christ—and they delight in these living stones.

He says they 'favour the dust thereof'. They delight in the very dust of this Zion, never mind the stones. God's true people delight in everything that belongs to the cause of the Lord.

The Psalmist goes on to say, 'So the heathen shall fear the name of the Lord.' God will work among the heathen and the heathen shall fear the name of the Lord. That is not carnal fear; that is not slavish fear. It's the fear which has respect and love for God in it—respect and love for God above all. It is a desire to love him above all, and to honour his great name. That is the fear of the Lord. It is called a clean fear. 'The fear of the Lord', says Scripture, 'is clean.' The fear of the Lord endures forever. It goes with you into heaven. It is seen too in the human nature of Christ, who worships God in his human nature, even in glory. The fear of the Lord which is clean and endureth forever is also in the angels, it's in all who worship God.

The Psalmist then says, 'When the LORD shall build up Zion, he shall appear in his glory.' When we see people building, we don't usually see them in their glory. We don't usually see beautiful clothing upon them, we don't see them wearing lovely garments or kingly garments. But this is a way of God displaying his glory, by bringing souls alive, making dead stones to be living stones, putting them into the wall. This reminds us of King David. He was not a covetous man, but in all his battles he took spoil from the defeated enemies. He took spoil from the Moabites, from the Edomites, from the Ammonites, from the Philistines, from the Syrians—from all the enemies round about. When David did this his great desire was to take the gold and the silver, the precious wood, the precious garments, the precious stones and to put it all on one side for the building of the temple of God, which was God's glorious building. David wasn't allowed to build the temple, but his desire was to see the temple built, the house of God, the place of true worship, the place of God's glory. David was a type—a picture—of Christ, who not only gathers the substance but who actually puts it all together.

In the days of Moses, Bezaleel and Aholiab were given the Holy Spirit to help them build the tabernacle of Moses in the wilderness. And the Holy Spirit worked not just through their minds and their memory but worked through their hands, through their fingers. He made their fingers adept and skilful,

## 5 The builder of Zion and his materials

and he gave them the eye needed for that, with the acuteness of mind and understanding which was necessary. But here you have the Lord himself, Christ the builder, who said, 'Upon this rock will I build my church; and the gates of hell shall not prevail against it.' The gates of cities were large structures. There was always a big space behind them, and usually the elders of a city would gather there, when they came together. Any public assembly was usually there, at the gate of a city. Even an army could gather there. But even if all the gates of hell were open and the armies were poured out, the gates of hell shall not prevail against it.

The Edomites used to say of the walls of Jerusalem, 'Raze, raze it quite.' To raze meant to bring down the walls completely. That was their desire. But the Lord builds for eternity. He built heaven and earth. Christ is the Creator of heaven and earth. 'All things were made by him, and without him was nothing made that was made.' These things vanish away, but here is a building for eternity—his blood, his suffering, what he has finished has made this certain. 'Thy kingdom hath none end at all, it doth through ages all remain' (Psalm 145:13, second version). This building is for ever. It is a building not made with human hands, but the maker and the builder of this building is the Lord himself. He planned it all, he makes it all, and it endures forever. In Revelation 21 we read of what John saw. He saw 'the holy city, new Jerusalem'—that is a name given to the Church—'coming down from God out of heaven, prepared as a bride adorned for her husband.' John looked for the origin of the Church and he saw it coming from God. It came from the heart of God, from the mind of God. The plan for it was all there. You remember that David was given a plan for the temple—it came from God. The plan of the Church was in the heart of the Lord from all eternity. It was in the covenant. John saw the new Jerusalem coming down from God out of heaven, and it came to the earth where it was built. Here we read that the Lord is the builder, and 'when the LORD shall build up Zion, he shall appear in his glory'.

Building was a favourite way of seeking glory among the kings and emperors. The pharaohs built pyramids and tremendous temples in Egypt. All these buildings were for the glory of the pharaohs. But they have gone, and you only have the ruins of the temples now, although the pyramids have lasted better. The pharaohs are now but dust and ashes. People have opened their tombs. Where are these powerful men? Just fragments, bones. They have gone, their souls are in eternity. They've no greatness at all. They died without Christ, without hope. Where is their greatness gone? There's no greatness now.

Solomon built the temple according to the plan that God gave to David. He also built the house of the forest for his first bride. These things would speak of his greatness. When the Queen of Sheba came she saw the glory of Solomon. She was used to great buildings, but she saw the way by which Solomon went out from his own place of residence to the temple. There was a special way built by which he went into the temple. The Word of God says that when she saw that there was no more heart left in her. She was so overawed by the glory of it all. It was built to a plan given by God from heaven, and he enabled people to carry it out. But above all, she was overawed by the glory of God. She questioned Solomon regarding the things of the Lord, who was pre-eminent.

I remember as a boy in school, we studied a poem about a great emperor, Ozymandias. It spoke of a man going through the desert. His foot kicked against a slab in the sand and he picked it up and he read upon it, 'My name is Ozymandias, king of kings: look on my works, ye mighty, and despair.' That meant, 'What I build is so tremendous that every other king and emperor will see it all and just despair.' But when the man looked around, there was nothing else. Just the sand and this

## 5 The builder of Zion and his materials

slab of stone. 'Vanity of vanities; all is vanity!' These buildings, what lasting glory will they give anyone? Telford was a famous builder in our land. We have churches on our own island built by Telford, and there are bridges and buildings on the mainland built by him. His name was illustrious, but he's gone to eternity and God will not give him according to the buildings he built. No, friends, it will be according to how we are, regarding Christ. If we know Christ, we will be glorified with him in his glory, but as for buildings, they are mere human vanity.

David spoke of the mercy of God, and he thought of the mercy of God as a building, the Church of Christ. 'Mercy shall be built up for ever.' The house of God—the building of God, Zion—will last for ever. It's all full of mercy, the undeserved favour and blessing of God. The forgiveness of sin, justification, sanctification, Christ as Saviour—it's all mercy. It's built up for ever. It's not something that will go once you have it. Mercy shall be built up for ever. David sang that, and he wrote it down in Psalm 89, so that we might sing it in all generations.

Now, the Church has a foundation. That foundation is Christ. It needed the best foundation. You see, this foundation is under the walls; it wasn't a broad foundation. Christ is the foundation. He said he would build upon this rock, and the gates of hell shall not prevail against it. He's called 'a sure foundation'. A city built on a sure foundation is what we have in the Church, and nothing was going to prevent Christ from building his Church.

We remember Nehemiah, who came out of the captivity. He was sent to Jerusalem by the emperor of Persia. When he came to Jerusalem, he was allowed to build up the walls: he was given the money, he was given the substance. But the enemies of the Jews were after him. They were trying to trap him, to kill him, to stop him, and they sent him various messages inviting him to meet them here and to meet them there, that they might carry out what they had in view. But Nehemiah said, 'I am doing a great work, and I cannot come down.' That is what Christ says about all his enemies, 'They want to spoil everything, but they cannot. I am doing a great work and I cannot come down.' Christ is the Lord, who is appearing in his glory as a builder of the Church. And oh, friends, to have the hands of the builder on our soul! When the hands of the builder come on our soul, very soon we will love righteousness, we will love the hands, we will love the builder, we will be joined to the living corner stone, Christ himself, and we will be living stones in Christ's building.

Solomon's temple was built without any mortar or cement being used. Nothing like that was used. The stones were built exactly to the specifications, and nothing made of iron was heard being used when the stones were fitted into their place. Nothing needed to be chipped off, so there was no sound of iron. The stones were ready, they were fitted into their place. We cannot always believe the things the Jewish scholars say, but they say that in Solomon's temple the blade of a knife couldn't come in between stone and stone. And many of these stones weighed tons. That's the work of the Lord, and that's his building.

## 2. The material of the building

Secondly, we should like to look at the material of this building. If you want to build a glorious building, you want good material—you want good stone, stone that is appropriate. But suppose there is no appropriate stone, no good stone. Suppose it's all rotten stone—and when they speak of rotten stone they mean stone that will disintegrate, it's not fit for buildings. Well, among men there was no stone fit for the building. Nothing but sinners. When God looked down from heaven high to see

## 5  The builder of Zion and his materials

if any were good, to see if any sought God as they were by nature, he said (Psalm 14:3),

> They altogether filthy are,
> they all aside are gone;
> and there is none that doeth good,
> yea, sure there is not one.

'No', he said, 'not one.' Not one that was doing good! There wasn't such a thing as a good man. They were all the enemies of God, as they were by nature. They had no desire for God. How could God build? Well, you see, this is the One who built heaven and earth by the word of his power. There was no material when he began to build. He built out of nothing. All that we see and all that we handle, all that is around us, all came from nothing. And it could go back into nothingness. But man cannot go back into nothingness. He's an accountable creature. He has to be accountable, he's a moral agent. He was made in the image of God. Men and angels are accountable creatures, they must go to be in the presence of God to give an account. They cannot go back into nothingness: that cannot be. When we consider the earth, the physical universe, these can pass away and go back into nothingness, but not accountable creatures.

God built everything from nothing, but he builds his Church from sinful people. To build from nothing might seem a problem, but God doesn't experience problems: he has infinite wisdom and infinite power. We might say, 'Here is the greatest problem ever. There was never such a problem as this one. How to build the spiritual Church out of the rubbish of an Adam, filthy human nature, sinful human nature, hateful human nature? How to build with that? How could he take the slime out of the slime pit to build a palace? How could he take the material that was in the world to build such an edifice? How could that be?' Ah, well, 'When the LORD shall build up Zion, he shall appear in his glory.' It is his glory that he can do that, and it becomes us to glorify him in all that. Yes, we can glorify him. 'Thy servants take pleasure in her stones, and favour the dust thereof.'

God builds. He has built, he does build, and he will build. He will finish the building, the top stone will be laid there, and it will sound out, 'All by the work of grace.' It's all of grace. 'Grace' means 'favour' or 'something given for nothing'. It is all of his grace, all of his favour; not of us. Our 'good works'—imagine: good works!—not any of that contributes to the building. God builds alone. Christ suffered alone; he builds alone. 'I will build my church.' Note: '*I will.*' He will have the glory, it will be his—the builder. When the gospel is blessed to a person, the builder is appearing in his glory in the experience of that soul—Christ is appearing to him in his glory. It is a glorious experience when a poor sinner is broken down and repents and believes.

And listen again, at verse 19. 'For he hath looked down from the height of his sanctuary; from heaven did the LORD behold the earth; to hear the groaning of the prisoner; to loose those that are appointed to death.' God hears 'the groaning of the prisoner', the one who is appointed unto eternal death. But the Holy Spirit has begun to work in that soul, and the sinner begins to groan before God in his agony of soul—a sinner, a lost sinner, turning to the Lord, weeping over his sin, desiring salvation, calling for mercy: a groaning prisoner. The builder is looking at that soul, and using that soul as part of his building material, building him into the wall. It is all the work of the Lord. The groaning is because the Holy Spirit is working in his soul, giving him to see his sin, giving him to hate sin, giving him to turn from it 'with full purpose of, and endeavour after, new obedience', looking to Christ, looking to the builder, looking to the hand. 'I cannot save myself. Let thy hand, O builder, save me. Grasp me, fit me into the building, knit me to Christ, make me as one of thy children.'

## 5   The builder of Zion and his materials

'To loose those that are appointed to death.' Sin ties, the devil ties, the world ties. But the Lord looses them. Oh, if the people in prison in Philippi were to read these words, they would understand it very well. When Paul and Silas were put into the prison in Philippi, an earthquake came from the Lord, the builder, and the doors of the prison opened. The doors were locked, but they all opened, and fetters opened, the chains opened, everything opened in the prison in Philippi. The prisoners were all free. Paul and Silas were free. The jailor had done everything he could to keep them prisoners. He even put the feet of Paul and Silas in stocks—wooden stocks, that fitted over the lower leg to enclose them. But all of that was unloosed, just as we have it here in the Psalm, that the Lord loosed those that were appointed to death.

You have it again with Peter and the apostles. Peter was in prison more than once, but let us look at one particular time he was in prison. James had been put to death by the sword by Herod, and Peter was in prison. He was going to be taken out the next day to be sentenced to death, but when they went to look for him, he wasn't there. He had been chained to two soldiers but yet the chains had opened, the gates had opened, he'd walked through them, right through the whole battery of gates into the street.

But wonderful as that is, it's not as wonderful as a poor soul being loosed from hell, from sin. God makes the prisoners free. They become free men in Christ. If he frees you, you're free. Ah, yes, it's a wonderful thing to trust in Jesus and to be made free.

The Lord regards the prayers of the people. He hears the groaning and he looses those who are ordained unto death. Yes, that's what he does! In verse 17 we read, 'He will regard the prayer of the destitute.' He will regard it; he will give it great respect. Who are the destitute? In our language, if you are destitute you have nothing. Absolutely nothing! But it says here that the Lord has great respect—great regard—for the prayer of the man who has nothing. It is the Lord himself who makes you destitute. So you come before him and you say, 'I have nothing, I'm not worthy, I can't praise anything I ever did or anything I have. All I can come with is my sin. "My sin I ever see." But of all else, I have nothing.'

The word 'destitute' is also the word for a shrub that grows in the desert. It was a useless shrub: you couldn't use it for anything. Most plants could be used for something. These people knew how to makes use of almost everything that grew, but this shrub had no use at all. It was just a weed; it was in the way. That's the word used: 'the destitute'. But the Lord has regard for the destitute, when he comes in prayer. 'He will regard the prayer of the destitute' and will not despise their prayer. The destitute person will despise his own prayer. He will feel, 'Well, my prayer is a worthless prayer, but whether it is worthless or not, I need to utter it. I *have* to utter it! I can only come as a beggar, as destitute.' The beggar has nothing. He's pleading for something because he has nothing. The only thing he has is hunger and need. So he comes with a need. That's how it is for the soul in whom the Lord works. He comes with a need, he comes with a desire, he comes with his emptiness to the fulness of the Lord Jesus Christ, and that is called faith. Faith is coming with your own emptiness to his fulness. 'Lord, I believe; help thou mine unbelief.'

There was a man who worked in this area many years ago, a man called MacBean. He was one of the Gaelic teachers in the island in the days when the gospel began to be blessed. He became an Inspector of Schools, then he became a minister. MacBean was preaching one day on Mary Magdalene, and he was using his imagination. He spoke of the devils being cast out of Mary Magdalene, as if all these devils fled and hid behind a wall and were looking out to see what had happened to

Mary Magdalene. In his sermon he had one devil asking another, 'Has Christ gone?' But he imagined another devil saying, 'Even if he has gone, if he has left his Word behind, it's hopeless for us.' Well, that's what Christ does. His Word is made precious to these poor people who are built into the wall of the Church. In that Word they have Christ himself. They have his mercy, his forgiveness, his justification, his sanctification, his presence, his promises. You have everything in the Word. Although he may seem to have gone, if he has left the Word in the heart, then the devils can't come back. Never, never, never!

It is the building of the Lord—a building made out of these poor materials. The prophet in the Old Testament speaks of the destitute man who didn't even have clothing, but that man was clinging to the rock. He came to the rock. He would never have come to the rock for it to be his clothing. That's the last thing he would do. But when he had nothing else, he came to the rock, and God gave him his clothing. Christ became his clothing. He was brought into the family of God. Friends, pride, human pride, spiritual pride, is the great stumbling block. It is in every human heart, even in the humblest of people as we are by nature before God, but God breaks it down. He has to break it down. They have to be made spiritually humble before God, to be as nothing, to be broken, to be desolate, to be beggars, to be empty. When that takes place, then the sinner sees the Lord in his glory. It is the Lord who builds up Jerusalem.

May God bless his Word. Let us pray.

## Concluding prayer

O gracious and blessed Lord, we beseech thee to be with us this day. We beseech thee to make thy Word precious to us. For we are on the way to eternity, from which no one can return. O Lord God, make us wise for eternity. Make us wise for our own souls. Make us wise with wisdom that comes from Christ who is the wisdom of God. Be with us in the evening exercise of worship. Bless thy worship everywhere. May a paean of praise rise up to the glory of thy great name from all parts of this earth. Give us to be a praying, praising people. Cleanse us. For Jesus' sake. Amen.

# 6

# Three lonely people

*25<sup>th</sup> January 2018, Lord's Day evening, Uig*

*I am like a pelican of the wilderness: I am like an owl of the desert.*
*I watch, and am as a sparrow alone upon the house top.*
Psalm 102:6–7

WE mentioned in the morning that this is a Messianic Psalm—it's about Christ. That's a wonderful thing, when you think of it. A Psalm that was written a thousand years before Christ came, and yet you can find in it the very thoughts of Christ in his humanity. The very thoughts he was going to have were revealed to us by the Holy Spirit, a thousand years beforehand. You have the same sort of thing in many other Psalms. For example, Psalm 22 is full of the thoughts of Christ when he was on the cross. Who would ever imagine that you could find such a Psalm, full of his thoughts when he was on the cross!

Psalm 102 is another psalm that reveals thoughts that Christ had in his humanity. There are very many places in the book of Psalms like that. Why then would people desire to lay the book of Psalms aside and begin to use hymns, made up by sinful men? Yes, maybe they were men saved by grace, but they were not led by the Holy Spirit to produce these hymns in an infallible, inerrant way. But this is the Word of God, and here the Holy Spirit is revealing things. Why would people lay that aside to sing something that is vastly inferior? We also have to remember that it was God who gave worship to fallen man and it is God who tells us how to worship. It is God who instructed this worship. Why then should we break away from God's instructions? Why should we turn away from the Psalmody, from the hymnary that God gave us, which is so precious and so full of Christ? There is no book in Scripture so full of the thoughts of the mind of Christ in human nature as the book of Psalms. It is a precious book. It is the book that God's people usually run to when they have trouble and trial. It is there with help for us in every kind of trouble and trial that we might have. God provides—let us make use of these provisions that God has made for us.

We should like just to look at this portion of Scripture. Taking it in its context, we should like to look at three lonely people. The first lonely person speaking in this Psalm is the Lord Jesus Christ. The second is the person who has been made lonely in this world by the Holy Spirit of God—someone who realises that he's a sinner and needs a Saviour. That person is made lonely by the Holy Spirit of God. And the third person we should like to say a little about is the one who is lost and who will be lonely for ever. We should like to speak about these things, with love in our heart for poor fellow sinners, for we are all on the way to eternity.

## 1. The Lord Jesus Christ

So first of all, Christ is here, saying, 'I am like a pelican of the wilderness: I am like an owl of the desert. I watch, and am as a sparrow alone upon the house top.'

# 6 Three lonely people

The first eleven verses of the Psalm are speaking about Christ's condition—how he's feeling. These words in verses 6 and 7 pinpoint his loneliness. He says, 'I am like a pelican of the wilderness.' A pelican tends to feed alone. It's in the wilderness, and it feeds alone. The owl comes out at night to hunt: it's on its own. The sparrow is used to having a flock around it but sometimes you see a sparrow on its own.

Christ says a great deal about sparrows, and so we might mention a little about that. He said, 'Are not two sparrows sold for a farthing?' Sparrows were netted, they were caught. Small birds were used as articles of food by the Jews, and they would sell them in the markets. You would think that if two are sold for one farthing that it would be four for two farthings. But no, it wasn't: you got four and you got one for nothing. You got five for two farthings. Christ also said that one sparrow does not fall to the earth without his heavenly Father. God has respect for every creature he created, including creatures which my eye and your eye cannot see. We are told by Christ that the sparrow that falls to the ground—the dying sparrow—does not die without the heavenly Father. He's the heavenly Father of his own people, but he still has respect for the life of a dying sparrow. A sparrow goes into annihilation: the spirit of the sparrow goes down into the nothingness from which it came. It only was only ever flesh—that's all—it had no soul, but still God has respect to it. Christ says, 'How much more value does God place upon one of you, his own children, than he places upon a sparrow!'

David also spoke of sparrows in Psalm 84. He was then in the desert. He wanted to get to the house of God, but he couldn't get to the tabernacle because of King Saul hunting him in the desert. David was a man of God and he desired to go to the place of worship. If the people of Uig and the people of Lewis and the people of Scotland had the same desire that David had, we'd have all of the churches filled to the brim. But of course we do not have that. However, David had that desire in the desert, and he said, 'My soul longeth, even thirsteth, for the courts of God's own house.' He also said that the sparrow found a nest, found a place in the house of God, in the tabernacle. David couldn't get to the tabernacle, he couldn't get to the house of God, but nobody would lay a hand on the sparrow that was hunted by people outside, if it came into the tabernacle. It was the same for the swallow that made her nest beside the altar. Nobody would lay a hand upon it either.

God's house was the only place in the whole land where nobody would touch the sparrow, where it was totally safe. They could nest there with impunity in the courts of the house. David envied the sparrow, a creature which has a short life of two or three years, which has no eternity, which has no comprehension of God. He envied the sparrow because it could nest in God's house when he couldn't get there to worship God.

We have Christ here in Psalm 102 speaking of his loneliness, as the sparrow all alone. It's used to a flock, a chattering flock that goes from place to place. It flits here and flits there. Christ says that he's like a sparrow all alone. He's not just speaking of one individual experience in that life, he's speaking of his entire life. He says he's like the pelican in the wilderness, the owl by night, the sparrow upon the housetop. It is as if he's saying, 'I'm all alone, that is my life.'

As we mentioned in the morning, Christ never asked anyone to pray for him. The disciples close to him couldn't understand his work—their ideas were so malformed, so wrong. His very mother believed (and blessed was the one who believed), and called him her Saviour in her song before he was born, but yet she didn't understand him. When he began to preach, his brothers and his mother came out to bring him home. Someone said, 'Thy mother and thy brethren stand without, desiring to speak with thee.' He answered, 'Who is my mother? Who are my brethren?' (Matthew 12:48). And he pointed around to all who believed in him, saying, 'These are my mother, these are my brethren.' He knew it was unbelief that made them want him to stop his work. They didn't seem to understand. He was God in the flesh, he was a man who was totally holy. He had all the holiness of the Godhead. It was the all-holy God who was walking through this sinful world, and dwelling among us, a sinful people. His mother was a sinner saved by grace. Joseph was a sinner saved by grace. His disciples were sinful men—yes, saved by grace—but still they had sin in thought, word and deed.

He was among them all the time, and the devil was conscious of him. The devil was turning the visible Church against him. The priests who should have glorified him hated him without a cause. The scribes, who copied the Word of God, they hated him. The lawyers, who made up the commentaries on the Word of God, they hated him too. The Sadducees, they hated him. The common people, they would say they loved him— but did they? They followed him for bread, for food, for the miracles. Yes, many seemed to praise him, but when it came to the end, Pilate asked, 'What shall we do with the one who is called Jesus?' And they cried, 'Crucify him! Crucify him!' He was brought before the highest court among the Jews, the court that looked after spiritual things and they asked him, 'Art thou the Christ?' They put him on oath, and he said that he was the Christ and that they would see him yet sitting on the throne of glory, coming with attending angels in the clouds of heaven. The high priest began tearing his clothes and speaking of this as blasphemy, because Jesus, being a mere man in the eyes of the high priest, was making himself God. Christ had called himself the Son of the Father, he had called himself the Son of Man, and the Messianic name, the Son of David.

Among the Jews, the sentence for blasphemy was stoning to death, and being hanged upon a tree after being put to death. But because of the Romans the Jews were restrained from stoning, but they managed to get Christ hung upon a tree. And as the Word of God says, 'Cursed is every one that hangeth upon a tree.' Those who blasphemed the name of God, after being stoned, they were hung on trees—hung, not nailed to the tree. Their hands were tied to the tree and they were hung there. When Christ was nailed to the cross—the tree—the Jews, his enemies, thought they were sending his soul to hell. They thought they were destroying him for ever.

Truly he was the loneliest. Yet, he was the one spoken of in the Old Testament who was to come into the world as a Saviour. The priests and the scribes and the lawyers and the Pharisees said they were waiting for him until he should come. But yet when Christ came, he could say, 'They hated me without a cause.' He came to his own, and his own rejected him, they refused him, they would not have him. 'We will not have this man to reign over us.' He was indeed lonely.

But there's another aspect to that. You see, Christ was the sacrifice—the one who would take away the sin of his own people, the sin-bearer. The guilt of his own people was laid upon him when he took our nature, from the womb. As his capacity to suffer grew, so his suffering grew. He was the 'man of sorrows, and acquainted with grief'. It was as if he was on the altar as the sacrifice from the very beginning. The disciples didn't realise that. Who *did* realise that? Who *could* understand that? But yet the Old Testament had spoken of it. He was the sacrifice. He was the burnt offering. The offering was offered up at the temple every morning and every evening. The lamb was offered up at nine in the morning and three in the afternoon, every day, and a double portion on the Sabbath. They would take a lamb, the priest would examine it to see that it had no faults in it, and then when it was killed, they would examine the inside of it—its organs—to see if there was any flaw, any disease, anything wrong internally. That was Christ. He was examined, and confirmed to be the totally holy Lamb of God. He said in one of the Psalms, 'Examine me and do me prove.' 'Try me, look at me. See that I am totally holy, without sin.'

The priests used to take the skin of the lamb and burn the lamb on the altar—the horns, the flesh, the internal organs, the hooves. Everything that belonged to the lamb, except the skin, was burnt to ash. There was a grating around the altar. If anything fell out onto the grating it had to put back onto the altar. It had to be turned into ash. Ash tells you that whatever it was, it had been totally burnt, totally consumed.

Christ entered total consumption, total destruction, he entered eternal destruction as the sacrifice. Of course he was lonely! The sacrifice was always lonely. Separate from the flock, on its own, devoured and destroyed. There were no friends for the lamb, just the fire, just death. These lambs were put to death. But Christ was a living sacrifice, Christ went through the greatest fire of all—the wrath of God, due to us for sin. He went through that as a living sacrifice. He never became unconscious before he died. He died totally conscious and went into death totally conscious. The lonely, lonely man! The sparrow on the housetop—all alone. 'I have trodden the winepress alone'—all alone.

There was never a lonelier one in this world than the Lord Jesus Christ. He was separate from sinners. He was put outside the flock. The other sparrows were not there. He was on his own. He had to go through what none else could go through. Yes, his suffering was deeper than the suffering of hell. Hell is fearful, hell is lonely, but none was ever as lonely as Christ. You have it in these words, 'My God, my God, why hast thou forsaken me?' and 'Eloi, Eloi, lama sabachthani.' 'Eloi' means 'strong', 'strength', or 'strong one'. 'My strong one, my strong one'—that is God. 'Why hast thou forsaken me?'

He then speaks to the 'why'. He answers it in verse 4 of Psalm 22. He says, 'But thou art holy.' It was an all-holy God who was laying the sin of his people upon Christ, that is, the guilt. That's the only way in which sin can be laid upon someone. You can't deal with sin as a concept, in the abstract. You cannot say, 'Here is sin, destroy it.' Sin has to be in a creature or laid upon a creature. Christ had the guilt of sin laid upon him. He was smitten as if he was the enemy of God, with an eternal smiting. It was eternal but because he was the eternal one himself, he was able to reach to the end of an endless eternity in the work that he did and accomplished.

The loneliness of hell is fearful. But think of the loneliness of Christ, the one who says that he is in the bosom of the Father, that he and the Father are one. The attributes of the Father are Christ's attributes too—what the Father has, he has. 'All that the Father hath is mine.' He was totally in the bosom of the Father and yet he is the one who was made the loneliest ever. Sin is hated by God, and he was bearing the sin of his own people, and God was going to put sin out of sight. That is the meaning of the scapegoat that was offered up every year. Two goats were offered: one was to die, the other had the blood of that one and it was taken away into the desert, into a place not occupied—where nobody lived. The scapegoat was sent there and left there in a place where nobody lived.

Christ went to a place where none ever went before, where none could go, an impossible place for anyone else. Christ went there, the loneliest of the lonely. No one could be more lonely than Christ, the Saviour-God. That is what is being stressed here. Christ was like the sparrow, all alone, all alone, all alone.

You can hear what he says in that loneliness. 'Hear my prayer, O LORD, and let my cry come unto thee. Hide not thy face from me in the day when I am in trouble. ... For my days are consumed like smoke, and my bones are burned as an hearth. My heart is smitten, and withered like grass. ... By reason of the voice of my groaning my bones cleave to my skin. ... Mine enemies reproach me all the day; and they that are mad against me are sworn against me. For I have eaten ashes like bread, and mingled my drink with weeping, because of thine indignation and thy wrath: for thou hast lifted me up and cast me down.' You see, a great element of Christ's loneliness was because of the hatred of God for sin. The face of the hatred of God for sin was turned upon Christ. He says, 'Thou hast lifted me up and cast me down,' as if he was taking a vessel, a clay vessel, and taking it up and then crashing it upon the ground, to break it and destroy it. Destruction was in his loneliness. It wasn't mere loneliness: it was loneliness with the wrath of God. And the wrath of God meant eternal hell, eternal death. He went further away than hell, deeper than hell.

We just have to bow our heads before what he says, and look to him in thankfulness that Christ took this upon himself gladly and willingly and lovingly for the sake of his own people, who were given to him in the eternal covenant. He drank the cup of damnation lovingly. He bore the sins of many. He died the cursed death of the cross. Oh friends, think of these things. Don't dismiss these things, think of them.

## 2. The sinner made lonely by the Holy Spirit

Secondly, we have the man who is made lonely by the Holy Spirit of God. We are in this world, we have our own friends and relatives, we have our own pastimes, we have our own way of spending our days and years—they pass on so rapidly. Life is so short. We have our own recreation, our own work. We have our own companions—they may be good or bad companions. We have our own habits—they may be good or bad habits—we may have habits of drink and drugs, immorality, thieving. We might be of those who condemn others, destroy reputations and things like that, or we may be respectable people. But it doesn't matter who we are. When God looked down to see if there was any—any!—that did good, what he said was, 'There is not one. They altogether filthy are.' Many, many people reject that. Ah, but what God says is the truth. We are all sinners under the wrath and curse of God as we are by nature.

But what does God do? How does God work? He works where the gospel is. When there is no gospel he doesn't work. Where the Word of God is not found, men and women are not made lonely by the Spirit of God. No, it's where the Word of God is. The Holy Spirit blesses the Word to the souls of men and women. What does he do? He makes them lonely in the world. They are in the world, they are without friends and relatives, and they are lonely. They realise that they have nothing, that they are empty, that they are sinners, that they have no God, no salvation. They begin to worry about their souls, they begin to read the Word of God, they begin to listen to see how they can be saved, and what it is to be saved. They begin to wonder how the Christians beside them in their family and in their church came to be saved. How does it happen? They listen to the preaching and the gospel is preached to them. Yet they say, 'The gospel is being preached to me, but I can't do what the minister is saying. It escapes me.'

They feel that they are getting lonelier and lonelier and more and more lost in the world. They are wandering in the world, not able to stop, not knowing how to react, or what to do, and they are lonely. They no longer have the same pleasure in the company they used to keep. They no longer laugh at the kind of things they used to laugh at, and people might think that they are becoming peculiar, becoming strange. They no longer go to the places where they used to go for entertainment. They

## 6 Three lonely people

no longer spend their time looking at the things they used to watch on the television. These things only drive it home more deeply to their souls that they are lonely. They cannot find what they are looking for in these programmes or in plays. They cannot find it in books. They cannot find it anywhere. They cannot even find it in the church. They read their Bible and they cannot find it. They are lonely. Their sins are there, and they don't know how to get rid of them. They are told how to get rid of them, they are told where to go, but somehow they are not able to go there. But they know that they are lonely. And they feel that there is nobody in this world so lonely as they are. Nobody!

They look at the sheep and they look at the cow, and they look at the dog and the cat, and they say, 'You're happier than I am. You know nothing about God, you were never meant to know about God. Your life is short and then you go to nothingness, but I am going to eternity. I am going to eternity, and I am lonely. I cannot find the friendship I need. I cannot find the love I need. I cannot find the forgiveness I need. I have been made lonely. It doesn't matter where I go, what company I'm in, I'm lonely. But in my loneliness I still want to hear the Word of God. I know there is something there, if I can only find it. I listen to preaching as I never listened before, because I know there is something there, if I could only reach it. I listen about Christ, the Saviour who can save from sin, and I know that if I can reach him, there is something there, before me.'

Then the devil speaks—or is it the devil? 'You are not meant to be saved. You are meant to be lonely, and you are meant to be lost in your loneliness. Lonely, with no friends who can help you, nobody you can turn to.'

Friends, listen to another side to all that. The Lord who makes sinners lonely, do you know what he's doing? He's stripping them of all self-confidence. They used to think they had some residue of goodness—that there was something left in them that was worth something. But the Lord deals with them by taking away every rag of their self-righteousness. He's going to strip them of all their own goodness, of all their own worth, of all their own value, until at last he brings them down to being sinners who have nothing. Nothing! Nothing at all but their sin. What a lonely, lonely man! He says, 'The only companion I have is my sin. I have no other companion but my sin.' It's the Holy Spirit of God who brings a man to that. He will not come to that by nature—no, never!

It's in the sinner's total weakness, in his total loneliness and helplessness and nothingness, that Christ in his fulness meets that poor sinner. That person has nowhere else to go. He's being guided, just like a blind man being guided and not knowing that he's being guided, and he comes to confront the Lord, to speak to the Lord, to address the Lord. He is not to go sideways, or anywhere else. He's face to face to face with the Lord, and that's the very thing that sinners avoid all their lives. They won't come face to face with the Lord until the Lord makes them come face to face with him. That is the best day in your life, when that comes about—the best day for the empty, lonely, lost sinner. Christ is the Saviour of lost sinners. The lost sheep was a lonely sheep. The sheep that becomes ill leaves the flock and goes to be by itself. The deer that is ill leaves the herd and goes to be by itself. God does that to the sinner. It's between you and your God. You cannot meet him as a group of people: it's as an individual. It is something personal between yourself and the Lord. The lonely sinner meets the Saviour who was lonely and who has everything that the poor, lonely sinner needs. The sinner needs a friend, and there is no friend like Christ in the human nature and divine nature. As he said to his people, 'I will be your God and you will be my people,' so he says to the sinner, 'I will be your God and you will be mine. I will marry you. Trust in me, believe in me. Weep, mourn, repent, believe!'

# 6  Three lonely people

Something comes alive there. It may just be like a spark. The sinner may be saying, 'Did I meet Christ or did I not? Perhaps I did, perhaps I didn't.' Then it gets stronger. 'I think that salvation has come under my roof. I think so. I think I have a friend who will not let me go.' It gets stronger and stronger, like a spark that begins to get brighter among the embers. With a draught it becomes a flame, becomes a fire.

The Lord works in that way. The child of God will look back and he will say, 'I was a lonely, lonely man. God made me lonely. But now I know that he has said to my soul, "I will never leave thee, nor forsake thee. I will never leave thee." Yes, when my father and mother forsake me, as they must do when they die, my God will never forsake me. He'll be with me in life, he'll be with me in death, he'll be with me in eternity. He's the Lord Jesus Christ, who loved me and gave himself for me. I know that now, but I didn't know it then. I came to know it and now I know all is well. The Church is married to him, and he to the Church. They're graven upon the palms of his hands, they're on the breastplate on the heart of the high priest, they are engraved on the jewels on the shoulders of the high priest. I think of his strength, his power. He has them in his power, he has them in his love. They will never be plucked out of his hand. Never, never, never. I will never again be lonely. I might feel lonely, I might feel that way, but I know that he will never forsake me. I know that. I believe that.'

Whatever happens in this world, that is a great situation to be in. Did the Lord ever make you lonely? Did he ever do that to your soul?

## 3. The loneliness of a lost soul

However, my friends, there's another loneliness and that is the loneliness of a lost eternity. You see, in this world men are not devils. They're fallen creatures in their totality—every part of us has been touched by sin—but we are not devils, and the reason is that the Holy Spirit is here in the world to prevent us from becoming devils. People don't seem to realise that. Devils are in the world tempting us, manipulating us. We're in their chains, we do the will of Satan. He's using our own lusts, our own sin, and he draws us. He uses various things to draw us, and to harden us in sin. He doesn't want us to be saved. He hates Christ and he hates the souls of men and women. He desires to destroy them, but they are not devils. He is the devil and the demons with him are all devils. But we are not devils by nature. Ah, some seem almost to be devils. When you read the papers you might think some people are devils. Christ called Judas a devil, but he wasn't a complete devil while he was in the world.

You see, the Holy Spirit strives with men and women. He enables them to do public good. They can love their children, they can love husbands and wives, brothers and sisters. The Holy Spirit gives us that. That's the restraint of the Holy Spirit. You sometimes see when husband and wife come to hate each other, where brother and sister come to hate each other, where close members of families come to hate each other, and you wonder how that can be. If the Holy Spirit withdraws restraints, that is what happens—hatred comes in. You can see it in nations too. You can see what happened during the last war—wiping out the Jews in Germany and people thinking nothing of it. The same kind of thing is taking place in the Middle East today with the activities of ISIS, for example. In the Bible, Pharaoh hardened his heart. Men can harden. Loving, kind people can become cruel murderers.

These things should warn us that we are all dangerous creatures if we are left to ourselves. But the Holy Spirit is there, and he's there especially where the gospel is preached among people who are not saved. The gospel has an influence even when it doesn't save them. It has an influence—a broad influence, a general influence. It makes people, in general, more moral in their disposition, in their deportment. When the gospel begins to go, then this darkness comes in more and more. You can see it in our own country. As the gospel begins to go back, to decrease, you can see sin coming in. You see the fearful, unnatural crimes that come in. But just think of it. If the Holy Spirit withdrew all his restraints from people, they would lose even the ability to show love and kindness and pity to their fellow creatures.

That is how it will be in a lost eternity. It all goes. The relationships we have here are only for the world. Our married relationships, our parental relationships, everything we have in our homes in the way of relationship, they go. It's no use a husband and wife saying to each other, when one goes, 'I'll soon be joining you,' as if they're going to continue the love they have for each other in eternity. They have natural love, but natural love doesn't enter eternity, natural relationships don't enter eternity. Christ said they would be as the angels, that 'they neither marry nor are given in marriage'. These things are not retained in eternity.

We need to have spiritual love, we need to know Christ. If we don't know Christ—if we don't have a spiritual tie, a spiritual love to the Lord—then there's nothing left but to be as devils in the lost eternity. There will be hatred for those whom we loved in the world. There's nothing left in the lost eternity but hatred—hatred for God, hatred for the Church, hatred for everyone. There is no love, there is no kindness. There will be nothing but loneliness, the fearful loneliness of a lost eternity. Everyone there is a unit. There is no relationship and no possibility of a relationship in a lost eternity. There are no cliques, there is no coming together as a flock of sparrows—it doesn't happen, it cannot happen. That's how it will be for people dying without Christ, without God, without hope.

The very works of creation are so intricate that we are without excuse. The animals, the birds, the insects, the fish of the sea, the shellfish—the tiniest creatures are all so intricate. There are miles of blood vessels in every person, and all of these things are so intricate. God says, 'You have no excuse. I'm telling you there is a Creator. I am telling you that I am, even there.' Then God says, 'In your very heart, you know it. You speak of good and you speak of bad.' How can you speak of good, how can you speak of bad if there is no God? There's no meaning in these things, if there's no God. The very concept of 'good' demands that there is a God. It's in the breast, it's in the conscience—so much so that some murderers have to confess because of their conscience. They have to tell that they're murderers even if they knew they were going to be put to death for it. They have to speak it out because of the conscience.

The conscience goes with us into eternity. The conscience goes with lost sinners into a lost eternity. If you are lost, how are you going to be when the condemnation is there within your own breast? You will say, 'I have sinned against an all-holy God. I have rejected the gospel. I refused Christ. I refused the Saviour. I trampled on the blood. I rejected the overtures made over and over again from the gospel pulpit in the name of Christ. I rejected them all when I heard, "Come unto me and be saved." I refused when I heard him saying to me, "Believe on the Lord Jesus Christ, and thou shalt be saved." I refused. He said, "Come unto me, all ye that are weary and heavy laden," and I refused. I rejected him. That's in my conscience. It's within me, I cannot quench it, I cannot do away with it. That is my companion in hell, that will never leave me, a condemning conscience, along with another companion: the wrath of God, the wrath of the rejected God.' Oh friends, consider: loneliness, loneliness, loneliness!

We live in a world where we pick up papers that speak of people being lonely—some old age pensioners die in their homes, and nobody knew they died, and nobody finds out, perhaps, for months, until somebody may happen to go to the house to check up, and finds them. An investigation may be made, and neighbours saw nobody coming or going for ages. The old person had no friends, no relatives: they were on their own. They were old and they were lonely. So society makes up its mind—well, people should be visiting them. People form various clubs and other things to attract old people because there are so many lonely people. But that loneliness is nothing compared to the loneliness of a lost eternity, It cannot even be called loneliness in comparison to what we experience if we die without Christ.

Dear friends, Christ died for sinners, and the gospel is for those who need Christ, those who need a Saviour. He makes them needy, he makes them lonely, so that they will approach him, seeking a relationship, a living relationship, an eternal relationship. Oh, that he would be to us a father, mother, brother and sister—that he would be everything! Christ said, 'Behold my mother, behold my brethren.' Yes, all of these people who believe in him, they are his relations.

Wouldn't it be good, now, if you and I were to trust in Christ? Christ knows how you are, he knows what is in your heart. He knows your situation. Nothing that is within you is hidden from him. He calls upon you to approach him to speak to him—to speak directly to Christ the Saviour, in the same way as those who were with him in the world, in the days of his flesh could speak to him. We can speak to him. Oh, come to the Lord Jesus, friend! May the Holy Spirit give you that! May he bless the Word to you! Let us pray.

## Concluding prayer

Gracious and glorious Lord, we beseech thee to help us, for we are of all men most miserable if we never come to know thee. But if we know thee, we will have thy friendship—the friendship of the Father and the Holy Spirit, of the Son, of the angels, of the Church of Christ. Ah, Lord God, put us among thy children; make us to have the spots of thy children. Bless us when we depart one from another. Grant to remember this congregation, we pray thee, if it be thy holy will to build them up, to restore them, to help them. Grant to be with those in office in the congregation, to be with thy praying people, to be with those laid aside, to be with young and old. Dismiss us with thy blessing. Take away our sins. For Jesus' sake. Amen.

# 7

# Help and guidance for the downcast

4th February 2018, Lord's Day, Achmore

*Thus my heart was grieved, and I was pricked in my reins. So foolish was I, and ignorant: I was as a beast before thee. Nevertheless I am continually with thee: thou hast holden me by my right hand. Thou shalt guide me with thy counsel, and afterward receive me to glory.*
Psalm 73:21-24

WE see the general outline of the psalm. The psalmist was seeing men of the world full of riches, seeming to get on so well in the world, seeming to be happy and to be full with what the world can give them. And as the servant of God he shunned many of the things that they would run after. Yet something came into his heart: envy. He started envying the very world. That is, until he went up to the house of God and there he realised how things really were, that these men were standing on slippery places.

We should like to take up two matters here.

1. First of all, how the psalmist felt in God's holy presence. He says, 'Thus was my heart grieved, and I was pricked in my reins. So foolish was I, and ignorant: I was as a beast before

thee.' That was how he felt in God's holy presence, after the thoughts he had about worldly men.

2. And then secondly, how the psalmist had God's help and wonderful guidance. 'Nevertheless I am continually with thee: thou hast holden me by my right hand. Thou shalt guide me with thy counsel, and afterward receive me to glory.'

## 1. How the psalmist felt in God's holy presence

We read in verse 21, 'Thus my heart was grieved, and I was pricked in my reins.' He was pricked in his reins. Farmers used to use a goad, a sharp pointed stick, when they were driving the oxen, especially young oxen that were not used to the yoke. Say, when they were ploughing and they wanted straight furrows, the ox may have tended to go to the right or to the left. Then they would put the goad into the flank of the ox, just touching it, to make it realise how it should go.

That is what happened to the psalmist. He says, 'My heart was grieved.' Grieved at how he himself thought, how he ended. Grief because he envied the world—he envied people who had plenty of the things of the world, who had good health, who had families that were complete, who seemed to be filled with the happiness of this world. The devil was using that to snare him, to draw him.

But when he went to the house of God, he saw the picture as it really was, the true picture. These people are in slippery places, they don't look to God. In verse 12 he says, 'Behold, these are the ungodly.' They don't have God. It doesn't matter what they have, they are ungodly, they don't have God. These are the ungodly who prosper in the world. They increase in riches, but they are the ungodly. The people of God have God himself as their riches. Their riches—their treasure—is beyond all comprehension. Yes, they live by faith, but this is the

## 7 Help and guidance for the downcast

snare that they're brought into: they look at things not by faith but according to the flesh. When we begin to do that, then the devil can set his snares for us, and we can begin to envy. That was what the psalmist felt.

He tells us what else he was thinking at that time. He says in verse 13, 'Verily I have cleansed my heart in vain, and washed my hands in innocency.' What a thing to think, that he had cleansed his heart in vain and washed his hands in innocency! 'In vain' means 'for nothing'. He thought he gained nothing by it. Just imagine a child of God coming to have thoughts like that! Well, we can have all sorts of thoughts in our sinful hearts: foolish thoughts, rebellious thoughts, worldly thoughts, lustful thoughts, dark thoughts. God has left us with that principle within us, and the devil keeps on trying to scare us and spoil us. The child of God finds it so difficult to come before the Lord in prayer, for example. He wants to pray with a clean heart. He wants to pray totally in earnest. Yet, at times, when he comes before the Lord, the devil begins to stir the pot. The child of God is conscious of all these things in his heart when he's speaking to the Lord. He's speaking to the fountain of holiness, and he feels it so very difficult. He feels so much shame before his Lord. He feels so unclean when he comes before his Lord in that state.

However, the psalmist tells us in verses 16 and 17 how he was brought to his senses. 'I went into the sanctuary of God; then understood I their end.' The sanctuary of God should be a place where our understanding is opened. Our spiritual understanding is opened when we gather to worship God. The Word of God does that, prayer does that, singing his praises does that. It's a place where God teaches his own people, where the Holy Spirit blesses the Word to them, where they come to realise more and more how things really are. This is how they have the proper balance in their lives. Oh, it's good to be in the means of grace, and it's good to turn to the Lord constantly in this world. We have so much spiritual opposition. It is not so easy for the child of God. No wonder he groans so often. No wonder he weeps in his heart so often. No wonder he feels that he's making no progress. No wonder he feels that he's full of darkness. And no wonder he feels that his life is made up of stumbling and falling. He's ashamed of himself constantly when he sees what he is in his own heart before the Most High.

There is something wonderful in all this, though. The psalmist is telling us how he was. He's being totally honest, he's not hiding it. By nature we hide things, and of course we cannot tell people everything about our sins, and our lusts, our inner thoughts. But the Holy Spirit made the psalmist to be totally honest. The psalmist spoke of his own weakness, and that was for the sake of the Church, because God's people go through experiences like that. They have to realise that the Lord understands that, that the Lord who searches the heart understands clearly how they are. God is giving them his own Word to help them. He gives them the experience of the psalmist to help them when they go through experiences of this kind.

We have that with David too, for example in Psalm 51. He spoke of his own great sin. He didn't hide it, and so the great sin of David went into the what the Church sings till the end of time. The great sin of David could have been hidden, and we might think that David would have had more honour if it were hidden. But no, God says, 'No, for the sake of the Church it has to be revealed,' so that the Church will understand how the Lord can take us up when we fall, how the blood of Christ can cleanse us, how we can find forgiveness constantly. If any man sins we have an advocate with the Father, Jesus Christ the righteous.

Moses tells of his own sin for the same reason. He doesn't hide it. Moses was the man of God, and yet he tells about the sin

## 7  Help and guidance for the downcast

of his brother and his sister. These were about the holiest people in the nation! It is all to help God's people. We are sinners, we slip, we slide. 'O wretched man that I am,' said Paul, for the very same reason, that he was conscious of this. Godly man as he was, and perhaps the godliest man that was in the world, still he was plagued by the plague of the heart.

The psalmist goes on in speaking of these things and how he feels in God's holy presence. In verse 22 he says, 'So foolish was I, and ignorant: I was as a beast before thee.' There are three things he says here.

He says first of all that he was foolish. In verse 11 we read about the worldly man who says, 'How doth God know? and is there knowledge in the Most High?' The fool says in his heart, 'There is no God.' Or as it is in the Hebrew, 'The fool says in his heart: no God.' He does not just say that there is no God, but he says, 'No God.' Not only that there is no God, but, 'I don't want to think about God. I don't want to think about his commandments. I don't want any thoughts in any way whatsoever to trouble me regarding God.' Oh, the fool, the great, great fool! The works of creation themselves clearly, clearly tell us about God. The very complexity of creation tells us about God. Just think of the wonderful way in which man is made up. It is said that if you took all the blood vessels in the human body and joined them all together, you'd go well over a mile. Who made these things? Who put the framework together? Who made the mind? Who made man capable of thinking of eternity, capable of thinking of God, capable of working out plans? The whole world is full of these things—so complex, so wonderfully made. God says, 'There you have the truth.' But the fool says, 'No. No God.' Their conscience inside also speaks to them of good and evil, but still the fool says, 'No God, no God.' The psalmist says, 'So foolish was I. How could I enter into that realm of refusing God? What was I doing?'

Then the second thing he says is, 'I was ignorant.' If you're ignorant, you know nothing. The psalmist says, 'What was I doing, entering into the realm of spiritual ignorance? How did my thoughts take me into that place?'

Then the third thing he says is, 'I was as a beast before thee.' The word he uses is 'behemoth'—a large beast. An animal—a beast—cannot know about God. It wasn't meant to know about God. It's meant to be in the world, under the rule of man. When they die, the spirit goes down, they disappear, they go. When an animal dies, there's nothing left but the flesh. It knows nothing about God, knows nothing about spiritual things, knows nothing about eternity, knows nothing about good or evil. That is how the psalmist saw himself. 'I was as a beast before thee. I was foolish. I was ignorant. I was as a beast. I saw these rich men and how they prospered. That's the kind of thoughts that come into my mind.'

These are the kind of thoughts that came into his mind. Yes, even though he was a godly man.

## 2. God's help and wonderful guidance

Then we have the true heart of this man—how he really is despite all these temptations. Despite all these thoughts, despite how impure he is, he has God's help and God's wonderful guidance in his life.

In verse 23 he says, 'Nevertheless'—that is, despite all that—'I am continually with thee.' You see what he's saying: 'Things come into my thoughts, temptations come, the devil puts things in me, the world draws me, my own corruption is there. I feel that the Lord is far away at times. But nevertheless I am continually with thee.' He's not saying that God is continually with him. No, that's not what he says. God is with his own people. God says, 'Lo, I am with thee alway.' He says, 'I will

## 7  Help and guidance for the downcast

never leave thee nor forsake thee.' But what the psalmist is saying is that he is continually with God. That's a great statement.

The psalmist speaks like that too at the end of Psalm 119. 'I, like a lost sheep, went astray.' 'I wasn't really a lost sheep,' he says, but 'like a lost sheep.' But he goes on to say that he did not suffer the Word of God to depart out of his mind. The Word of God was with him all the time, and he could say, 'Thy servant seek, and find.' That's what you have at the end of Psalm 119, which is full of the praise of the Word of God, the precepts of God, and the guidance of God.

It's good to be able to say, 'I am continually with thee.' 'I can't turn away from the Lord, I can't turn my back on the Lord, I can't put Christ out of my life. I've no desire to do that. I can't but keep on turning to him and calling upon him and seeking his help. I am continually with thee.'

Then he says, 'Thou hast holden me by my right hand.' This is what is behind it! 'Thou hast holden me by my right hand. Thou art holding me. The grip that the Lord has upon my soul is a grip that Satan cannot break, and the corruption of my heart cannot break it, and the world cannot break it.' Nothing can pluck them out of his hand. God holds onto his own people.

Indeed, what the psalmist says is, 'Thou hast holden me by my right hand'. God is taking hold of my hand: not just my hand, but my *right* hand. Now, the right hand is normally the stronger of the two. Normally you would use your stronger hand—the right hand—to grasp hold of something, or to maintain yourself or to help yourself.

Here the Lord is taking hold of the psalmist's right hand. It's like the Christian who has faith. By faith he takes hold of God.

But think of a child. When his father is taking him by his right hand, the child's hand is inside the father's hand. The child in his own way is taking hold, but it's really the father's hand over the child's hand that is taking hold. Still the child could say, 'I'm taking hold,' but also his father is taking hold.

Well, everything is inside the hold that the Lord is taking of us. He will never cast off his own. He will never let them go, whatever happens. That is the psalmist's comfort. He is conscious of the holiness of the Lord. He's conscious of the fact that he's not worthy of being upheld. He's conscious of the fact that he's worthy of being cast away because of the thoughts that he has, the things that arise in his heart. All his corruption troubles him. But at the same time, he has faith and he can say, 'I am continually with thee.' He can say, 'Thou hast holden me by my right hand. I'm not upheld by my own right hand: no, I'm upheld by the Lord. I live by faith, by the strength of the Lord. All the power of God is behind my keeping. Whatever happens, I'm upheld by the power of God.'

The three men in Daniel's day were threatened with the furnace because they would not worship the king. They refused and they said that they would not do it, even if they died in the furnace. They didn't die, but supposing they had died, even then they would still have been being led and upheld. Our bodies and our souls are in the hands of the Lord at death, and the time will come when body and soul will be restored once again to be with Christ in his glory.

It is good to have a consciousness of the Lord. The child of God should seek to promote that by making use of the means, especially prayer and thinking of the Lord. A consciousness of the Lord helps us, and keeps our feet from sliding, if we are conscious of the Lord being there, close to us, near to us.

# 7  Help and guidance for the downcast

I once read of a shoemaker. There was a man he much admired—a man of integrity, a godly man. The shoemaker was a Christian, and he said that he kept that man's picture before him on his bench where he worked. He said, 'That man's integrity, that man's godliness, has always helped me. When I think of that man and what he was, it helps me.' But think of the God of that godly man! Think of God being before you, on the bench, on the desk, in the home, in the workplace, in the street, wherever you go. If your thoughts are in the Lord, it helps you when temptation comes and worldly thoughts come, when trouble comes and trial comes. It's good to know that the Lord is there. He keeps you, he helps you.

Here is another illustration. There was a little girl who was afraid of the dark in her bedroom. In the darkness of the night she came out of her bedroom and went to her mother's bed. Her mother said to her, 'My bedroom is just as dark as your bedroom!' 'Oh,' the little girl said, 'but you're not in my bedroom, and I want to be with you.' A closeness to the Lord is what every child of God should be seeking constantly. And that's what the devil and the world seek to loosen.

Anyway, we come to this: 'Thou shalt guide me with thy counsel, and afterward receive me to glory.' Two things are left to look at: being guided with God's counsel, and being received to glory. If you're not guided by his counsel, you'll never be received into glory.

The psalmist says he's guided by God's counsel. He used to be guided by his own counsel and by the counsel of the devil and by the counsel of the world. But a change came into his life, and he began to be guided by the counsel of the Lord. He began to listen to the Word of God, to what the all-holy God was saying. He began to desire to please God, to show love to the Saviour. He began to desire to grow in grace and to grow in holiness. He desired to grow in love to the Lord and to sinners. He wanted to grow. He wanted to be guided as he went through this world with all its different circumstances and complicated circumstances. He wanted to be guided because he didn't have the requisite knowledge or wisdom. He felt he was a fool, an ignoramus, a beast. He needed the counsel of the Lord.

The human heart is so proud. When people give advice, many just react against it. They're not going to be guided by other people—they have their own wisdom and common sense and so on. That might be appropriate at times, but in spiritual matters it is not appropriate. We are really ignorant, we are really foolish, we are really acting as beasts until we are guided by the counsel of the Lord. The Word of God is so precious, and the Holy Spirit uses the Word of God to lead you in your mind and heart as you go through this world, if you look to the Lord for guidance and help. He is our eyes in the wilderness. In the wilderness the children of Israel were led for forty years by the Shechinah. He went before them, and they could all the see the pillar of cloud by day and the pillar of fire by night. The Lord went before them: where he went, they went. He led them in an uncharted way through the wilderness with hope. There was no way, nothing to indicate how they should walk, no signposts. There was nothing like that, but he led them by his right hand, his glorious arm. He led them through the wilderness.

That's what the Lord does for his people with his counsel. Yes, the world will laugh, the world will mock, the world will think that you are a fool, the world will think that you are ignorant. But God's people have wisdom that the world doesn't know, and their wisdom is to listen to the counsel of the Lord. They are led by the Spirit and by the Word, and the Spirit blesses the Word to them. So it's good to read the Word and to meditate upon it. It's good to know what God is saying to poor sinners, what he is saying to his own people, the encouragement he is giving them, the help he is giving them. The Word they receive to uphold them is like a staff. Jacob said, 'With my staff I passed over Jordan.' He was crippled, but still he went over Jordan, and we see him on his deathbed leaning upon his staff and worshipping God. The Word of God is our staff. Let us lean upon it, let us worship God leaning upon it. Let us be led by his counsel, not by the counsel of men.

Then the psalmist says, 'And afterward receive me to glory.' That's a wonderful thing. Christ elsewhere says, 'I go and prepare a place for you: if it were not so, I would have told you. And if I go and prepare a place for you, I will come again, and receive you unto myself; that where I am, there ye may be also.' What you have here is the fact that he will receive us: 'Receive me to glory.' Christ said that he would come again. When the child of God dies, Christ said that he comes again for him. But he says more than that: he says that he will receive them as well as coming for them. He receives them, like somebody standing in the doorway of heaven, the doorway of glory, to welcome them. They don't just go through the doorway into glory with nobody there to greet them. No, the one who loved them with an everlasting love, he's there for them. He is their true heaven, their true glory. They are going to Christ. They are going to be like him and to be with him. It is just how the Jews received their guests: the kiss on the cheek, the oil on the head—that is, the Holy Spirit on the head, and the washing of the feet. Your shoes are taken off and you're in the house without shoes in the comfort of the house, as if the house is your own. That was the Jewish reception of guests, and that's only a faint picture of the reception of his own people. 'Receive me to glory.'

The Hebrew word 'glory' is the same as the word 'weight', something heavy. Glory is a weight. It is sometimes called a weight of glory, a glory of glory. This glory is beyond all our comprehension. People ask, 'What is heaven like?' We cannot tell. We have symbols, we have hints here and there, but all we know for sure is that Christ is there, and that Christ will take his people to be with him there, and the glory is all there. God's people are going to glory, and God's people are glorified. They are inside that glory. They are brought into it in some wonderful, glorious way, to have a fellowship with Christ that they could not have here. Although the psalmist was continually with the Lord here, he will be more with the Lord in heaven—in glory—than he ever was here. They will be totally like Christ, within the limits of creaturehood. They will be totally sinless, they will be holy. They will know God's people, every one of them, better than their own family in this world. Their mind is open, their understanding is open, their mental grasp is far, far greater and their spiritual grasp is far greater.

Oh, friends, to be able to say that he will receive me—me!—to glory. You see, we are all different. We have personalities, and your personality will go with you into eternity. You'll always be conscious of your own personality, no matter who's with you or where you are. You'll always be conscious, that you're a 'me', your own person, your own self, your own personality. And how wonderful it is to think of Christ receiving me to glory!

Paul had something like that when he spoke about the 'Christ who loved me'. He loved me!—my person, my sinful, sinful, sinful person. Christ who loved me, the chief of sinners. Christ loved me, and gave himself for me. So, you see, your person—your own personality—isn't wrong, it always will exist. And to have Christ receive me to glory, to his glory, to himself, is a wonderful, wonderful thing. Oh friends, may we all have that! May that be our portion!

May the Lord bless his Word. Let us pray.

7  Help and guidance for the downcast

## Concluding prayer

Bless thy goodness to us, O Lord, we pray thee. Go before us, guide us and lead us. Teach us how to walk in thy holy way. Be with us on this Sabbath Day. Help us to worship thee, in public and in private. Take away our sins. For Jesus' sake. Amen.

# 8

# The promise of the Holy Spirit

4th February 2018, Lord's Day evening, North Tolsta

*And I will pour upon the house of David, and upon the inhabitants of Jerusalem, the spirit of grace and of supplications: and they shall look upon me whom they have pierced, and they shall mourn for him, as one mourneth for his only son, and shall be in bitterness for him, as one that is in bitterness for his firstborn. In that day shall there be a great mourning in Jerusalem, as the mourning of Hadadrimmon in the valley of Megiddon. And the land shall mourn, every family apart; the family of the house of David apart, and their wives apart; the family of the house of Nathan apart, and their wives apart; the family of the house of Levi apart, and their wives apart; the family of Shimei apart, and their wives apart; all the families that remain, every family apart, and their wives apart.'*
Zechariah 12:10–14

ZECHARIAH is prophesying after the captivity was over. The children of Judah and Jerusalem had been carried off into Babylon. They had now been allowed to come back and to begin rebuilding the walls of Jerusalem and the temple. You have Zechariah speaking about Christ and his benefits, and the great blessings that the country was going to have when the time of Christ would come. He speaks of that in various ways as you go through this prophecy, including in this chapter. It's not always easy to discern, because he's using Old Testament language to speak about New Testament ideas and blessings. For example, In America, when people saw trains for the first time, they called them iron horses. It was a new thing to speak about, and they didn't have the word 'trains' but they had the word 'horses'. It's the same kind of thing when the prophets in the Old Testament are speaking about the New Testament. There are new concepts, new ideas, and they use their own vocabulary and the concepts of the Old Testament in speaking of these things. We have to understand that.

The prophet begins, 'The burden of the word of the LORD for Israel.' The burden comes from 'the LORD, which stretcheth forth the heavens, and layeth the foundation of the earth, and formeth the spirit of man within him'. That is the Creator. The prophet has a burden from the Lord, the Creator. It is his duty to bring his burden to the people of Judah and Jerusalem, and to open and display to them the word of the Lord in prophecy.

That's what he does here in this chapter. For example, he uses Jerusalem as a picture of the Church of Christ. He says, 'I will make Jerusalem a cup of trembling unto all the people round about, when they shall be in the siege both against Judah and against Jerusalem.' The gospel was going to prosper, and those who tried to destroy it in those days would be themselves destroyed, under the hand of God. That's how it worked out in providence. He speaks of the terror 'in that day'. Five times in this chapter he says 'in that day'. And the day he is speaking about is the day of the gospel, when the gospel will appear among them, when Christ will finish his work, when people will be blessed and begin to believe in Christ as Saviour. He says, 'In that day,' speaking of these great blessings.

Again, Zechariah speaks of the Church of Christ as being weak. He speaks of it as being like a tent. In verse 7 he says that the Lord 'also shall save the tents of Judah first. In that day shall the LORD defend the inhabitants of Jerusalem; and he that is feeble among them at that day shall be as David.' Here he is speaking of the strength of the grace, of the blessings that will come upon his own people. They are like people in a tent, and they are feeble people. The Church is low, the Church is weak, but despite being weak, somehow it survives and grows. Somehow it seems that against all appearances, still the Church grows and becomes stronger and stronger. We see that as we go through the chapter.

We shall look at three things.

1. In looking at these words of verse 10, we should like to speak first of all about the promise of the Holy Spirit being poured. 'And I will pour upon the house of David, and upon the inhabitants of Jerusalem, the spirit of grace and of supplications.' You remember John the Baptist speaking of that. 'One cometh after me', one 'who was before me'. He said that Christ would baptise with fire and with the Holy Spirit, that Christ was going to baptise when he poured out the Holy Spirit. That's what John was speaking about, and that's what Zechariah is speaking of here.

2. Secondly, there are the blessed results of that pouring. 'They shall look upon me whom they have pierced, and they shall mourn for him, as one mourneth for his only son.'

3. Lastly there are the recipients of that blessing and the extent of the blessing. 'The land shall mourn, every family apart; the family of the house of David apart, and their wives apart,' and so on.

8   The promise of the Holy Spirit

## 1. The promise of the Holy Spirit

'I will pour upon the house of David, and upon the inhabitants of Jerusalem.' The 'I' here is Jesus Christ, he is the one who will pour. 'I will pour,' he says—not, 'I will sprinkle.' He could have said that if he had chosen to. He suffered, he died, he rose again, he went to heaven and some days later, at the time of Pentecost, he poured the Holy Spirit upon his disciples. They began to speak in other languages, and people who had come to the Jewish feast from all over began to hear the gospel in their own language. It didn't matter where they came from. They heard Galilaeans, men who were mocked because of their accent. They heard Galilaeans, who had no scholastic attainments, nothing in the way of education, just the common education the Jews had. Yet they were speaking with all these tongues, fluently. They were making no mistakes in preaching the gospel, because the Holy Spirit was poured out. There was a mighty, rushing wind and cloven tongues of fire appeared upon the heads of these disciples. Peter also preached, and the gospel was blessed, and three thousand people believed on that day. Three thousand!

It soon went up by another five thousand. It then began increasing here and there, and began spreading out from Jerusalem to the rest of the land. Of course, then the persecution began, but that only scattered the fire, and it began taking flame all over. Then it went into Asia, into Europe. The disciples and the apostles were sent out to various parts, sometimes to die. They preached the gospel and they suffered. No power of Satan could keep it back. The Lord tied Satan in a measure at that time. The world was full of the power of the devil at that time. Many were devil-possessed. The devil was around to do many things in that day, when Christ was in the world. We see that when we read the gospels. The devil had fearful power in that day. But he was unable to keep back the gospel when the Holy Spirit was poured out. That is what Zechariah is speaking of here.

It is Christ who pours out the Spirit. He says, 'I will pour upon the house of David, and upon the inhabitants of Jerusalem.' That means the house of David, the royal family, the descendants of David. 'I will bless them. I will pour my spirit upon them, and upon the inhabitants of Jerusalem, the spirit of grace and of supplications.' We all know what the pouring of the rain is. And we read about oil being poured upon the head of the high priest—not just put on here and there, but poured.

Here is the great pouring: the pouring of the Holy Spirit. That proved that Christ was accepted by God. That proved that he was on the right hand of God, that he had the power. Jesus Christ, the God-man who was in this world, had a life of humiliation and suffering. That same Jesus, the God-man, was then so exalted that he could pour the Holy Spirit, the third person of the Godhead, upon sinners in this world. That's the promise, then, that Christ made through Zechariah. That is the power, and nothing could keep him back. It all began there in Jerusalem, a figure of the Church, as it is very often in Scripture, using Old Testament phraseology to convey a New Testament concept.

Then Zechariah explains about this Holy Spirit. He calls him, 'The spirit of grace and of supplications.' 'That's the spirit I'm going to pour.'

The Holy Spirit is the spirit of grace. Now, 'grace' is the same word as 'gift'. A gift is something you get for nothing. The spirit of grace was not anything that people were going to earn or going to buy: it was something given, just out of the goodness and mercy of the heart of the Saviour. He just poured it on sinners—on dark sinners, on rebels, on those who had opposed Christ, on those who had crucified him. He just poured it upon them. This Spirit is given freely, for nothing. When you say it's for nothing, it means you don't pay anything for it. And not only this, but you didn't deserve it. When you receive the Holy Spirit in your heart, you're going to praise the Lord for ever and for ever, because you didn't deserve it, yet you received him for nothing.

He's called not only the spirit of grace, but also the spirit of supplications. Supplication is something that a beggar does. To supplicate means to beg, to plead for something. If you're in need, if you have no money and no home, you're in rags and you have no food and your children are suffering, you'll go anywhere to beg for food for them, to beg for clothing, to beg for necessities. Well, when the Holy Spirit comes into the heart of a man, that man becomes a beggar. He doesn't go to men, but he goes to the Lord to beg.

How does he begin to beg? He says, 'Have mercy upon me, a sinner.' The publican in the temple was a saved man when he said that. Christ said that about him. When you come to the Lord Jesus, you begin to beg for him to have mercy upon your soul, because you see that you cannot live without him. It means everything to you, to be redeemed by him. You come to him with all your heart.

Then when you think back on it, after a while, you will say, 'It was the Holy Spirit who made me come that day, with that prayer, with that begging! I have nothing. I have nothing, Lord, but sin. I have nothing to offer. I am not worthy of the least of thy mercies. All I'm asking for is mercy—mercy, pure mercy. I can pay nothing for it.' The Holy Spirit brings that out. Did you ever have that in your experience? Ah, it would be a good thing if we all had that in our experience!

## 2. The results of the Holy Spirit being poured out

Then we see the blessed results of the Holy Spirit being poured out. He says, 'They shall look upon me whom they have pierced, and they shall mourn for him, as one mourneth for his only son.'

'They shall look upon me whom they have pierced.' It is Christ who is speaking here. He says that they will gaze upon Christ. 'They shall gaze upon me whom they have pierced.' We know that when Christ died, a soldier put a spear through his side, into the heart, just to make sure he was dead—and he *was* dead. But this passage is not talking about that. Instead, it is speaking of my sins there in the sufferings of Christ. What I am worthy of—eternal destruction at the hands of the Lord, eternal hell, eternal hatred, eternal fire. What I am worthy of because of my sin. 'Against thee, thee only, have I sinned,' and my sin was laid upon Christ. My sin was aimed at God, my sin was aimed at the glory of God, at the throne of God. 'Against thee, thee only have I sinned.' It was God's law I broke, not man's law. That's how I have to look at it: 'I've broken God's holy law. I'm a sinner from the time I came into this world. I've kept on, as it were, piercing Christ. All my sins, as it were, passing upon him.' When you believe, you see it that way. He bore the wrath of God on behalf of his own people.

'They shall look upon me, and they shall mourn.' They shall mourn, they shall repent, they shall hate sin. How will they hate sin? They have faith. Yes, of course they have faith. You'll never hate sin until you have faith, you'll never repent until you have faith, you'll never mourn for your sin until you have faith. Yes, without faith the conscience might condemn you for something you did wrong, but that doesn't make you hate sin. You still live as a sinner without Christ until you are born again, brought alive, and then you have faith in Christ. You look upon him, and from the time you begin to look upon

## 8 The promise of the Holy Spirit

him, you look upon him for ever—in life, in death, in eternity. He is the one that all eyes in heaven see. He is the centre of all attention in glory. Every eye—whatever kind of eyes we have had, or will have—every eye is fixed attentively upon him for ever and for ever. He's full of the glory and goodness of God. He is the one to whom we will look for ever. And repentance, someone has said, is like the tear in the eye of faith.

Faith and repentance go together. As you gaze upon sin, as you gaze upon Christ, you see your own sin in that light, and you abhor your sin. You abhor what you see in yourself as you come to see more and more of the preciousness of the Saviour, who loved you and gave himself for you and suffered gladly for you. Yes, you see the one who was pierced, the one who was made a curse, who suffered and died. It is my sin passing upon him.

Then he goes on: 'They shall mourn for him, as one mourneth for his only son.' That's to show how deep the mourning is. It is not superficial mourning. Just think of the Jewish family: they all had a piece of ground in Canaan, and the ground was left to the family. It went to the eldest son, and their hopes were fixed upon the eldest son. Now, supposing the eldest son died, just think of the mourning there would be. Oh well, friends, mourning is a common thing. Death is a common thing. It is a common thing if you have a son lost or a daughter lost or a dear one lost. Zechariah is making use of this mourning to speak about the spiritual mourning God's people have in faith as they look at Christ and hate their sin. They mourn, and the agony of that mourning, he says, is like the mourning for an only son.

It is true mourning, it is true repentance. They hate sin. Sin is that which should not be, but they still have sin within them, a sinful principle. That is so difficult for the child of God. He hates what he sees within himself. 'That which I would not,' said Paul, 'that I do,' and he says that he did not do what he would wish to do. 'O wretched man that I am!' he says. This terrible situation! The godly person in the world is in agony of soul, mourning because of what is within him and what he does in thought, word and deed. They shall mourn and be in bitterness for him, as one that is in bitterness for his firstborn. He shall be in a spirit of bitterness against sin. 'The harm sin does, the harm sin has done to me, the harm sin has done to mankind, the harm sin has done to the world, and all the sin that is around me as well as the sin I find within myself. I feel a spirit of bitterness against it. I hate sin but at the same time, "My sin I ever see."' That is what he says.

Now, notice what Christ says. 'I will pour … and they shall look upon me whom they have pierced, and they shall mourn for him.' Who's the 'me' and who's the 'him'? Well, very often in the Scripture you have the Lord going from the first person, 'me', to the third person, 'him'. He speaks of 'me'—that is, himself—then stands back and he speaks of the 'him'—still meaning himself. He speaks of the 'him', but it's the one person all the time—it's the Saviour, it's Christ all the time.

'In that day', he says, 'shall there be a great mourning in Jerusalem, as the mourning of Hadadrimmon in the valley of Megiddon.' There's going to be a great mourning in Jerusalem, when the Holy Spirit is poured out, when these thousands begin to believe. Men and women will begin to grieve as they never grieved before. They never grieved before because of their sin, they never grieved because they sinned against God, they never grieved because they sinned against the one who loved them and gave himself for them—until now. It's a great, great mourning that will take place in Jerusalem on the day of Pentecost and in following days.

They must have mourned very greatly at Hadadrimmon in the valley of Megiddon. In the history of Israel, a very sad event happened in the valley of Megiddo. There was a godly king of Judah whose name was Josiah, and Scripture calls him 'good king Josiah'. He was a godly man, and he drove out idolatry and sodomy from the land. He did other good things at various times, and he caused great blessing to come upon the people. There was a kind of revival in those days under good king Josiah. But then Pharaoh Necho, king of Egypt was passing by with an army. He said that he wasn't coming to attack Judah but going elsewhere, to oppose the Babylonians. But Josiah went out to fight him, and Josiah was killed in the valley of Megiddo. He was pierced with many arrows and he died. The whole nation mourned for that man. They mourned for good King Josiah as they had never been seen to mourn for any other king. Josiah's servants brought back his body and they had special services in their mourning for that king. The Holy Spirit makes uses that as a picture to describe the Saviour's death. Christ was pierced with many, many arrows when the sins of his people were laid upon him. And Zechariah is saying that the mourning they had for Josiah at Hadadrimmon is similar to what will be seen in Jerusalem on the day of Pentecost. When the Holy Spirit is poured out, it will resemble the mourning at Hadadrimmon in the valley of Megiddon. It will be like that. You will see people, thousands of them everywhere, weeping, mourning, sorrowful because of what they are—great sinners. They have sinned against the Most High and now they desire to live to his glory. Now, they hate sin and mourn for sin, and they keep on mourning.

Rowland Hill and John Bunyan and John Newton found repentance—sorrow for sin—so sweet. It wasn't just sorrow for sin. It was a sorrow for sin that turned these men to Christ. That was their repentance—not half a repentance, but a full repentance—a sorrow for sins that turned them to Christ. These saints of God at times felt as if they might like to take repentance with them, even to heaven! The reason for that was the sweetness of turning to Christ. It was so sweet to be at the feet of the Saviour, pouring out their heart to the Saviour, receiving the mercy, the love of the Saviour. Of course, repentance doesn't enter heaven, but in heaven they do have love for the Saviour. He will show his love to his people in heaven as he never showed his love to them in this world. They will be sinless then, and able to embrace his love. Their understanding will be opened, their mental and spiritual capacities will be enlarged, and they will be able to enjoy the blessing of the Lord as they could not enjoy it here. Oh friends, to be among them! That's the mourning, then, as of 'Hadadrimmon in the valley of Megiddon'.

### 3. The recipients of the blessing

Now a little about the recipients of this great mercy and this pouring. 'The land shall mourn, every family apart.' The mourning at Jerusalem will be so great that people will say, 'The land is mourning.' Wouldn't it be wonderful if the island of Lewis began to mourn, if they could say on the television, on the radio, in the newspaper, that the whole island of Lewis is mourning! But the reporters wouldn't put that in, because they themselves wouldn't be mourning for sin. They don't believe in that. They can't accept that you can have families and an island with so much mourning for sin in it that you can actually say the island is mourning for sin.

But just think of the island here, when the *Iolaire* went on the rocks and over two hundred perished. The whole island mourned. The whole island was under that deep shadow. If only our island were turned to the Lord in true repentance, in true mourning for sin, how blessed that would be! And how people would love each other. Yes, grace does that. It brings people to love each other. God's people love each other. Our best days as an island were when God's people desired to gather together. To speak about who? About Christ! Christ, the great topic of worship, the great topic of speech, the great centre for their worship. They never tire of Christ. 'Tell me more about Christ, give me more of Christ, make him more precious, bless him more and more to my soul.'

'The land shall mourn, every family apart.' Notice this apartness. He says, 'Every family apart; the family of the house of David apart, and their wives apart.' The families themselves begin to divide when this mourning comes in. You see, it's a personal matter. You can have a congregation and somebody there is blessed by the Holy Spirit, and he turns to the Lord. But he does it as an individual: the rest of the congregation might be totally untouched, and this individual alone might be mourning before the Lord—repenting savingly, because repentance is a saving grace. But in Zechariah's prophecy we have these families. The families are apart from other families, and even inside each family, they are apart. The wives are apart from the husbands, they're all going to be by themselves.

I remember hearing about the revival in Snizort on the island of Skye. When it took place, so many were weeping in the church, and it is said that men and women headed for the trees that were growing nearby. They wanted to be on their own, to deal with the Lord on their own—to be behind a tree or behind a rock, away from others, to be apart, on their own, just themselves and the Lord. The gospel does that when it deals with you, in your heart. It puts you apart. It's different if the whole family comes to repent in the same way together, but for every individual, that's how it works out.

When you have a flock of sheep and one is sick, very often it goes to be by itself. When you have a herd of deer on the moor and one is sick, it goes to be by itself. It's apart. When you have a poor sinner into whose heart the arrow of the Lord has gone, who has been touched by this spiritual baptism of the Holy Spirit, then he goes apart. He's on his own before God. 'Have mercy upon me, a sinner. Upon *me*.' Yes, he'll think of his family—father, mother, brother, sister, children and all the rest—but at this time, at that very moment, when he goes apart, he has to think of his own soul. 'Have mercy upon me, a sinner.'

Notice it says, 'The family of the house of David apart.' That's the royal household. In the royal household it's the same thing—you go apart. It's not a different kind of salvation that you have in the royal household. If the Queen is saved, it's the same kind of salvation she will have as the beggar has or the man on the dunghill. There's no difference. God doesn't make a difference like that.

Then it mentions the family of the house of Nathan—that's the prophet, Nathan. Then it mentions the house of the family of Levi—that's the priest. And then it mentions the family of Shimei—that's the common man. So whether it's the house of royalty, whether it's the house of priesthood, or whether it's the house of the prophet, or whether it's the house of the poor, destitute man, it makes no difference. The work of the Holy Spirit is one. It's the same—it puts them all apart. It separates you from everybody else. All the families that remain—everyone—every family apart, their wives apart.

Ah well, friends, Zechariah is in glory. His hope in these things is now sight. He understands these things as he never did when he spoke of them. He may not have understood all that he was saying. The prophets themselves, we read, were looking into the things that the Lord gave them. Searching where Christ was, that's what they were really doing. Peter tells us it was 'regarding Christ'. The portion we have taken in this chapter has Christ. But the great thing is, do *I* have Christ? Do *you* have Christ? How are we placed on the way to eternity?

The Holy Spirit came to this island as well. The pouring reached Europe, and the islands where we are. Yes, and the

# 8  The promise of the Holy Spirit

Reformation was part of that pouring. It still goes on. The pouring still goes on, and the great concern is, has it passed us by to a great extent? Is it just a few drops that we are going to have? Or will it be like a pouring?—not just a sprinkling, but a pouring?

And are we earnest? Do we know Christ? Are we earnest in our prayers for ourselves, and are we earnest in our prayers for others? When you think of eternity, when you know that each one of us must go into eternity, are you not earnest? If we die without Christ, there is only the blackness of the darkness of hell for ever and for ever. There is no mercy there, no gospel there, no pouring of the Holy Spirit. We should be earnest about that. When God's people are not earnest, the world will see that. When God's people are earnest, the world will see that as well. The world will begin to worry when God's people are earnest, but when they are flippant, and when they never speak of these things among the world, then the world says, 'Well, it can't mean very much to them if they never speak of these things, never mention these things, never tell me about where my soul is going.'

There are people in North Tolsta who are mourning today like the mourning in the valley of Megiddo. But they are a happy people. They have a happiness although they have a grief. They have a grief that the world does not know, a spiritual grief because of sin, but they have a spiritual happiness because of Christ. You would think that these two things couldn't go together, but they *do* go together. They are found together in repentance. These happy mourning ones thank the Lord that they were made to mourn for sin.

Some people say, wrongly, 'Surely the mourning must come before salvation.' This is how these people work it out: 'I've got to mourn for my sin, and then I turn to Christ.' The true mourning for sin—the *real* mourning for sin—is a saving act, although the sinner who begins to truly mourn for sin might not know that. But when he's mourning for his sin, he's looking to the Saviour for mercy, as one that has been turned that way—to look to Christ alone for salvation and to hate his sin. That one is saved already. But instead, these people have the wrong idea, that you mourn for a while and then after that, when you've been sorrowing and sorrowful enough, then you begin to trust in Christ. It's not like that: the two things are together, you don't separate them. Without faith, you cannot please God. Without looking to Christ as your own Redeemer and Saviour, you're not going to please God. Whatever kind of mourning you have, if it doesn't put you to that, you're not going to please God and you don't know salvation. Yes, people will mourn in hell and people might mourn bad things they have done in this world. That's remorse. We can be remorseful—the conscience does that, but that's not the same as turning to Christ in your mourning. So let us then examine what we have, and let us pray that we might have what is true, what is real, what is useful, what is helpful for ourselves and for our children. May our children go apart, may our wives go apart, may we go apart, and may we know Christ as our Saviour.

Let us pray.

## Concluding prayer

O gracious and glorious Lord, we beseech thee to bless thy Word to us. Make it precious to us, who are on the way to eternity, that the Lord Jesus might be above all other treasures in our eyes. Oh that he might be supreme, that he might be the One in whom we trust, that he might be the One to whom we will be married for evermore. Ah, Lord God, thy promises are deeper and higher and more full than we ever realise. Give us to embrace them by faith. Grant to put us apart this evening, looking to thyself. Give us journeying mercies. Cleanse us. For Christ's sake. Amen.

# 9

# No room in the inn

19th May 2018, Lord's Day morning, Leverburgh

*And she brought forth her firstborn son, and wrapped him in swaddling clothes, and laid him in a manger; because there was no room for them in the inn.*
Luke 2:7

WE see that this account of the Gospel was written by Luke, who also gave us the Book of Acts. He was one who was used by the Lord. He set out everything in a very careful historical manner in Acts, just as he did in the first three chapters of this Gospel.

In chapter 1, verse 5, he says, 'There was in the days of Herod, the king of Judaea, a certain priest named Zacharias.' So he's giving it a historical setting.

In chapter 2 he says, 'It came to pass in those days, that there went out a decree from Caesar Augustus, that all the world should be taxed. And this taxing was first made when Cyrenius was governor of Syria.' Many used to say there was no such person as Cyrenius. The enemies of the gospel would seek to dispute the facts of history. But it's not so long ago since evidence was turned up out of the ground showing that there was indeed such a man as Cyrenius as a governor of Syria.

Then when you go to chapter 3, at the very beginning, Luke says, 'Now in the fifteenth year of the reign of Tiberius Caesar, Pontius Pilate being governor of Judaea, and Herod being tetrarch of Galilee, and his brother Philip tetrarch of Ituraea.' He puts it all in a historical setting. There's no way of saying this didn't happen. Even the worldly man has to recognise that this is history. What Luke says are things that can easily be confirmed.

But we are speaking not just of these historical matters, we are speaking of the most wonderful thing that took place in time. Jesus Christ, the second person of the Trinity came through the curtain between eternity and time and took to himself the nature of man. There was no other kind of man but sinful man, and Christ took to himself the nature of sinners, yet without sin. He came to save his own people, whom he loved with an eternal love and to whom he would send the gospel to bring them in. That's why we have the gospel—to bring people in. 'Preach the gospel to every creature,' said Christ. His people are here and there, and without the gospel they're not going to come in. But preach the gospel to every creature, and they will come in.

We read here that Christ was born at a time when Caesar Augustus ordained that all the world should be taxed. The taxing was not actually made then, but everyone had to register then for the taxing. It came into the heart of the emperor and his counsellors in Rome that the whole world—the world that was in the empire—should be taxed. Everybody had to go to his own city, and so Joseph went to his own tribal city. He belonged to Bethlehem, so he went to Bethlehem. And at that time Mary was great with child. The Word of God had said a long time ago, through Micah the prophet, that Christ should be born in Bethlehem. 'Bethlehem … out of thee shall he come forth … that is to be ruler in Israel.' 'Bethlehem, out of thee shall come him who is to save his people.' And so it just

## 9 No room in the inn

happened in the plan of God. that when Joseph went to Bethlehem to register, Mary had the child. It was all in the plan of God: Christ had to be born in Bethlehem. Joseph had to go to Bethlehem. He didn't leave Mary behind: he took her with him, and there she had the child in Bethlehem. Caesar Augustus had his own plans for taxing, for raising money. That's what *he* thought of, but he didn't know that God had greater plans—to send his own Son into the world through Bethlehem. Bethlehem means 'the house of bread'. It was the house out of which would come the manna. Christ is the bread of life which, if a man should eat, he would never die. If you believe on Christ, you will never see eternal death.

So Bethlehem had to be the place where Christ was born. The time came, which the prophets speak of. Daniel speaks of the year. Jacob in Genesis, even before that, speaks of the sceptre: 'The sceptre shall not depart from Judah, nor a lawgiver from between his feet, until Shiloh come.' Shiloh was the peacebringer. The sceptre of rule was the Word of God. The kings had departed, but the sceptre would not depart from Judah. The Word of God would not be taken away from them until Christ came. It would still be there. The Jews were so careful, copying out the Word of God. Every time their copy contained a mistake, they destroyed that parchment. The man who was copying never tried to repair a mistake. He wasn't allowed to do that. If he got a figure wrong, a letter wrong, anything wrong, there was no repairing or attempting to put anything right. It was destroyed. It was the Word of God they were copying. This is how careful they were when they made copies of the Word of God. The sceptre, the rod of rule of the Church of God, would not be taken away until Shiloh would come. He came, and the rod was still there, the sceptre was still there, the Word of God was still there. By and large, the priesthood had departed in their hearts—the Pharisees, Sadducees, lawyers, scribes. But the Word of God was still kept, copied out so carefully.

Shiloh came then, as it was prophesied. When he came, he came at night-time. You never know when a child is going to be born—will it be during the day or during the night? Christ came during the night. When a child is born in the Royal Family, the whole country knows about it. In fact, the whole world now knows about it. If a new prince is born into the world in London, the whole world knows about it. Well, *this* child had been spoken of in the Old Testament, the Messiah who was to come. The Jews said they were waiting for him. Daniel told them when he should be expected. But yet, when he came, who recognised him? Where were the priests who should have been crowding in Bethlehem, waiting for him? Where were the scribes? Where were the lawyers who made the Scripture commentaries? The scribes who copied out Scripture? Where were they all, who should have been waiting for the coming of their Messiah? Where were they? They weren't there!

This darkness was not only in Bethlehem: there was a darkness upon the spirits of men in all the land of Judaea. There was no one to proclaim his birth. There was no one to come with satins and silks. No one to lead him to a palace. When he was born it was in the darkness of Bethlehem. His mother after birthing him took him up and laid him in a manger, in the feeding trough of animals. That's all she could find that seemed suitable. We don't even know if he was born in the stable or not. He might have been born outside or he might have been born inside. The Word of God doesn't tell us. All we know is that she took him up and she laid him in the feeding trough, in the manger. She laid him there. 'There was no room in the inn.' No doubt, as well as Joseph, many others who belonged to Bethlehem had come to register for the taxation. So there was no room in the inn. And when the time came, the Messiah came into the world—in that dirt of the stable, the filth, the smell. No hygiene, no cleanliness in the surroundings. That's just the way the world was: full of sin, no spiritual hygiene, no spiritual cleanliness, yet he came into the

## 9 No room in the inn

world. His mother wrapped him in swaddling clothes. Every child was swaddled like that. He was wrapped with his arms by his side and the cloths wrapped round him. Thirty-three years later Joseph of Arimathea and Nicodemus swaddled him again. They put the winding sheet around him, and they laid him in the grave. He had finished the work given him to do. And so he was laid to rest in the grave. Not in a manger, but in a stone sepulchre. Such are the ways of the Lord.

There were no crowds to proclaim him. Where were the multitudes? Where were they all, with their palm fronds? Where were they all? They weren't there! Just Joseph and Mary, and the babe in weakness. The babe that couldn't feed itself, couldn't clothe itself, couldn't cleanse itself, couldn't stand. The human babe newly born is totally helpless. And the Lord Jesus Christ entered into that state. He humbled himself. The Lord who created all things by the word of his power. He spoke to nothingness, and from nothingness the whole universe came into being. That is the very One here, who, newly born in our nature, can do nothing for himself. He humbled himself. That's where it began, and that's how he continued, until he humbled himself even unto death, the accursed death of the cross.

Just imagine if the night could speak! For God could give the night speech, if he desired, just as he made the ass speak, and he could make the very stones speak. And if the night were to speak, what a story it could tell of what took place in Bethlehem! The Holy Spirit has revealed what we need to know and here we have it placed before us in Scripture. Nobody was there but themselves. There was no room in the inn. The Lord of glory came unheralded into the world, in utter poverty and degradation and weakness and darkness.

We should like to look at our own souls—our own hearts—for a few moments, in the light of what we have here. Let me look at my heart, and you look at your heart. We can divide up the heart: we can make it an inn, or we can make it a stable. You can make it what you like. But there was no room in the inn. Yes, make it an inn, and see if there is room in your own heart for Christ.

## 1. The heart

So, first of all we can go to the heart room in the inn of our soul, the room where we love. We love our own. Husband and wife love each other, mother and child, father and child, brother and sister. Love is there in the heart. You can say today, 'There is love in my home. There's love in my heart.' But is there love for Christ in your heart room? The Word of God has said, 'Ye shall love the Lord your God with all your heart and with all your soul, with all your mind, with all your strength.' That is, you will give the Lord love, as you give love to nothing else or anyone else. But you know what Scripture says about men and women and children, as a whole? That they 'loved darkness rather than light, because their deeds were evil'. When it says their deeds were evil, 'deeds' means the thoughts, the words and the actions. Consider the evil that is in the heart, the lusts that are in the heart, the degradation, the darkness that is in the heart. People don't want to think about Christ. I met a man the other day. I spoke to him about churchgoing. He doesn't go to church. He came from one of the villages in Lewis. He never went to church after he left the Sabbath School. He doesn't want to talk about eternity. He doesn't want to spend his time even thinking about these things. We speak of the heart loving Christ, but no, he doesn't know about Christ. He didn't want to hear about Christ.

That's the story of many: no heart room. Is there room in the heart for Christ? Is there room in your own heart for Christ? Did your heart ever call out for Christ? Did you ever seek the Lord Jesus, that he might occupy your heart, and take it over,

## 9 No room in the inn

and rule in it, and sit on the throne of your heart? Heart room has to be prepared by the Holy Spirit, so that the Son of Glory might come in and reside there forever. Imagine having the heart where Christ lives forever. Forever! That's what the child of God has. Christ will live there forever. The child of God knows the love of Christ. It has been shed abroad in his heart, and his only mourning is that he doesn't love Christ as much as he desires.

It's good to desire to love Christ. But some may say, 'There is no room, at present anyway. There's just no room.' The door is shut. Indeed, if the door is shut fast, the door is bolted, completely closed, then there's no room. 'The room is full. It can't take Christ. I love many things. I desire many things. My heart goes out to many things, but I'm sorry but at present there is no place for Christ.' What a tragedy! That room was made for him. God created that room in Adam for the Saviour, for himself. What a tragedy that is!

I read once of a lad who left the Highlands and went off to sea and left a widowed mother behind. He never wrote, but she was waiting for him to come back. He came back eventually, but when he got there the house was desolate and the neighbours told him that she had passed away a few years before. They told him where the grave was, and he went to the grave. He said that what he was saying over the grave was, 'Mother, mother, I *did* love you, although I went away. I *did* love you.' Ah friends, let us *show* our love. Christ said, 'If ye love me, keep my commandments.' It's how the life is, how the heart is, how we live.

And you know, if Christ doesn't have the heart spiritually, who really has the heart? I'll tell you who has the heart. Satan has the heart. He has it in a subtle way, so that you do not recognise that he has it. He puts things before you, that you run after, that you desire—the things of the world, the things of pleasure and joy, the things that entrance you and draw you and ensnare you—and you do not know that you are worshipping him through these things. People give their hearts to worldly things, and they have no time for the gospel. They are taken up with other things. They don't know it, but Satan has their heart. Yes, but their eyes will be opened. One day their eyes will be opened in hell. They will not worship Satan then, but in hell it will be too late. Too late! They can't then say to the Lord, 'Come into my heart, take over my heart, rule over my heart.' No heart room. Closed. Bolted. No room.

## 2. The ear

Then there is also the ear room. Christ said, 'Take heed how ye hear.' That is, make sure that you *do* hear the gospel when it's given to you. Hear with all the hearing you have. It is so important that the gospel be heard by you. Yet Christ said not only, 'Take heed *how* ye hear,' but he also said elsewhere, 'Take heed *what* ye hear.' We are willing to hear all sorts of things. If we hear somebody slandering somebody else, we might stop there for ten minutes, or quarter of an hour or more, to hear these juicy tales. Maybe it is something darker, unworthy to be spoken of, but still we stand there to hear it. We can speak to our neighbour, we can speak to a friend on the phone and spend an hour, we can listen to people here and there, we can hear and hear and hear. That's how we spend our time in the world: hearing. We went to school, where we learned what we were hearing. Before we went to school we learned to speak because we were hearing. It's all through hearing. In a sense we are what we are through hearing.

But when the gospel comes, the devil seeks to stop our hearing. 'You can listen to it, but don't listen too carefully. Don't take it to heart. Don't listen earnestly. Don't hear the things that speak of the judgment of God and your sinfulness. Don't hear these things that speak of the eternity that is before you.

Don't hear it, just skim over it.' It's like somebody listening to a radio or a television indoors and there's a knocking on the door. But they won't listen to the knocking. They don't even hear the knocking. They're too entranced by what they're hearing. They're taken in by it. It thrills them. They don't want any interruption. They don't want anybody to break in upon what they are listening to. The devil is quite willing to let you hear all sorts of things in this world—all sorts of things, as long as you won't hear the gospel, or at least as long as you don't hear it too well. He doesn't mind you hearing, coming to church. It might worry him; it does worry him. He studies each one of us. He studies you. He knows how you listen and how you don't listen. The devil is studying all that, and his minions, the fallen angels, are studying with him. They are always there where the gospel is preached. And they're trying to work in your minds, your imagination, to make you drift away so that you don't listen too well. They're afraid you might hear.

Just think of Legion. The devil saw the ship crossing the sea and he caused a storm to come on the ship in which Christ was, as if trying to stop him. But the ship went to the exact place where Legion was. He was full of devils and no man could bind him—even the chains on him, he broke them. He spent his time among the dead, crying and cutting himself with stones. The devil's trophy! But Christ went there and he spoke to him and he drove out the devils. The man ended up 'sitting at the feet of Christ, clothed and in his right mind'.

'Hear, and thy soul shall live.' Did you never hear the sweet tones of Christ speaking to your soul? 'Believe in me, and thou shalt be saved. Come unto me.' Did you never hear him speaking to you? Or did you blot out the voice? Did you refuse to hear? Did you say, 'I'll hear you later on'? And then did your hearing ear became more and more deaf? Your ear became less and less able to hear as you went on, because of the hardening process.

Well, that is the great question. Is the ear now closed? Is the ear room closed? Yes, heart room is closed, ear room is closed. The door is closed. You can listen to all sorts of things, but you cannot listen to Christ. Ah, it's as if to say, 'I'm sorry, for the present, that room is closed and can't be opened.'

### 3. The eye

But then, what about eye room? Were the eyes ever tired of seeing? No, never. We are told that the fool looks to the ends of the earth. He looks everywhere—it doesn't matter where—he looks at anything and everything. The eye doesn't tire of seeing. But here is Christ. 'He is like a root out of the dry ground: he hath no form nor comeliness; and when we shall see him, there is no beauty that we should desire him.' Christ didn't have physical beauty. That's what Scripture is telling us. Christ didn't have the physical beauty that would draw people, deliberately. But he had spiritual beauty, the beauty of his character, the beauty of God, and so the spiritual eye can see Christ and can say, 'He is altogether lovely. My beloved is white and ruddy, the chiefest among ten thousand.'

But like fools we look everywhere apart from looking to Christ. Maybe we even read the Word of God sometimes. The Bible is a biography. If known and understood, it's the biography of Christ Jesus. Yes, Christ is seen through shadows in the Old Testament. The sacrifices were Christ really—Christ in shadow. The temple was Christ in shadow. The altar was Christ in shadow. The prophets were Christ in shadow. Everyone anointed with oil was the Messiah in shadow. The whole Old Testament is full of Christ. In the New Testament he has come out of the shadows.

Have you ever seen the beauty of Christ? You know, when someone has seen the beauty of Christ, his great desire is that everyone else can see what he is seeing. Can you see him? Can't you see the beauty of the One who loved his own and gave himself for them, and went deeper than hell, to suffer in the room and stead of his own people? Christ poured out his soul unto death, to glorify the Father and to save his people. Look inside, to see the beauty of Christ. See the beauty in his heart. See the beauty in his works. See the beauty in his actions. See that he is the beautiful One.

In the book of Revelation, the Lord speaks to a congregation which seems full of blind men. He tells them to take eye salve: medicine for the eyes, ointment for the eyes. They needed that. We need the Holy Spirit to open our eyes and open our minds. We need the Holy Spirit to implant faith, which gazes upon Christ. People then wonder, 'Why didn't I see that before? Why didn't I see the beauty of Christ before? Why wasn't I entranced by him before? Why wasn't he the altogether lovely One for me before this?'

What a pity, to go through the world and never to see the beauty of Christ! What a pity to be under the gospel, and to be reading the Word of God, and not see Christ! The eye can go through Scripture, going through pages, chapters, books, the whole book, time and time again. Ah yes, it's all very well talking the talk. That's not walking the walk. It's all right speaking around Christ, but when you know Christ, when you see him as he really is, then you'll speak in a different manner. You'll then speak experimentally as one who has seen Christ, as one who has seen the Lord.

You can imagine what happened after Christ died and rose again and ascended. Maybe twenty, thirty, forty years later. Let's say 70AD when Jerusalem and the temple were destroyed. Imagine somebody there, telling others, 'I was a witness of the gospel. I saw Christ. I remember Christ. I saw him.' The disciples spoke that way. 'Whom we saw,' they said. 'We looked upon him with our eyes. We handled him.' That's how John speaks of him. 'We handled him. We put our hands on him. We saw him, God in the flesh! We saw him. The wonder of it all! And we loved him.' That's their own dear Saviour. The disciples loved him so much that they went out to die for him, preaching the gospel, dying one after another.

Ah well, perhaps you say, 'I'm sorry, but I don't see that. There's no room in the eye room, for eye room is closed, it's bolted, the door is fast shut. No, I never saw the beauty of Christ.'

## 4. Time

Take the last one then—time room. Time is short. God created time. There was no time in God. God was eternal. He created time because it related to the universe and the world and creatures, and they all need time. They need seconds and minutes and hours. They need time that passes from moment to moment. God is not like that. God exists in every moment. To him it's always the present. He has no beginning and no end. And he's equally present in all parts of the universe eternally.

But we are different. We are in time, and time is limited. People may speak as if matter is eternal—evolutionists may speak in that way. But their eyes will be opened yet. They have no excuse. God will never excuse them. Nature tells about God. It's a strong witness about God.

Well, you say, 'I'm so busy.' Do you have family worship? 'Well, no, I'm so busy. I work all day. I work so hard. I need to get to bed. I need to rise early in the morning. I've got to care for people. I've got to do things. My time is taken up, my diary is full.' But strangely enough, there has been enough time to look at the television. We have time for the newspaper. We have time to do various things we desire to do, but strangely

## 9 No room in the inn

we have no time for the most important thing of all—the salvation of our own souls.

Now friends, we are given time to worship today, and we appreciate that, and we are thankful for it. We're thankful when we see people who gather in the house of worship, who give that time to the things of the Lord, who give the Sabbath to the Lord, as it were. But that's not good enough. You see, you've got to have a saved soul. Have you given time to the salvation of your soul? Have you given time to come to the feet of Christ, to pour out your heart to him? To call upon him in spirit and in truth? Did you give that time? It's all very well walking around the door of salvation. It's one thing to walk about the door of heaven, but it's another thing to enter the door of salvation. Will there ever be time in your experience when you will say, 'I believe in thee, O Lord Jesus, as my Saviour'? Will there ever be time in your experience when you begin to praise the Lord for having mercy upon your soul? Will there ever be time in your experience when you come to weep over sin, and hate sin, and love righteousness? Will there ever be time in your experience when you come to see that the world is nothing compared to Christ? Oh, consider time room! Will you ever have that space of time, that part of time that's so precious?

I remember in the Army, lads gathering together in the evening in the barracks, saying they were killing time, and they'd take out a pack of cards to kill time. Imagine such a phrase: 'to kill time'! They were just bored. They didn't know what to do with the time they had on their hands, so they brought out a pack of cards and began playing cards. Imagine 'killing time', when time is so precious!

The Lord says, 'Seek ye first the kingdom of God, and all these things you need in the world will be added unto you. But seek ye first the kingdom of God.' This is what time should be used for, ahead of everything else. Yes, we want our children to have work, and to have health and strength and a long life, if that be the will of God. But above all else we want them to have Christ, even if their lives are short. We want them, in time room, to come to know Jesus as their God and Saviour—we want that above all else.

Yes, we can read many books, we can see many programmes, we can go to many places, we can get to know the world pretty well, but unless we come to know Christ during the time we have in the world, our time here will be a waste of time. We have wasted our time. Wasted! Vanity! 'Vanity' is the word 'emptiness'. Our lives will have been vanity and vexation of spirit, all coming to nothing. After all our striving, after all the things we sought for, after all the things we wanted, if we didn't come to Christ we have nothing. Job said, 'Naked came I out of my mother's womb, and naked shall I return thither: the LORD gave, and the LORD hath taken away; blessed be the name of the LORD.' Why did he say, 'Blessed be the name of the LORD' when he seemed to have lost everything? Because he hadn't lost everything. He still had Christ as his Saviour. He had the Redeemer as his Saviour. So he could say at the end of losing everything, 'Blessed be the name of the LORD.'

I have heard of a castle somewhere in Scotland, and it is said that in that castle there is a dungeon, and on one wall of stone is written, 'No hope.' People who were enclosed in that dungeon died there. They had no hope, and one man wrote 'No hope' on the wall. No hope! If we die without Christ, if he never enters our soul, if there's no room in the inn of our soul for Christ, then what will happen to us? There's a museum in America with a number of jars, and a notice says these jars constitute the chemicals and the gases that make up the body of a 140-pound man. But a human being is not just chemicals and gases. A human being has a soul as well as a body. A

## 9  No room in the inn

human being has an eternity. If we know Christ, the body is as saved as the soul.

Christ came into the world in darkness, and when he came to the end of his life on the cross he was in darkness, such darkness that he called out, 'My God, my God, why hast thou forsaken me?' He came in darkness and lived in darkness to save his own people, to save sinners, to save people from heathendom— to save, we hope, your own soul.

Is there room in the inn? Or do we leave today saying, 'There is no room in my inn.' Ah, friends, we will know darkness then, if there is no room in the inn. But may God bless his Word. Let us pray.

## Concluding prayer

We pray thee, gracious One, to bless thy Word to us. Give us to be thankful for the goodness of the Most High for thy dealings with us and the help given to us. We pray thee, O Lord, to keep us. May we be of those who come to know thee as our dear, precious Saviour. Oh, may the gates of heaven be open before us. May we see Christ as the gate of heaven. May we see Christ as heaven itself. Be with us and cleanse us. For Jesus' sake. Amen.

# 10

# Remember Lot's wife

19th May 2018, Lord's Day evening, Leverburgh

*Remember Lot's wife.*
Luke 17:32.

IN Genesis chapter 19 we read of the end of Lot's wife, how she was turned into a pillar of salt. The Dead Sea is full of salt, and even nowadays, if there is a strong wind there, you can see trees and other things being covered with the salt and becoming like peaks of salt. But what happened here was a volcano putting out fire and brimstone, pouring out the salt. Lot's wife became a pillar of salt. 'Remember Lot's wife.'

We should like to say a little first of all about her marriage; then secondly, something about her dwelling place; and then thirdly, something about her judgment—that she was made into a pillar of salt.

## 1. The marriage of Lot's wife

This woman married Lot, the nephew of Abraham. When Abraham left Ur of the Chaldees he was called by the Lord— by the Lord Jesus Christ as we call him today—the God of glory. Abram was the name given to him then when God called him and Lot out of Ur, that evil city where the people worshipped idols. God called them out, not telling them where he was taking them. Abram did not know where he was going when he came out. A strange thing that, to come out and not know where you are going. Not only so, but he was going outside his own native place. He would be exposed to many enemies, many tribes, many peoples who would gladly attack him for his flocks and for what he had. But Abram did not really come out, not knowing where he was going. He was going to the Lord. He was going to God. He was going to the One who called him out. He was going to the God of glory. That's where he was going. And even when he was promised the land of Canaan later on, what he looked for was a heavenly Canaan. His heart would not be satisfied with a piece of ground: he needed Christ, he needed heaven, he needed glory, so he looked for an heavenly country.

Abram took Lot with him, his nephew. We don't know when Lot married, we don't know who he married, we don't know what her name was, we don't know who she belonged to. We know nothing of these things about this woman, except that she was Lot's wife and at the end she became a pillar of salt. Yet she's used by the Lord to teach you and to teach me.

Marriage is meant to have its own joys. God gave two institutions to man before man fell. The two ordinances God gave mankind were the Sabbath Day and marriage. God did not take these ordinances away when man fell. He left them to man. He left the Sabbath Day, because we needed the Lord. We needed his fellowship, we needed this day set apart for the Lord. Adam needed it, even when he was sinless, and much more when he became a sinner. God also left mankind with marriage. It says in the Bible that when Jesus returns again at the end of the world, there will still be those who are 'being given in marriage'.

Of course, the devil would like to take away marriage. The devil doesn't want marriage. In our day and generation, young folk sometimes do not marry, they simply come together. There used to be a law that would make them marry if they came together, but they have to take vows now according to the law, either at a Registrar or a place which is counted lawful by the law of the land.

A marriage took place yesterday, between a prince and a woman from America. But why do we have marriage anyway? 'Well,' you say, 'it's so that we might have a measure of happiness together, sinful as we are. So that we might learn not to be selfish, but to look after each other and to be kind to each other.' We are basically selfish, you see, and the marriage tie is meant to help us in this. And when you bring up children, you have to sacrifice something of yourself. There's a teaching here, not to be selfish, certainly. But above all, marriage is meant to teach us about Christ, about heaven, about salvation. You don't have children very long. In a few short years they leave you, and if you did not teach them when they were young, it's too late when they are gone. There's nothing left then but to pray for them. We're meant to teach them, we're meant to pray with them, even when they are tiny, even in the cradle. We are meant to pray with them and for them.

In the great eternity there is only one marriage. That is the marriage of Christ and his people. All his people are called his Bride. As well as that, all of the redeemed, all his people are called the family of God, the sons and daughters of God. Marriage is meant to be used with that end in view. But, you see, people use everything for their own selfish or worldly ends. Friends, you who are married, see that the Bible has a central place in your marriage: it cements, it ties together, it brings about blessing.

Lot was a good man, a godly man, and this woman was married to him. He was with Abram, and they went together to the land of Canaan. Their flocks grew, they prospered, they had wells, they had servants. Abram had three hundred and eighteen trained servants. We don't know how many Lot had; we don't know if he had any. But he was with Abram, and everything seemed to be going so well. But then the split came between Abraham and Lot, because the men who were herding the cattle and the sheep and the goats began to quarrel over pasture. Now, the land was promised to Abram, and not to Lot. Lot had no promise from God, but Abram, who had the promise of the whole land for his people, gave Lot his choice: 'You go in one direction, and I'll go in another. You and I are brothers in the Lord, and we must not have quarrels because the heathen will see it; it will bring down the cause of the Lord. So you go in one direction and I'll go in another.' Lot chose the best pastures, which lay towards Sodom and Gomorrah, two of the five cities of the plain. That was the best place in the whole country for sheep and cattle, and Lot chose it. He could have taken any place—there was lots of pasture—but he chose the best, and so they separated.

## 2. The dwelling place

The second thing we have here is the dwelling-place of this lady married to Lot. They came towards Sodom—not *into* Sodom, but *towards* Sodom—to the pastures. They lived in tents. We do not know, but it may be that she was pushing her husband towards these fine pastures. After all, it meant more sheep, more cattle, more wealth, more power. Maybe she was pushing, maybe she wasn't, but anyway they came close to Sodom.

Then we find them *inside* Sodom. Instead of living in a tent, they're now living in a house. Since Abram left Ur of the Chaldees until he died, he never lived in a house. Nor did Isaac, nor did Jacob. They all lived in tents. But here is Lot and his wife, and they're in a house. How did they get a house in Sodom? They were wealthy enough to buy a house, that was easily done. But then, is that all that matters? Economics, how you get on in the world, money, wealth, place, cars and houses: is that all that matters? These things do matter. We do not say they don't matter. They matter, but the thing is this: nothing—nothing at all—should come between us and the things of our souls. Nothing!

Lot and his wife went into Sodom, a city given over to extreme wickedness. They were living among the people in that city. In the Word of God Peter says that God turned the cities of Sodom and Gomorrah into ashes and made them 'an ensample unto those that after should live ungodly; and delivered just Lot, vexed with the filthy conversation of the wicked: (for that righteous man dwelling among them, in seeing and hearing, vexed his righteous soul from day to day with their unlawful deeds).' This is what the Word of God says about Lot, that he was just and righteous. What was he doing there, then? He was vexed from day to day. He felt the agony of hearing what they said and seeing what they did in that fearful city. So why did he stay? We do not know. You wonder if his wife wanted to stay. Had she some influence in the decision to stay? Whether she had or not, they stayed. That was their place. And they had a family. Some of their daughters married men of that city. You would wonder that there would be such a thing as marriage there. They brought up children there. It would have been far better if they had never gone near that city.

We must think of our children. We must warn them of what is ahead, of the dangers of marrying unbelievers. It is true that unbelievers can be converted. But when you marry, it's not just a matter of your feelings and your heart; it's also a matter of the head. Where are you going to end up? What kind of children are you going to have? How will they be brought up? What will be their faith?

So Lot and his wife were in a trap in Sodom. And how was he going to get out of it? He still had two daughters at home. Through time, as things were going, they too would marry into Sodom, as far as we can see. The whole family then would be married into Sodom. Married, entrapped.

What kind of city was it, then? Well, we know, we've read about it. But how had they come to be so evil? How did that come about? Well, Ezekiel tells us. 'Pride, fulness of bread, and abundance of idleness was in her and in her daughters, neither did she strengthen the hand of the poor and needy.'

The first thing he says was 'pride'. It was a proud city. Because they were wealthy, they were full of pride. You can see that: 'pride, fulness of bread'. They had no worry about food. Most nations worried about food. When the harvest came they hoped they would have a full harvest to last until next year. But in that place they had fulness of bread; their land was so good.

They also had 'abundance of idleness'. The land was so fruitful. Everything grew so well, and that meant that they had abundance of idleness, a lot of time for themselves. And you say, 'Maybe that would be a good thing, a lot of time for ourselves.' That is why people go on long holidays. But you know, friends, it's not really a good thing to have too much time for ourselves. It is good for us to work six days a week and to rest on the Sabbath Day. I don't mean people should slave, but they should be occupied with duties. Yes, it is good to have a rest of days, of holidays, but not to go to excess and idleness.

Well, the people were idle, and then they began to follow each other into various things. You see how young folk who never work get caught up in gambling, drugs, immorality, all sorts of things.

The people of that city had 'pride, fulness of bread and abundance of idleness was in her and in her daughters, neither did she strengthen the hand of the poor and needy'. Notice that. They had no time to help the poor and needy. The best nation for looking after the poor in these days was Israel: God made laws for them. But these proud people, with fulness of bread and idleness, plenty of wealth and plenty of opportunity, they never cared for the poor and the needy.

Lot and his wife stayed there, in that city with its own amusements, its own pastimes. The people were all full of the filth of the world, the immorality of the world, the lewd talk of the world, the lewd practices of the world. And you know, sin carries on and on and on. You can't say to sin, 'Stop here!' There's no stopping of sin. It cannot stop. It doesn't obey any law. It doesn't stop for law, there are no boundary lines. It goes on and on until God stops it. And God *will* stop it.

## 3. The judgment

Then there was the judgment. The people of the city gathered around Lot's house, the dwelling they had chosen. They wanted to have carnal knowledge of the angels. How far would sin go? Even when the angels smote the men with blindness, they still tried to find the door. You would think that when they were smitten with blindness, they would become afraid or terrified and would retreat. But no! They were given over to that sin. And God wiped them out. These two angels were given that work. God uses his angels in providence. He uses his angels for sicknesses. At times we see that in Scripture. God uses angels for plagues, for winds, for storms, for volcanoes. When we read about volcanoes, wonder about the angels. When we read about earthquakes, wonder about the angels. God uses them. They are instruments in his hand—mighty instruments, but they are nothing compared to God who uses them. They are holy angels doing his will, and God's will is a good will, it's a holy will, it's a just will.

Remember Lot's wife and the judgment. The angels said to them they should leave early in the morning. So they left early in the morning. The Lord had given them these two angels to help them. The two angels had four hands between them, and they took hold of the hands of Lot and his wife and his two daughters. But before they left, Lot had gone to the homes where his daughters were married. He wanted his daughters—his married daughters—to be saved, and also their husbands and whoever belonged to them. He went and spoke to his sons-in-law. But his sons-in-law thought that he was joking. It wasn't that *they* were making fun. No, they thought that *Lot* was making fun. They thought that this serious matter was merely Lot joking. There's no fun in the judgment of God. But we wonder about Lot's disposition. He was a godly man, he was a just man, his soul was vexed with their evil deeds. But could he have been of such a nature that he would be joking in the way he spoke to them, at times? We don't know. When he did speak to them at this time they thought that he wasn't serious, and so they wouldn't take him seriously. It wasn't going to happen. He was only saying it in fun.

It's not easy when you speak to people and tell them there's a heaven and a hell, and that if they do not believe in Christ as their Saviour, they're going to be lost, and then you see them smiling at you. They think you're soft in the head, or you know nothing. They think, if you were wise enough, you'd be an atheist; if you were wise enough, you'd believe in evolution. So they look down at you: you're just one of these who know nothing, swallowed up with religion, that foolishness. And so they go on. And they perish. And they go to hell.

It's a fearful thing to go to hell. It's a fearful thing to think of yourself going to hell. Your eyes opening in hell, and there's no way out. Never, never, never! You are punished for your sins forever and forever, and your sins just keep growing. You never pay the debt. It's not payable: it's so great, and it's increasing. All you're doing is sinning and sinning and sinning in a lost eternity.

Well, Lot and his wife and his two daughters came out of the city. Then the volcano began. The brimstone and the fire came on Sodom and Gomorrah and Admah and Zeboim. These four cities were covered and wiped out. They all perished, all of them. They all went into eternity at that time. Meanwhile Lot and his wife and the two daughters were outside, and Lot had pleaded to have this one city saved—Zoar, which means 'small'. It was a tiny city, and God gave it to him, spared it for his sake. But Lot didn't know that: he ran to the mountains.

Then Lot's wife looked back. She was coming behind Lot, and the Word of God tells us that she looked back. We don't think it just means that she glimpsed back. 'Look not behind,' the Lord had said. He says that to each one of us regarding Christ. 'Believe in the Lord Jesus Christ and thou shalt be saved. But do not look back.' And Paul tells us that if we desire to look back or go back, an opportunity would be given us. But those who are truly saved never want to go back. What will they go back to? What is there to go back to? The world? Its pleasures? But I have Christ!

Lot's wife had daughters married in Sodom who perished, who were plunged into a lost eternity. What a thought that is! It may be that Lot himself would glance that way, hearing the volcano with its terrible noise and the terrible heat behind him. But his wife looked back with her heart. You see, she never left Sodom in her heart. She never left that home she had, in her heart. She never had the same kind of heart that Lot had.

## 10 Remember Lot's wife

He desired the things of God, but she seemed to desire the things of men. Her heart looked back. Yes, that was her life, that was her place. It was now destroyed. But Lot went to the mountains. Yes, Lot had sinned in Sodom, but Lot's wife looked back. God made her a pillar of salt. The salt engulfed her and piled upon her, and she became a pillar of salt. A mount of salt. Buried in salt. Dead in salt.

The destruction of Sodom and Gomorrah had reached her because in her heart she belonged to Sodom and Gomorrah. Remember Lot's wife, dying in the salt and going to a lost eternity. A lost eternity! 'Remember Lot's wife.' She would remember. She *does* remember in eternity. In her lost eternity she remembers that she was married to a godly man. She remembers that. She remembers the day they went to Sodom. She remembers the day they came to live in Sodom. She remembers all these things that took place. She remembers the warning of the angels. She remembers godly Abram. But she's in a lost eternity.

In a lost eternity you are given over completely to sin, nothing but sin. There is no love in hell. No love is possible in hell. No love for the husband you had and the wife you had. None. It's gone. The children? No, no love. No love for anybody. Love does not enter hell. There is no regard for anyone, no desire for anyone, just sheer hatred, total sinfulness. Hatred of God. Hatred of Christ. Hatred of Lot. Hatred of Abram. Hatred of the children. Yes, hatred: that is all. Hating the devil. Hating God. Nothing but hatred.

'Remember Lot's wife.' Her body engulfed by the salt will have a resurrection. It may have been destroyed by the burning brimstone and salt that came upon her. It doesn't matter. There will be a resurrection, both of the just and of the unjust, and she and Lot will stand before Christ at the great judgment throne. Lot will stand on one side, among the sheep, and she will stand among the goats. They will never, never, never have any relationship of any kind evermore. Oh, husbands and wives, love each other in Christ! Brothers and sisters, love each other in Christ! Parents and children, love each other in Christ! Seek that Christ would be brought into your life, that your life might be a true life, a blessed and eternally happy life, a glorious life! But without Christ it's a life better not lived.

In this world, the ungodly laugh and joke, they make cracks, they live lives of pleasure, they seek to fill their lives with pleasure. They don't want to take heed of what you say regarding their souls. But where will it end? In the same place where Adam might have ended.

I don't think Lot's wife would have been an old woman. It doesn't matter what age she was, but you remember Lot's wife. 'Remember Lot's wife.' Set up a post in your memory, plant it in your memory, and remember Lot's wife. You see, it might be used by the Lord to turn you to the Lord Jesus for salvation, if you think of it, if you dwell upon it, if you take it to heart. 'Remember Lot's wife.' Yes, a nameless woman. We don't know who she was, but there she is to be remembered.

Lot fled. He lost everything that he had, all the wealth he had, and fled with his daughters to a cave in the mountains. He fled to commit shame with them. Yes, the influence of wickedness followed him. Then the Word of God ceases to speak any more about Lot. It leaves him there. Yes, he was a good man, but the Word of God has no more interest in his progeny. It only carries on now with Abram, who became Abraham.

## Application

So, remember Lot's wife. Where will your own life end? Where will *my* life end? What will it be like? It doesn't matter. If you know Christ, everything is well: you have Christ. But going to bed tonight and seeing the darkness coming, and never knowing if you will see tomorrow, surely that itself should cause fear and torment, and cause you to cry loudly to the Lord Jesus. You speak to Christ! Never mind what people say or what people think: it's your soul and it's one precious soul to have. One precious soul! Call on Jesus Christ, speak to him, pour out your soul to him. He knows who you are, where you are. He knows your needs, and he can meet with them, and be your God and your Saviour. May he grant it.

Let us pray.

## Concluding prayer

Gracious Lord, grant now to be with us and to bless us this Sabbath evening. Go with us to our homes and give us journeying mercies, we beseech thee. Bless this Sabbath day to our souls. Make the day as one of the days of the Son of man in our experience. Bless, we pray thee, the pastor expected to begin a charge here, be with him and make him a great blessing in the congregation. Uphold the elder here in the congregation and bless those who pray, those who go on their knees before thee to pray for the congregation. Put thine arms around them, gracious Lord. Take away our sins and wash us. For thine own blessed name's sake. Amen.

# 11

# The time of Paul's departure

10th June 2018, Lord's Day morning, Tarbert

*For I am now ready to be offered, and the time of my departure is at hand. I have fought a good fight, I have finished my course, I have kept the faith: henceforth there is laid up for me a crown of righteousness, which the Lord, the righteous judge, shall give me at that day: and not to me only, but unto all them also that love his appearing.*
2 Timothy 4:6–8

PAUL is writing to Timothy, this being the second letter to Timothy, who was his own convert. He called him his own son in the gospel. Timothy's mother was a Jewess; his father was a Greek. You can see that Timothy seemed to have a grasp of both worlds—the Gentile world and the Jewish world. But as a young man he came to know the Lord as Saviour, and he now came to preach.

Timothy began to preach in a day when the life of those preaching the gospel was very uncertain. It was the same at one time in our own nation, in the time of the Covenanters. Most people of course don't read about these things nowadays. They don't know that there was fearful suffering in our land because of the gospel, and men and women were put to death in the Killing Times. The Covenanters refused to wor-

## 11  The time of Paul's departure

ship using the rites that Charles II introduced. This shows the intolerance that comes in when people depart from the faith of God, and persecution that is used to try and force people to worship in the way that the persecutors worship.

Timothy lived in a day when the Jewish Church was persecuting believers. The Jews had rejected Christ. Timothy was preaching in a day when Nero was emperor. Nero was a monstrous person on the throne of Rome. He seemed to be out of his mind at times, and the devil was working through him. Nero put so many of God's people to death. It was during his reign that Paul was put to death. I tend to believe that Timothy too must have been put to death after a while. But the Word of God doesn't speak of that. The Word of God is there to speak mainly of salvation for sinners. That's the stress for you and for me.

At the time he was writing to Timothy, Paul was in prison. He had been in prison already and he spoke already of being released from prison. And now he's in prison in Rome for the second time, and he makes it very evident in the words of our text that he's about to die. Nero the judge will condemn him, and he will die.

So this last letter that he wrote to Timothy was perhaps the last letter that he ever wrote. He says to Timothy, 'I charge thee therefore before God, and the Lord Jesus Christ; … preach the word; reprove, rebuke, exhort with all longsuffering and doctrine. For the time will come when they will not endure sound doctrine; but after their own lusts shall they heap to themselves teachers, having itching ears.'

He's prophesying what is going to happen to the Church. Nowadays people look around and they say, 'We see the Church of Christ fragmented, broken up—denominations here and there. In the old days we'd have one congregation, say, in Tarbert, one congregation in Stornoway, one congregation here and there. Not a village with a number of congregations. That's how it used to be.' The apostle Paul had the same experience, and he saw that things were going to change. He saw that there would be people with 'itching ears'. They couldn't endure sound doctrine, they couldn't endure being told they were sinners, they couldn't endure being told of the judgment seat of Christ. Yes, they could endure being told that everyone was going to heaven, they could endure being given comfort all the time, but not being rebuked while exhorted. That has come to Scotland as well. People have itching ears and so they heap up to themselves teachers who suit themselves, ministers who will soothe them on the way to a lost eternity.

Ah friends, the apostle saw that coming upon the generations following his own one. Never mind what has taken place in our own land, the same thing takes place everywhere the gospel is planted. The devil begins to work immediately, and the corrupt heart of man begins to work.

Paul said to Timothy, 'Watch thou in all things, endure afflictions.' Then he spoke about himself to Timothy. Of course, Timothy could visit him in prison, and Paul expected him to come. But for now he says to Timothy, 'I am now ready to be offered, and the time of my departure is at hand.' These words are in the present tense: 'I am now ready to be offered, the time of my departure is at hand.' Then he speaks in the past tense: 'I have fought a good fight, I have finished my course, I have kept the faith.' Then he speaks of the future: 'Henceforth there is laid up for me a crown of righteousness, which the Lord, the righteous judge, shall give me at that day: and not to me only, but unto all them also that love his appearing.' Let us then look at what Paul says of the present, the past, and the future.

# 11   The time of Paul's departure

## 1. The present

First, the present. 'For I am now ready to be offered.' The word 'offered' is really something that refers to sacrifice. So he's saying, 'I am now ready to be sacrificed.'

Every Christian, according to God's Word, is a kind of sacrifice: a spiritual sacrifice. Every Christian gives himself to the Lord. He tells the Lord that he belongs to him, and all that he has belongs to the Lord. But of course, Paul is here speaking about his death. He would be put to death by the Romans. As a Roman citizen, he would be decapitated. He would not be crucified. To be crucified, you had to be brought down to the status of a slave. As a slave, you would be scourged, and then you would be crucified, as happened to Christ. They would always scourge a slave. Christ was brought down to the status of a slave. But Paul was a Roman citizen, and Roman citizens were put to death by being beheaded. But Paul didn't particularly speak of that the manner of being put to death. That didn't seem to occupy his mind at all when he says, 'For I am now ready to be offered.'

The word 'offer' here is the word 'drink offering', 'libation'. And why does he speak of that? In the Mosaic order of sacrifice, the last thing to be done was the pouring out of the libation, the drink offering. When you saw the wine being poured out, you knew the service had come to an end. That's what Paul is speaking of. 'I am now ready to be offered.' The sacrifice was come to an end. You have the same with the Lord Jesus Christ, where it says about him that 'he poured out his soul unto death'. He poured out his soul, that is, he came to death itself, the very end of the sacrifice.

Of course, sacrifice is an act of worship. Since the time Paul came to know Christ, in a sense his life became a kind of worship. There are so many who think that the Christian only worships when he goes to church or when he has family worship, but the Holy Spirit is within him as the Spirit of worship and the Christian can cast arrows of prayer out to heaven as he walks the streets. He can think upon the Lord and his mercy. A worshipful spirit is meant to be within the heart of every child of God all the time. If Christ is so important, if the Lord is all-important, then our minds should be turning that way constantly.

For Paul, it was all over now as far as this world was concerned. But the worship would not be over at the point of death, when they put him to death. When the drink offering was poured out, Paul's worship would not come to an end. He was going to glory. He was worshipping in death, and he would be worshipping in heaven. He will never cease to worship. Paul today is worshipping in heaven, gazing upon Christ and seeing God in Christ, and worshipping God as he was never able to worship him in this world: without sin, without spot.

Paul was ready. Some people say to us, 'Well, I would like to go to heaven, if I was ready.' That is because they're conscious of indwelling sin and sinful thoughts. But the readiness of the Christian is given him by the Holy Spirit when the Lord's time comes. When the Lord's time comes it doesn't matter what we are doing, whether we die outside in the street, or in our bed, or during our work: we are made ready. The Holy Spirit makes his own people ready. When they die, they are made totally holy at that point. They are ready to enter glory, to be with Christ, no matter the feelings they may have had while they walked this world.

Then the second thing Paul says regarding the present is: 'The time of my departure is at hand.' 'The time is at hand, it's here, it has come: the time of my departure'. He's going to leave this world, he's going to leave the strife, the trial, the persecution.

# 11 The time of Paul's departure

He had spent time in prison, not only in Rome, but also at other times. Felix kept him two years in prison. He had suffered greatly. He had been shipwrecked, spent a day and a night in the sea, had been beaten seven times with rods, scourged, chased from city to city, with persecuting mobs seeking to stone him. One time he was stoned, they thought he was dead, but the Lord didn't allow him to die then. But now his time had come, and he says, 'The time of my departure is at hand.'

Now, the word 'departure' is a sea-going word, a naval word. It's a word that belongs to sailors and fishermen. It really means a ship departing, leaving the quay, leaving where it was anchored and tied, and now going away. It's like a ship leaving the quay forever, from the place where it was tied up for a number of years. When the ship arrived, the anchor was let down, there were ropes here and there, there was a gangway plank. Those on board had come off the ship, they mingled with those of the country to which they had come with the ship. They maybe spoke a different language and had different kinds of clothes. They were a different people; they were unknown by the people of the land. But now it's the time for departure.

It is like that for Christians when it is time for them to leave the world. They knew they were a different people, but now the time of departure has come. They were in the world, in a sense. The world knew them not, but the world recognised something that was different. These were people who desired to glorify Christ, and to have a godly walk. They had an interest in gathering together to worship the Lord, an interest in the words of God in the Bible, in prayer, in godly conversation. The pleasures of the world had no taste for them. They lost that taste: their taste was now for the things of God.

So the time for departure has come. They were long enough in the world, but they are now on board ship. There is a whistle, and the ropes are thrown this way and that way, and they separate from the quay forever. They go to their own land.

Paul could say, 'The time of my departure is at hand. I'm leaving this world. I'm leaving the ministry. I'm leaving the apostleship. I'm leaving Timothy, I'm leaving Luke, I'm leaving all the saints I knew in the world. I'm going home to my own country, to my own place that Christ has prepared for me. The time of my departure is at hand.'

Friend, when your time comes to leave this world, how will you leave it? Will you leave it looking to Christ or will you leave it without Christ? I knew of two men on their deathbeds. When they were spoken to about their souls, they both said in Gaelic, '*Tha e ro fhad' a-nis,*' which is, 'It's too late now.' Imagine a person under the gospel, hearing the gospel, reading the gospel, seeing the gospel in the lives of other people. Just imagine that person under the gospel—forty, fifty, sixty years—coming to a place where they say during their last minutes, '*Tha e ro fhad' a-nis.*'

You and I will come to the end in this world. We must leave it. But where are we going? Where are we going to spend eternity? Friends, what will the world give you? What treasures is the world going to give you? What great joys and what great pleasures? Put it all in God's scales, weigh it upon his weights, not upon the scales and weights of this world. The greatest treasure you can have is Christ as your Saviour. Then the day of one's death is better than the day of one's birth. The death of the saints, we read, is precious in God's eyes.

## 2. The past

Then Paul speaks of the past. 'I have fought a good fight.' This man had been a wicked man. He had been the cause of many of God's people being sent to prison and put to death. He was supervising when Stephen was put to death. I don't think he got over that. I think an arrow of conviction went into his soul then, although not savingly. He called himself the chief of sinners, because he didn't know anyone in this world who hated Christ as he hated him before he was changed. But still, he says here, 'I have fought a good fight.' Christ had mercy on him. It doesn't matter how sinful you are, the blood of Jesus can cleanse you, can save you. Christ is a present and willing Saviour. Why do we not speak to Christ? Why do we not come to Christ and cry to him in our souls and call upon him? He's the same Christ who walked the streets of Jerusalem.

Paul says, 'I have fought a good fight.' This is the man who says, 'Put ye on the whole armour of God, that ye may be able to stand in the evil day.' He knows that there's a Christian warfare against the devil, against the world, against the flesh. It's inside him, as well as outside. If it was only outside, it wouldn't be so bad, but it's inside as well because the old principle is still there. That principle is still there, working to bring up evil and rebellion in the heart. Grace has to war against all that, internal and external. It's a fearful warfare that Paul's talking about.

When we think of warfare, we tend to think of the First World War and the Second World War, and all the other wars in the world. The world is full of war. This is not just because of the sinfulness of men, but also because God is punishing the world. The world doesn't recognise that. The newspapers talk about all of these wars, but the newspapers do not talk about the good fight. You can open any newspaper you wish and it doesn't cover the good fight. It's not there. It's not on the television either. You don't find it mentioned among people. They don't want to speak about it. They don't even understand it. They don't know what you're talking about. But it's the fight of faith.

Paul lived a life of faith. He followed Christ, and so he went through this spiritual warfare. He could say, 'I have fought a good fight.' He suffered intensely for the sake of Christ in every way. Even if people don't make you suffer, the devil will make you suffer, and your own heart will make you suffer. So, friends, do we know anything about this good fight in our own experience?

'I have finished my course.' The apostle Paul was used to the arenas of Rome, and the Olympic Games and other games. They had these competitions constantly. The emperor Nero began putting Christians to death during these games. The athletes used to run and wrestle and have various other competitions. Saying 'I have finished my course' speaks of the running competition, like on a racecourse. It wasn't an easy race. He began to run that race outside Damascus when the Lord Jesus Christ met with him, when he came to believe in Christ. That day he began to run his race. There were many obstacles, but he ran it, 'looking unto Jesus, the author and finisher of his faith'. He ran it looking at Christ.

It can be very difficult to run your race, even naturally. The legs become weary and the lungs become full of fire, and the body craves to stop. Everything in the body is craving to stop, but you must carry on until you reach the end. But Paul says, 'I have finished. I have come to the finishing line.' It's good to be among those who run that race.

Paul was looking unto Jesus. They say, if you run a race—say a sprint—every inch is important, so you have to keep your eye on something ahead of you. If you don't keep your eye on one object, then your course tends to waver a little from side to side. But if you keep your eye on one object then you go straight, you don't lose inches on the way. Paul kept his eye on Christ. The closer you come to Christ, the better you see him and the more you are like him.

Well, Paul finished the race. It's over, he'll never run it again. And will you run it? Will I run it? Are we running it? Oh friends, are we running this race? Or are we just wandering through the world without knowing how it's all going to end? Not really understanding the meaning of our lives. Never fully happy, knowing there is something missing but never being able to put our finger upon it. But it's Christ that's missing. We were made for God. And until we find him, there is always something missing. We'll never find what we crave for, it's not there. We can laugh and joke, we can drink, we can try drugs, we can try immorality, we can do anything we like, but we cannot give happiness to ourselves. We've got to know Christ to know what the meaning of a real happiness is. Many a young person went out for pleasure and when they came back at nighttime and were by themselves in their bedroom, they just wept, because despite all the pleasure they enjoyed, they never came to happiness. We need Christ.

Ah, Paul says, 'I have kept the faith.' Some will say, 'Well, that is the grace of faith.' Certainly, once you have the grace of faith, you'll never lose it. Christ said to Peter, 'I have prayed for thee, that thy faith fail not.' Peter could never lose his faith. He could deny the Lord, but he never lost his faith: it was there all the time. He went out and he wept, and faith was in that weeping.

However, I do not think Paul is speaking of the grace of faith when he says, 'I have kept the faith.' Rather, it's something like what we call the Confession of Faith, that small book that takes together the teaching and doctrine of Scripture and puts it in a small compass to make it easy for us, so that we can learn about the teaching of Scripture. That teaching is in the Confession of Faith, and as a church we make use of it. Paul had his own doctrine, his own confession of faith and his own teaching. He kept to that teaching: he didn't let it go. Others let it go, but he didn't let it go.

We live in a day when churches are letting the faith go. They are adding to the teaching or taking away from it. They are letting it slip through their fingers, out of their hands. Paul was faithful in his preaching all the time. 'I have kept the faith.' He could have said, 'I didn't change my preaching before Nero. The preaching I used for the common man was the same kind of preaching I used for the great man.' Ah, how many would be like that?

### 3. The future

Then Paul goes on to speak of the future. Oh, the future, friends! My future, your future. I must die, I must give account of my stewardship. And you must give account of it, the same as myself. There will be no ministers' collars then. We'll have no crowns on our heads then. We'll not be called prime ministers then or officers then. We'll just be before the Lord in our own characters, as we are.

Paul says, 'Henceforth there is laid up for me a crown of righteousness.' 'This is what is before me. Something is laid up for me, set apart for me. It has been kept in a special place for me. It has been preserved for me. Nobody can do anything about it—to take it away or to change it. This crown of righteousness is there: it's meant for me, it's laid up for me.' It's a crown, because we are kings and priests unto God.

'Henceforth there is laid up for me a crown.' He calls it a crown of righteousness. Now, when we speak of righteous-

## 11  The time of Paul's departure

ness, normally we are speaking about the righteousness of Christ. Christ kept the law perfectly and he sacrificed himself to meet with the breach that was made in the law. He's a repairer of the breach. He glorified God in our nature by working out a perfect righteousness in our nature. He had a righteousness as God, but that didn't have to do with this. He took our nature, and in our nature he worked out a righteousness that would be for sinners. He bore the sin of many. He worked out that righteousness under the justice of God and he satisfied the justice of God.

But that's not what Paul means here when he says 'a crown of righteousness'. You see, when you come to know Christ as your Saviour you desire to have what is called a righteous walk, a holy walk. You desire to live to God's glory. Everyone in this world who lives by faith, and who walks by faith in the world, will have a crown of righteousness laid up for them.

Now, what about that crown? What is he going to do with it? It's laid up for him. It's his, but it's not his. He's going to take his crown, his own crown which is laid up for him, and he's going to throw it at the feet of Christ. We'll ascribe glory and honour to Christ, because whatever we have in our walk in life, whatever grace we had, whatever conduct we had, it was all of grace. It was all from Christ. Christ earned it all for me. I could never have walked with the fear of God and the love of God in my heart unless Christ had died to earn that for me. He ascended up on high, he received gifts for men, even for the rebellious. The glory is his. Throw the crowns at his feet—not at his head, but at his feet. He has his own crowns on his head, but give the glory to him, put it all under his feet.

Who's going to give him the crown? He says, 'The Lord will give the crown to me.' 'A crown of righteousness, which the Lord, the righteous judge, shall give me.' It's the Lord who has laid the crown up for him. It is the Lord who has kept it for him. The devil can do nothing about it, and the world can do nothing about it.

When athletes competed in the Olympic Games, they received crowns. But they were usually crowns of leaves. Yes, they were given prize money as well, but usually a crown of laurel leaves—a fading crown. The wooden part of it would last. They would keep that and show it to their children, saying, 'This is something I received as a young man when I ran in the Olympic Games. I received it from the hand of the emperor.' But here is something far better, 'a crown of righteousness, which the Lord, the righteous judge, shall give me'. It's a reality. It's not a fading leaf: it's a glory. It's the Lord, the righteous judge, who will give it to me. At the Olympic Games and other games, they could have judges who weren't righteous judges— judges who would cheat. Maybe they favoured their own relatives or their own townsmen, or whatever. But here it is the Lord, the righteous judge, the just judge who will give me the crown. What a wonderful thing that is!

Paul goes on to say that Christ will give it to him 'at that day'. He doesn't say, 'He will give it to me when I die.' He doesn't say that because he doesn't mean that. He uses this phrase a few times. We don't find him in this letter speaking about his death, as such. He doesn't seem to mention death except in other terms. But he says, 'At that day.' It seems it was a phrase he liked to use. And when he says, 'At that day,' he means the day of resurrection. That is the day when he will rise out of the grave in his body, and all of the Church will rise with him who died, and those who are left alive at the end. Some of God's people will be left alive at that day. They will not die, but they will all ascend to be with the Lord in glory. That is the day of resurrection—when the body and soul will be fully saved, glorified, sanctified. My body will then be sanctified, the same as my soul. My body will be glorified, like unto his glorious body. My soul will be made like unto his soul. I can never be Christ,

## 11  The time of Paul's departure

but within the limits of my creaturehood, I will be made like unto him. And at that day, at the glory of that day of resurrection, I will give my soul and body to him, and to him alone.

On that day some will rise to everlasting glory but others, friends, will rise in a different way—never desiring to meet with their bodies again. Those who destroyed themselves by committing suicide will have to meet their body again. Those who were killed in warfare, those who were swallowed up by death in some way or other, those who were destroyed with atomic bombs, whose bodies were just vaporised. It makes no difference: the Lord who took Adam out of the dust of the earth, who made all things out of nothing, will resurrect all, great and small. We must all stand before the judgment seat of Christ. Oh, when I rise, will I rise in the image of Christ? Or will I rise in dread and fear—fear, such as I never felt in this world, before the great holy God, who will judge us all?

Then Paul goes on and says, 'The Lord will give the crown not to me only, but unto all them also that love his appearing.' The crown is not just for me but it's for all those who love his appearing—that is, his appearing at the end, when he will resurrect all and judge all.

There are some who look to the appearing of Christ. We have seen people on their deathbeds longing for Christ. We have seen that, but here is one who doesn't just long to meet Christ when he dies. His longing was beyond that. God's people love his appearing, when he will appear at the end and they will meet him body and soul. The body coming out of the grave will be a heavenly body, and it will be reunited to the soul at last. Job has already been dead four thousand years. How much longer will the world last? We don't know, but after these thousands of years when Christ appears, the soul and the body will come together. But if we do not know Christ as our Saviour, we will not love his appearing.

Oh, friends take it to heart! We desire everyone to know Christ, to seek Christ as your Saviour. Take it to heart! Without Christ you have nothing, and if you have Christ you have everything. If Christ is yours, God is yours, all things are yours.

Paul spoke of the present, he spoke of the past, he speaks of the future, and now he has gone. He's waiting now for this day when the crown will be given him. Will you and I be there beside him, receiving the crown at the same time? Will you and I be there to give Christ the glory and the honour for all he has done? May it be so! May that be in your experience.

Let us pray.

## Concluding prayer

Gracious and glorious Lord, we beseech thee to bless us. Give us to put our hope and confidence and trust in thee. Stir up thy strength and might, we pray thee. Come near to us, we pray thee. We by nature run from thee; we by nature stay away from thee. We are Adam-like, hiding ourselves in the trees. That is our nature when we hear the voice of God. Let us hear thy voice efficaciously. Bring us out in the open before thyself, bring us out as seeking, trembling, poor sinners. Bless thy Word to us. Take away our sins. Be with us in the evening exercise of worship. Cleanse us. For Jesus' sake. Amen.

# 12

# Trial, deliverance and preservation

10th June 2018, Lord's Day evening, Tarbert

*At my first answer no man stood with me, but all men forsook me: I pray God, that it may not be laid to their charge. Notwithstanding the Lord stood with me, and strengthened me; that by me the preaching might be fully known, and that all the Gentiles might hear: and I was delivered out of the mouth of the lion. And the Lord shall deliver me from every evil work, and will preserve me unto his heavenly kingdom: to whom be glory for ever and ever. Amen.*
2 Timothy 4:16–18

SOME would like to call this letter the last will and testimony of the apostle Paul. It was written in prison to Timothy. Paul had been incarcerated in prison already, then released, and then arrested again. Now he's in prison and as he says in this chapter he knows that he's going to die. He doesn't know how soon, but he knows that it will be very soon.

The time of his departure has now come. People might wonder why God allowed a man like that, who was so useful in the vineyard, to be put into prison so often and kept in prison so long. But that is the Lord's way. Paul was the one the Lord sent into Europe with the gospel. He brought the gospel to

Europe, and we are indebted to this man, Saul of Tarsus, who was also called Paul.

The name 'Paul' means 'small'. He didn't have a commanding presence. He didn't depend upon that. He didn't depend upon on how well he could speak. He didn't depend upon his education. He depended upon one thing, and that was the blessing of the Holy Spirit upon his preaching. He went to Europe with the gospel and now we see him in the prison in Rome. Nero the fearful tyrant was the emperor—the emperor who blamed the Christians when Rome went on fire and who sought to gather them where he could find them, and put them to death in the arenas in various ways.

Paul wrote this letter close to the end of his days, while he was in prison. The Lord used him in prison. In prison he could write. He wrote to Timothy and asked for parchments from him, so that he could write and send letters. We have a lot of teaching in Scripture that came from the prison, and it is precious. This was God's way of making him stop other work, so that he could write. In prison he prayed. In prison he bore the churches on his spirit. In prison he could weep and rejoice, before he died and went to be with Christ.

Here Paul says, 'At my first answer no man stood with me.' What he means by his 'first answer' is his first trial. It was now over, and he was going to be tried for the second time, where he would be condemned and die.

We should first like to say a little about his first trial, when no man stood by him. Secondly, we should like to speak about the Lord standing with him. And thirdly, about the assurance he has regarding the future: 'The Lord shall deliver me from every evil work.'

# 12 Trial, deliverance and preservation

## 1. Paul's trial

Let us look at his first trial, the first examination he had before Nero. What a terrifying experience it was for people to meet with Nero as their judge! The law didn't matter, it was what Nero said that counted. He was a cruel monster of a man. Yet all of these things were in the Lord's hands.

Paul says, 'At my first answer no man stood with me.' Nobody was there with him. Where were all his friends? Where were all the Christians? He says there was no one. No one to plead his cause, no one to witness on his behalf, no one to give him any assurance. There was just no one. It reminds us of the Lord Jesus when he was taken from the garden of Gethsemane to be tried. Peter had said that although all should forsake him, he would never forsake him. Peter said that he would follow him, even unto death, and all the rest of the disciples said the same thing. But yet in the garden of Gethsemane they all forsook him and fled. We know from prophecy that he was to tread the winepress alone, but just think of all men forsaking him!

When Paul came to Rome, he was brought there as a prisoner. The Christians in Rome heard he was coming, and they went to the outskirts of the city at Appii Forum to meet with him, to pray with him. When Paul wrote to the Romans he told them that their faith was spoken of throughout the Christian world. They were such a people in these days. The Roman church was a faithful church at one time. We can see what it became later, but at that time it was faithful. Paul could praise it, and he could praise their faith throughout the earth. But now things look different—all men seem to have forsaken him.

Paul mentions Demas. 'Demas hath forsaken me, having loved this present world.' Demas forsook him because he loved the present world; he didn't love the world to come enough. Most, perhaps, would think that Demas was not a saved man at all. He was a preacher, and he's commended by Paul elsewhere, but he forsook him at this time as he loved this present world. Demas wanted to live: he was afraid to die, afraid of Nero, afraid of others. Whether he was in Christ or not, we don't know, we cannot tell.

Paul then mentions another one who forsook him. In verse 14, he says, 'Alexander the coppersmith did me much evil: the Lord reward him according to his works.' Probably at one stage this Alexander would have been covering wooden idols with copper. Then he was converted, if it was a true conversion. He preached with Paul. But then he began to preach heresies, things that were wrong, and elsewhere Paul says that he delivered Alexander and another person unto Satan because of their blasphemies. They lost their church membership because of it. Being delivered to Satan means being delivered to the kingdom of the world, being put out of the church membership and left just in the world. That's what Paul meant by Alexander being delivered to Satan. The purpose for that was so that he might learn not to blaspheme or to say things that were wrong. But he didn't learn that, and so Paul says about him here, 'Alexander the coppersmith did me much evil: the Lord reward him according to his works.' He leaves him in the hands of the Lord. It is the Lord who understands everything, it is the Lord who is going to judge.

So these two men left, but why did they leave? They were against Paul. And then elsewhere he mentions two other men who preached against him, Phygellus and Hermogenes. He says that all they in Asia had turned against him. The church in Asia seemed to have turned against Paul because of the teaching of Phygellus and Hermogenes.

# 12  Trial, deliverance and preservation

So you see how things were for Paul. Not only did he have Nero on the throne but the church of Christ was in such terrible throes and trials. There was dissension and trouble and strife in the Church of Christ, and that's what Satan wants. He takes brethren from loving each other and being knit to each other. He wants to have them at each other's throats—against each other. He does everything to destroy the cause of the Lord. Paul saw that when he was in prison, writing to Timothy and speaking of these things to Timothy. And it's not only that. 'At my first answer no man stood with me.' The very terror of Nero would keep people from coming to witness on Paul's behalf. If you witnessed on his behalf, the danger was that you yourself would be arrested and would be in the same danger as the apostle.

Where Timothy was we do not know. Paul was writing to Timothy, and Timothy is coming to the prison to see him. Timothy is going to take fearful risks. Another man was with Paul now that he is writing, and that is Luke. 'Luke is with me.' But where was Luke when he had to witness the first time? We don't know. But whatever happened then, now Luke was with him. You must remember that people were terrified. You've got to realise that they had families as well—they were in terrible straits, and they had to keep their heads down. It wasn't that they didn't love the Lord and didn't love Paul, but they didn't witness at a time when Paul was seeking for witnesses. Whether Nero would listen to any witness or not is another matter altogether. What Paul is saying is that they weren't there. Yet he prays, 'I pray God, that it may not be laid to their charge.' This is his prayer. 'I don't hate the brothers who did not come to comfort or witness on my behalf, or to speak up for me. I don't hate them, I'm not grieved at them.' Rather he prays for them, that this may not be laid to their charge. You see, he loves them. He loves God's people. He knows they are weak people, that it is easy for man to be afraid. Death and torture make people afraid, so he's praying for them, and he says that to Timothy.

There's another matter here. The apostle Paul is tasting of the very cup that he himself gave to others before he was converted. He had been a man of cruelty as well. Before he was converted, he really thought he was serving God in having Christians put in prison and put to death. Stephen testified to the Sanhedrin—the spiritual court of the Jews—of the evils they had done in crucifying Christ, and such like. They dragged Stephen out of Jerusalem because they wouldn't crucify a man inside the holy city—it had to be outside the city. That is why Christ was crucified just outside the city. They were evil people. When Stephen was dragged out, Paul was there, supervising it all. He kept the coats of those who were stoning Stephen—they were laid at his feet. Paul wanted Stephen to be stoned to death. Stephen was a very godly man, who preached the gospel to them and was praying for them when they were stoning him, praying to the Lord Jesus for his very enemies. Paul had men like that put to death and he thought he was serving God. And now he was getting a taste, as it were, of what he himself had done to others. He was now partaking of the very cup that Stephen had drunk from. That then was what took place at his 'first answer', the first time he came before Nero.

## 2. The Lord stood with Paul

Then Paul tells us that there was one who stood by him. 'Notwithstanding the Lord stood with me, and strengthened me.'

He now had Luke, and Timothy was going to come to the prison, bringing books and parchments and Paul's coat. The winter was coming, and Paul was cold. He was getting old as well. He must have been somewhere around sixty years of age. He wasn't old in our terms, but in their terms he was old. This was about 66AD, four years before Jerusalem was destroyed by the Romans.

However, no one had been there the first time and we do not know the whys and wherefores of that. Perhaps some people were far away. Perhaps some people couldn't get to Rome to witness in any case. Perhaps Timothy was preaching somewhere. But whatever was true, 'the Lord stood by me'. If the Lord stands by you, that's everything.

It's strange that it's when you go through troubles that the Lord seems to come closer to you. John Bunyan was twelve years in prison, and he had great anxiety. He was worried about his blind daughter. Who would look after her? Who would look after his wife? Who would care for his family? But he says quite plainly that he never felt the presence of the Lord as he did when he was in prison. When he was in prison and worrying for his family, it was then he was able to cast himself wholly upon the Lord, and he had the presence of the Lord there as he never had it before.

We've heard that about God's people time and time again. Sometimes they had the presence of the Lord in times of a great illness. Daniel's three companions were cast into the fiery furnace. Nebuchadnezzar was so angry he demanded that it be heated up further. His servants who threw Daniel's companions into the fire died—slain by the fire or its fumes or whatever. But Nebuchadnezzar saw Daniel's three friends walking in the fire, and one with them like unto the Son of God. No smell of burning was ever to come from their clothing. And that was the best day they ever had in this world. The best day—when Christ was with them, walking with them. Oh, what fellowship! Oh, what great blessing in their great, great trouble! You find that is how things are when you go through Scripture and read about the experience of God's people.

Paul goes on to say, 'The Lord stood with me, and strengthened me.' Elsewhere he could say, 'When I am weak, then am I strong.' 'I am what I am, by the grace of God. In me, (that is, in my flesh,) dwelleth no good thing,' but 'I am what I am, by the grace of God.' He says here that he was strengthened, 'that by me the preaching might be fully known'. He was strengthened to preach. He wasn't going to stop preaching. It didn't matter where he was. It didn't matter, should he be in a court of law. He was taken prisoner originally by Felix, and Felix brought Paul before him to try him. But Paul never tried to defend himself. You would think he would plead for his life, but that wasn't how he reacted. He began to tell Felix about the things of eternity, and it was Felix who began to tremble when Paul spoke. Felix, the judge, began to tremble—not Paul, the prisoner. Paul wanted to preach, he needed to preach. Men and women were going to perish unless they came to know Christ. Then when Felix was removed as judge and Festus took his place, again Paul was brought before Festus, and again he preached. The call went out, 'Paul, thou art beside thyself!' Yes, 'Much learning doth make thee mad!' He was called 'mad' because he preached during his trial.

Elsewhere in this epistle we learn that when Paul came to Rome he was given a cell by himself. He was able to hire that cell thanks to his friends. I think they were the people of Philippi, his favourite congregation, the first congregation he had in Europe. They were sending gifts to him all the time and he could hire a better prison cell with the money they sent him. He was chained to a soldier all the time he was in prison, but he was allowed to preach. The slave of Philemon was converted when he came to hear him. The gospel that Paul was preaching in prison actually entered the household of Caesar himself. There were those who belonged to the emperor's family who came to know Christ because Paul was in prison and preached in prison. The gospel spread like that.

## 12 Trial, deliverance and preservation

He says the Lord strengthened him, 'that by me the preaching might be fully known, and that all the Gentiles might hear'. The gospel he preached in the prison in Rome began to spread through Rome, the capital city. Nobody knows how the congregation of Rome began, nobody can speak of anybody going there to preach the gospel to them. Probably Christians from various parts of Rome just came together. Likely they had heard the gospel in Jerusalem at the time of Pentecost, and then came together. Now here was Paul the apostle preaching the gospel. He was given knowledge that other men didn't have. He had an understanding of the Word of God that non-apostles did not have. And the gospel began to spread through Rome and even through the emperor's family. That's how God works.

Paul had desired to go to Rome with the gospel. He spoke of it, but he never dreamt that this was the way in which he was going to preach the gospel in Rome. The gospel, friends, is the good news, the good tidings for sinners, that 'Jesus Christ came into the world to save sinners'. He died in the room and stead of sinners that 'whosoever believeth in him should not perish, but have everlasting life'. The gospel we have is the gospel he had. It's the only gospel. It's for you and me, that we might believe and be saved. When Paul went to heaven he was going to meet people who belonged to the emperor's family as well as others from all spheres of society.

Paul then goes on to say that he preached, 'that all the Gentiles might hear'. 'And I was delivered out of the mouth of the lion.' He didn't die the first time: he was delivered out of the mouth of the lion. The lion didn't devour him. The Lord Jesus himself in Psalm 22 speaks of being delivered out of the lion's mouth. The devil would have destroyed him, if possible. Of course, we have a difficulty here in understanding exactly who or what the lion was. There was Satan anyway, who would have devoured and destroyed him, and would have prevented Paul from preaching, if he could have. He didn't manage, and Paul came out of the prison that first time.

There were also the Jews who hated Paul. They would have destroyed him if they could. There were also pagan people, who worshipped idols—Rome was full of idol worship—and they would have destroyed him. He had many, many enemies who would have destroyed him. But it didn't matter which mouth it was, it was 'the mouth of the lion'. And he was delivered out of the mouth of the lion. He was like Daniel, who was in the lions' den. They threw him into the den where the lions were. And he said that an angel from God closed the mouths of the lions, and they couldn't touch him. And now here was the apostle, and 'the mouth of the lion' did not destroy him. He came out of prison.

In prison that first time, he had told them to prepare lodgings for him: he knew he was going to come out. He knew how and why he was delivered. His time hadn't come. The Lord Jesus Christ was in heaven on the right hand of glory; he was the High Priest interceding for him and for all of God's people. Jesus was interceding so that the devil and the world could not destroy him. They could not bring Paul to death before his time. There is a time, there is a place, there is a means. And Paul knew that the Lord in heaven was looking after him.

### 3. Paul's assurance

Then we see Paul's assurance for the future. 'And the Lord shall deliver me from every evil work, and will preserve me unto his heavenly kingdom: to whom be glory for ever and ever. Amen.' The Lord is the deliverer from every evil work, but was Paul not to die? Was he not to come before Nero again and be put to death? He didn't know how he would die. He might be made a torch, as many Christians were, covered with tar, tied to a post and set on fire. He might be put before

## 12 Trial, deliverance and preservation

two horses, tied to them, and they would be driven apart and he would die as his body was broken. Or he might be in the arena with wild beasts. But whatever might happen he said, 'The Lord will deliver me.'

How could Paul speak of being delivered? Well, you remember the three who were cast into the fiery furnace. Nebuchadnezzar told them that they would be cast into the furnace if they did not worship the image that he had made. The three men said that the Lord would help them and that even if the Lord did not preserve their lives and allowed them to go into the fiery furnace, they would not worship the image. You would say, 'How is the Lord preserving them, then?' Well, the body and soul are in the hands of the Lord and he's going to bring the body and the soul into glory.

We have different ways of dying but we are in the hands of the Lord. If you know Christ, your body and your soul are in his hand, nothing can pluck the body or soul out of his hand. You can suffer death in very, very different ways but none can pluck the body or the soul out of his hand. Scripture tells us that we are united to Christ by the Holy Spirit. The soul is united to Christ. The body is equally united to Christ, and Christ said, 'None can pluck them out of my hand.' And Christ also said, 'None can pluck them out of the hand of my Father.' It's the same hand, the divine hand. They are not pluckable. It's not possible that they could be plucked out of his hand. In that way they are preserved, they are to be kept 'from every evil work'. The devil would desire to have Paul in hell, to have Paul lost, to have Paul utterly and everlastingly destroyed. But it couldn't be, it couldn't happen.

The Lord 'will preserve me unto his heavenly kingdom'. That's where Paul was going; he knew that. This present world lies in sin, and the god of this world is the devil. The devil uses various things to make people worship darkness instead of worshipping God. But Paul is being preserved unto the heavenly kingdom.

Wouldn't it be good now if you and I could say, 'I am being preserved, and whatever happens to me in this world, I am being preserved unto his heavenly kingdom'? Not preserved unto the kingdom of this world. These things pass, but 'thy kingdom hath none end at all, / it doth through ages all remain'.

The everlasting kingdom is the place where his people are his brethren. They are the brothers of Christ. They can call God the Father their Father. Christ brings them close to God, as their representative. He prepares them a place that the angels cannot approach to, as they are not the sons of God. The angels have not been bought by the blood: they have not been saved. The angels have been kept, but not saved. But here's a family who were sinners, black sinners, and they're saved, they're cleansed, they're sanctified, they're glorified. They have a kingdom, they have a closeness, a proximity, to the Father. That's the heavenly kingdom, the glorious, glorious place Paul knew he was going to, and that took away his fear, that took away his worry.

Foxe's *Book of Martyrs* used to be a book people commonly read in Scotland. It is about the various martyrs put to death just before the Reformation. These people were tortured simply because they said Christ was their Saviour and Christ was the Head of the Church, and that they believed in Christ. They were tortured and put to death at the stake. I've been going through that book recently and what amazed me was that many of them may have had fears and so on, but when they were brought to the stake and the fire was lit around them, you read there, time and time and time again, how their fears seemed to go. They saw heaven just moments away, and they praised God and sang his praises. People around them were converted through these things. They saw how these martyrs died, how they were praising Christ. And their persecutors would very often beat drums, to deafen people to the sound of their singing and their preaching as they died, and their speaking to Christ as they died.

Ah, friends, it's a wonderful thing to be preserved unto his heavenly kingdom. It's his kingdom and it's a heavenly kingdom, and Christ treats his own people as no one ever treated them. He took them from the miry clay, he put their feet on a rock, he put a new song in their mouths. He loved them with an eternal love. He does everything for them. He gave himself for them. He suffered agonies deeper than those of hell for them because he loved them, and they never knew that he loved them until they came to believe in him and trust in him. That is our prayer, that among ourselves many, if not all, would trust in Christ as Saviour.

Paul concludes: 'To whom be glory for ever and ever. Amen.' This is how he finishes up, praising the Lord. In this last letter he seems to have written, he seems to finish up praising the Lord. He does not speak of the fear of dying, but he praises the Lord, 'to whom be glory for ever and ever'. He could say, 'To whom be glory,' thinking of Christ and praising Christ in the prison. It may have seemed like madness. You wonder how the soldier who was chained to Paul would react to all this. He was with him night and day. He'd be with him when he was praying, he'd be with him when he was writing, he'd be with him when he was speaking and preaching. What a privilege to be chained to Paul! We do not know whether that soldier came to know Christ or not.

Here Paul praises Christ, 'to whom be glory'. We cannot add to his glory, but we can acknowledge it. We can praise him—that's called giving him glory. You'll never praise him unless you know him as your Saviour. It's no use saying, 'I'll praise him,' without knowing him as your God and Saviour. That's not praise at all: that's falsehood.

We sing, but do we sing from the heart? Do we praise from the heart? Are we glorifying him from the heart? Or is it something mainly from the mouth? Think of these things, friends. Earnestly think of these things, because you and I are on the way to eternity.

Then Paul finishes up by sending his greetings to friends, here and there. This is the end, so he sends greetings to them. 'Salute Prisca and Aquila, and the household of Onesiphorus.' Salute them. 'Erastus abode at Corinth: but Trophimus have I left at Miletum sick.' He says to Timothy, 'Do thy diligence to come before winter.' We don't know if Timothy came in time or not, if he came with the coat in time or not before Paul died; if he came with the books and the parchments. Paul wanted the parchments to write. Did he write any other letters or not? We don't know. This is the last record we have of the writings of Paul.

'Eubulus greeteth thee, and Pudens, and Linus, and Claudia, and all the brethren.' They are greeting Timothy. 'The Lord Jesus Christ be with thy spirit. Grace be with you. Amen.' He finishes with 'Amen.' 'Amen' doesn't mean 'the end'. Many think that 'Amen' at the end of a prayer means 'the end'. But prayer doesn't end. If you're a true believer in Christ, the spirit of prayer is in the soul all the time. You don't say, 'My prayer's finished and that is that, until I begin to pray again.' 'Amen' just means that you are setting your seal on what you have said already, that it is the truth. 'I'm certifying that what I have said is the truth. I'm setting my seal to it: it is so, that's the reality, that's the truth. Amen.' And what he says here is *all* truth.

Oh, friends, many, many thousands in the world have come to be blessed through the writings of Paul, and through this letter and through these words that we've had as a text. Men and women have been saved; they have come to know the Lord Jesus. And who knows but that God might have given us this text tonight for the sake of a soul, a precious soul on the way to eternity. We are all private individuals. We all have our own thoughts. We all have our own reasonings inside our hearts, and the Lord knows how you are in your heart tonight. He knows that. Oh friends, seek Christ! Speak to him, call upon him, pray to him, ask for mercy—the sweet, gracious mercy, the forgiveness, the blessing of the Lord Jesus.

May he bless his Word. Let us pray.

## Concluding prayer

Gracious and glorious Lord, we beseech thee to be with us, to help us and to guide us, and to dismiss us with thy blessing on this Sabbath evening. Oh, may it be one of the days of the Son of Man for us! And may thy Word throughout the whole world be blessed. May there be rejoicing in the presence of the angels, rejoicing in the heart of the Saviour over sinners repenting. We pray thee to bless thy Word to ourselves. Give us journeying mercies. Do not let us forget what we hear. Give us to meditate, give us to pray, give us to seek thee early, earnestly and fully. Cleanse us for thine own gracious name's sake. Amen.

# 13

# Paul's experience of the law

1st July 2018, Lord's Day morning, Achmore

*For I was alive without the law once: but when the commandment came, sin revived, and I died.*
Romans 7:9

THE epistle to the Romans is the most theological writing that we have in the Bible, the most theological of all the letters that we have in the New Testament. When you come to this chapter, there are many who say that we just cannot understand what it is talking about. But that tells us that they must have had teachers among the Romans who were able to understand the letter and who were able to explain the various things to the people in the congregations regarding this letter. We needn't think that we are superior in our understanding of the Word of God to those who lived two thousand years ago in Rome. It was a wonderful congregation at one time.

We don't know how the congregation at Rome began. There's no record of any apostle going there with the gospel and starting a congregation. But it was the capital city and no doubt many Jews lived there. No doubt there were a number of converted Jews who would have been at the feasts in Jerusalem, especially at Pentecost, when the Holy Spirit was poured out.

# 13  Paul's experience of the law

No doubt some of the multitudes on the day of Pentecost came from Rome. And when they came together in Rome they would worship together. They wouldn't have needed an apostle to go to begin a congregation there. It developed and became a fine congregation for a time, although eventually, because of the world and the devil and the flesh, it turned into something else. But the church in that city was a pure church for a good many years. People reckon that it was a good church up to close on four hundred years. We ourselves have to take warning when we think of these things.

Let us come to what we have here in verse 9. We have first of all a strange life: 'For I was alive without the law once.' Then we have a strange visitation: 'The commandment came.' And then thirdly, a strange experience: 'When the commandment came, sin revived, and I died.'

## 1. A strange life

The apostle says in the first place, 'I was alive without the law once.' Now the man who's speaking here is Paul. And Paul was brought up under the law, meaning both the Ten Commandments and also the ceremonial law, the law they used for worship, for every approach of the priests to God, for tithing and so on. His whole life was under the moral law and the ceremonial law. But he says, 'I was alive without the law once.' And that seems a strange thing to say when he had been under the law.

Paul was taught the law as a boy. As a man it was explained and expounded to him. He says that he sat at the feet of Gamaliel, a doctor of the law. So he was well instructed in the law. He could tell you everything about the law. He knew so well what was in the law. And he had an iron control of himself. People couldn't fault him in his law-keeping. So zealous was he to keep the law that he persecuted the Church of

Christ: he was willing to go to Syria—to Damascus—to arrest Christians there and to bring them back to Jerusalem to be tried, imprisoned and put to death. He was so zealous for the law.

We have seen children brought up under the law, in a sense. They were taught the Ten Commandments, and the Catechism questions on what each commandment requires and forbids. We have known a number who sat an examination in which they had to repeat the whole Shorter Catechism, receiving a Bible as a prize for doing that. We have known others, and as they grew up, sitting examinations in the Sabbath School regarding various parts of Scripture, receiving prizes because they were proficient in that.

The apostle Paul knew the law exceedingly well. He says to the Galatians, 'I profited in the Jews' religion, above many of my equals in mine own nation, being exceedingly zealous of their traditions.' He knew the laws. He knew the teaching about them. He knew all the traditions. He was zealous. He says he profited, he came on above the majority of those who were with him, if not above all.

But now he says, 'I was alive without the law once.' You see, the hope he had under the law was a dead hope. He thought that by keeping the Ten Commandments and the ceremonial law outwardly, all would be well, he would be saved. It never occurred to him that it was a matter of the heart—not a circumcising of the flesh, but a circumcising of the heart. That didn't seem to occur to him.

When the Jews disputed with Christ regarding these things, they said to him, 'We have Abraham as our father. We are the children of Abraham. And Abraham had all the promises.' They were keeping the law. What Christ was saying to them, they just couldn't follow. They said, 'Abraham was our father,' and they went on to say, 'God is our Father.' And Christ said that if God was their Father, they would know him—Christ—because he was the Son of God and he was sent out by God. The Jews couldn't follow that. They had a dead hope. They were under the law, and they thought that keeping it outwardly was enough to enable them to claim God as their Father.

But, you see, the apostle Paul speaks of different kinds of sinfulness. Some people are sinners 'without the law': they just love sin, and that's it. They won't look at the law or try to keep it at all. But the Jews, he said, were 'under the law', and thought that by keeping the law they would get to heaven. But the Word of God doesn't tell us that a sinner can be saved in that way. It tells us the very opposite. Adam was meant to keep the law when he was an unfallen man—he was meant to keep the law of God and therefore to have a righteousness. But a sinner who begins to keep the Ten Commandments in order to work out a righteousness is still a great sinner. In fact, he is an even greater sinner than someone who is totally without any law at all, because he has the law of God, though he doesn't understand why God has left the law with him. He doesn't understand that the law is there to teach him about sin, about his own heart. He thinks that by keeping it he'll get to heaven.

There are some people among ourselves who think that by keeping the law of God they will get to heaven. But the Word of God goes against all that. It tells us that that is a vain hope. The hope these people have is a mirage, something they think they see, an image they have in their mind. It's all false. The devil said to man before the fall that if he ate of the fruit, 'Thou shalt not die,' and after man sinned the devil keeps on telling him, 'You are not dead.' But man *is* dead. He's dead to God as he is by nature. He doesn't understand the law. He doesn't love God. He has no delight in the law. He has no delight in keeping the commandments. Keeping them doesn't give him fellowship with God. He doesn't understand that he's condemned and lost, and that by seeking to keep the law to get to heaven, he is only sinning more and more against God.

Paul thought he had the law, and yet he did not have the law at all. He wasn't obeying God at all, because for sinners the first commandment is, 'Believe on the Lord Jesus Christ, and thou shalt be saved.' That's where the keeping of the law begins for a sinner, not in keeping the Ten Commandments or the traditions of the Jews. It's not like that.

'I was alive without the law once,' Paul says. 'I was among it all. I was brought up under it. I was taught the commandments. I was at the feet of Gamaliel. But still I was alive without the law. There was something about the law I didn't understand. I didn't understand its spirituality, that it was dealing with my heart. I thought the outward was what the law commanded—that if I wore certain garments, that if I had my phylacteries on my arm and on my forehead, and if I kept all the feasts, if I gave my tithes, if I went to Jerusalem twice a year to the feast, if I went to the synagogue, if I kept the Sabbath, if I prayed outwardly—I thought that was it! If I could say Abraham was my father, that was it! But I was alive without the law. I didn't understand.' As he says elsewhere, 'I did it ignorantly and in unbelief.'

That's how Paul was: doing things ignorantly and in unbelief. And yet there are people in our own churches under the gospel who still think that the way of salvation is just in keeping the Ten Commandments. But a sinner is condemned, and under the curse of God. How can the sinner do away with that curse? How can he do away with the condemnation? He cannot even keep the Ten Commandments, but sins against them daily in thought, word and deed. How can he be so foolish?

But people are like that. Educated people. People with degrees. People who have been brought up under the gospel, who were instructed in their parents' homes all their days. It's because of sin. Sin blinds the heart. Sin takes away our spiritual understanding so that we think that we can get to heaven by merely keeping the Ten Commandments. That door is closed. It is an impossibility. There is only one man who ever kept the Ten Commandments, and that was the Lord Jesus Christ. And he did more than keep them: he met with the curse of the fall of man so that he might open a new door in himself.

## 2. A strange visitation

Then Paul speaks of a strange visitation. He says, 'When the commandment came.' That seems strange, because he had the commandments. He had them all. He knew them all off by heart. He could teach people about them, and he did that. But he says that the commandment came, as if light had come into the soul, as if he now understood something about the commandment that he never understood before.

With some people it comes like lightning: the understanding is opened immediately. 'Those who sat in darkness have seen a great light.' With other people it's like a gradual sunrise: diffused light, stronger light than sunlight, getting stronger and stronger.

When the commandment came, the light came into Saul's darkness. Before that he was like somebody who was in the darkness in a den of lions. He thought he was totally secure. He didn't know he was in danger. He didn't know his true situation until the daylight came, and then when he looked, he was in a den of ten lions. Every commandment was like a lion, every commandment condemned him. His eyes were opened to see that he was condemned. There was no way out of the dungeon where he was. He was now with the ten lions. The light had come because the commandment came.

The commandment came in a wonderful way. It came with authority as it never came before, with utter and total authority. Greater than the authority of Caesar, greater than the authority of a parent. It came like a commandment from Sinai. The commandments that came from Sinai made the people quake and fear. They could not bear the voice from Sinai. They ran from it. When the Lord spoke the Ten Commandments from Sinai they had to flee from that. It was too much. They told Moses that he could deal with the Lord for them and that he would reveal it to them, but they couldn't bear God's voice. 'Speak thou with us, and we will hear: but let not God speak with us, lest we die.'

But when the commandment came to Paul, he had to bear it. He couldn't avoid it when it came with its great authority. The hand of the Lord was stretched out to him. The hand of the Lord with ten fingers of fire came to his soul in a way that the law never came before. There was no way in which he could avoid that. The scales fell from his eyes, and he knew he was condemned.

What was the difference then? He found out that the command was spiritual, that it dealt not just with outward acts, but it had to do with the motives of the heart. He found out about the motives of his own heart. In verse 7 he speaks of that: 'I had not known lust except the law had said Thou shalt not covet.' He says that that commandment, 'Thou shalt not covet', came to him strongly. It had to do with the heart—not just with the hands and the feet and the outward acts, but with the heart.

Paul had been there at the death of Stephen. He had been in charge. He had kept his eye on the clothing of the witnesses who had stoned Stephen to death. He had desired to see Stephen stoned. He was a murderer. But the law came to him, and he began to understand the law was dealing with his motives, with his heart, with the inward man and not just the outward man. So when Christ met him outside Damascus and said to him, 'Saul, Saul, why persecutest thou me?' he also said to him, 'It is hard for thee to kick against the pricks.' The Jews would use a goad, a sharp stick, when they were driving oxen for ploughing, or whatever. If a young ox wasn't used to ploughing it wouldn't tend to go straight along the furrows. It might try to rebel, to kick, to go its own way. But the goad was there to be put into the flank, to make it turn this way or that way and to make it go forward. The pricks of the goad Christ referred to were in Paul's conscience.

When Paul was on the way to Damascus he knew that something was wrong with him. The law had now come. It had visited him. He was seeing things in a different way. The prayers of Stephen when he was dying no doubt had something to do with that. Seeing a child of God dying, and loving his persecutors, those who were putting him to death, and praying for them that the Lord would not leave their sin to their charge—no doubt it had an effect on him. Saul heard the speech of Stephen, he saw the life and death of Stephen, and now his conscience troubled him. Something was wrong with him. The law was going inwardly. The law was going into the motives, the desires. He couldn't keep it out. The devil couldn't help him keep it out. The world couldn't help him keep it out. It was there, and Christ said, 'Why are you kicking against the pricks? It is hard for you to kick against the pricks. The goad is going into you and you're reacting out against it. You're lashing out against it.' It reached his conscience. And there Christ met with him and there he dealt with him. And there he became his Saviour.

The Ten Commandments become a kind of accusation against the sinner. When the Holy Spirit begins to deal with him, the Spirit shows him that he is a sinner. You can see a parallel with the children of Israel in Egypt. The ten plagues began when

Moses came into Egypt. The slaves in Egypt didn't know the trouble they had when Moses came. Then the plagues began, and Pharaoh made things difficult for them. They could no longer make up the tally of bricks, they were no longer given straw to help them. And they protested. They were suffering. But then, it had to be like that. Moses had to be a saviour to take them out of Egypt. A picture of Christ. The ten plagues had to be there. Just in the same way, the law had to work. The ten fingers of the commandments had to be there. The law came. This visitor came: 'The commandment came.'

### 3. A strange experience

Then Paul speaks of his strange experience. He says, 'Sin revived, and I died.' Did he not have a sense of sin before? Yes, of course he had a sense of sin: he had a conscience. But he didn't see sin as he should have seen it. Natural man can see sin. Natural man has a conscience, but it's the conscience of a dead man. He doesn't seek the glory of God. He doesn't see the heinousness of sin. But the Holy Spirit lays his reach upon him, and his conscience helps him in many ways. Under the gospel, the conscience can be made more tender, but that's not the same thing as a man being brought alive.

Paul says, 'Sin revived, and I died.' 'I died. I knew I was condemned to death. I knew I was finished.' Did you hear that? He was on the way to Damascus, and it all came to a head when Christ met with him. He was a dead man: condemned by sin, on the way to hell, despite all the teaching he had. Despite thirty years of instruction! It had all seemed in vain. But of course it wasn't to be in vain. As soon as he was converted he was able to preach the gospel. He had such a knowledge of Scripture! He was able to prove that Christ Jesus was the Messiah spoken of in the Old Testament. When he spoke to the Jews, he had it all off by heart. But at this time, he died, he says. It's as if all the graves had opened. The sins that were buried and put away, as he thought, now rose out of the graves. And he was the one who was dead. He was the one that was condemned. Every sin that he ever did, great and small, seemed to rise up against him, to condemn him. The Word of God condemned him. There seemed no way, no hope. No hope! The old hope was dead.

That's how it must be. That's how the Lord works. He destroys the carnal hope. He destroys the old hope. He destroys the old way of salvation that you nurtured in your heart. It is false. It has to be destroyed. And that's what happened with Paul.

Paul found himself dead under the law. Verse 10 says, 'And the commandment, which was ordained to life, I found to be unto death.' The commandment was ordained to life. What does that mean? Before Adam sinned, he was spiritually alive. By keeping the commandments he was working out righteousness, so the commandment was ordained to life in the experience of Adam. But this wasn't holy Adam: this was sinful Paul. So he says, 'The commandment which was ordained to life, I found to be unto death. When the commandment came sin revived, and I died.'

Then he says in verse 11, 'For sin, taking occasion by the commandment, deceived me, and by it slew me.' How can we understand that? How can sin take occasion by the commandment? Well, this is how sin worked in his soul. Sin, the devil, and his own sinful heart said, 'Keep the commandments and you'll be alright, you'll have eternal life!' So sin drove him to seek eternal life by keeping the commandments. So he says, 'Sin, taking occasion by the commandment, deceived me.' The sin of his own heart deceived him. Sin said to him, 'Keep the Ten Commandments and you'll be alright!' So sin itself deceived him, and his own sinful heart deceived him, and by the commandment slew him. He found himself slain, slain by sin. Dead. Condemned. He had sought to be a faithful servant. He had an iron will. There was no one like him who worked to promote the cause of the Jews. But all of that was now finished. When he met Christ, it had all come to an end.

Paul was dead as far as the law was concerned. The law of God slew him. He had no hope. That's when he met Christ. 'Who art thou, Lord?' He knew he was the Lord. But it was all such a great puzzle. Yes, he knew it was the Lord but, 'Who art thou?' 'I am Jesus of Nazareth whom thou persecutest.' Paul hated Jesus of Nazareth above everyone else. 'I am the chief of sinners,' he said later, because there was no one among the Christians who had a history like his, in hating Christ. But he said, 'I did it ignorantly in unbelief.'

Where the law slays you and leaves you dead, that's when faith comes in. That's when Christ operates. You have to lose your own self-sufficiency. 'I found mercy.' And lying on the ground, Paul said to Christ, 'What wilt thou have me to do?' That is, 'What is thy will? I desire nothing but thy will.' That is the best place to be. He fell there before Christ as a lost sinner. He rose on his feet as a saved man and an apostle. 'I will send thee,' the Lord said to him. An *apostolos*, the Greek word for a messenger. 'I will send thee.' The Lord would make him an apostle to the Jews and to the Gentiles. He would send him to the ends of the earth. A changed man! Well, Christ was the one who changed it all. At Pentecost they began calling out, 'Men and brethren, what shall we do?' Peter was preaching to them, thousands of people who depended on the keeping of the law to be saved. And thousands of them were in this same condition that Paul was in here. The law only slew them, condemned them.

What must we do to be saved? 'Believe on the Lord Jesus Christ and thou shalt be saved.' That was the only way. There is no other way. That is the first commandment. That is the keeping of everything. If you believe in Christ as your Saviour, the wonderful thing is that you are justified. That is, God looks upon you as if you had kept the law and also satisfied the broken law. That is the work of Christ. God looks upon you as if you had done the work of Christ. We are accepted in the beloved—accepted in Christ, identified with him. Ye are one with him. His justification that he worked out is your justification. And it becomes yours. It is laid to your charge when you believe on the Lord Jesus Christ. And Paul rose as a servant of Christ. He could say, 'For me to live is Christ, for me to die is gain.'

Ah friends, it's all there. There's a great deal in Romans you may say you cannot understand. But you can understand these things. You've got to think, you've got to stop. You take small bit after small bit, and you put it all together, and understanding grows with that.

Three strange things, then. He was 'alive without the law once'. The strange visitation: the commandment came, and it came in a special way. And then the strange experience: that sin revived in his experience, and he died. But the strangest thing of all is that he found Christ. Or, as he himself puts it—a better way to put it—he was found by Christ. Christ found him.

Oh, friend with a precious soul, has Christ found you? Has he found me? That's what really matters. Am I in Christ or am I out of Christ? Are we wrestling for the souls of others as well as thinking of our own? Is the Lord going to bless the gospel among us? Or will he allow us to go back and back to harden? Will he depart from us? Will he refuse his saving power in the future among us because we are such a sinful people?

May the Lord then bless his Word. Let us pray.

## Concluding prayer

O gracious and glorious Lord, to whom else can we go? for thou hast the words of eternal life. There is no one else to whom we can apply. There is no other door, no other gateway into glory. And many are deceived in our own land. They think they are on the way to heaven and they are in places where nobody warns them that they are not in the way to heaven. And there are others who refuse to hear such voices which say they are not on the way to heaven and that they are taking the wrong road, because man is blinded by sin. O Lord God, remove the scales from many in our land. Visit us in a day of mercy and in a day of spiritual preparation, we beseech thee. Bless us in our various places—our homes, among our friends, in our church, in our missions, in our island, in our nation. Oh, visit us in a day of power, we beseech thee. Stretch out thine hand in saving power. Touch us in our hearts, we pray thee. Work faith in many hearts. Work repentance in many hearts. Draw nigh to us. Bless thy Word to us, and cleanse us. For Christ's sake. Amen.

# 14

# Comfort to the sorrowing Church

1st July 2018, Lord's Day evening, Uig

*But Zion said, The LORD hath forsaken me, and my LORD hath forgotten me. Can a woman forget her sucking child, that she should not have compassion on the son of her womb? Yea, they may forget, yet will I not forget thee. Behold, I have graven thee upon the palms of my hands: thy walls are continually before me.*
Isaiah 49:14–16

ISAIAH was a prophet sent to the people of Judah. After Solomon's death when Rehoboam became king, you remember that the tribes broke up. A separation came in. Judah and Benjamin adhered to Rehoboam, and the other ten tribes separated and went on their way. The ten tribes had been carried off into captivity before Isaiah was born. Now he was sent to warn the two tribes which were still ruled by the house of David that, if they were idolatrous and immoral and Sabbath breakers as the ten tribes had been, they too would be carried off into captivity. Before Isaiah died, he prophesied that the two tribes would be carried off into captivity. He also prophesied about the great captivity of sin and the great return from captivity through Christ for sinners. That's the background.

The first part of this chapter deals with the Lord Jesus Christ. God the Father is saying to him, addressing him as Israel, 'Thou art my servant, O Israel, in whom I will be glorified' (verse 3). In reply Christ said, 'I have laboured in vain, I have spent my strength for nought, and in vain: yet surely my judgment is with the Lord, and my work with my God' (verse 4) He had come to his own people, the Jews, and the Jews as a people had rejected him. Yes, the Church began in Jerusalem with many thousands of Jews, but as a people they rejected him. So the Lord replied, 'Though Israel be not gathered, yet I shall be glorious in the eyes of the LORD. It is a light thing'—or a small thing—'that thou shouldest be my servant to raise up the tribes of Jacob.' It is as if he said, 'That's a small matter compared to what I have in view for you.'

Verse 6 continues: 'And to restore the preserved of Israel: I will also give thee for a light to the Gentiles, that thou mayest be my salvation unto the end of the earth.' That was a great consolation given to the Lord Jesus. The Jews rejected him, they crucified him, but he knew that his work would be blessed to the ends of the earth. He knew that they would come from all parts of the world, to believe in him. There are millions of believers today, and in every generation, who trust in the Lord Jesus. That's what we have at the beginning of the chapter.

Coming to verse 14 we see the Lord's people, as they often are, a depressed people, brought very low. After they were carried off into captivity, the cause of the Lord became very low. From time to time in various places the Church of Christ will say what Zion said, 'The LORD hath forsaken me and my Lord hath forgotten me.'

So we will look first at this sorrowing of the Church. Then we learn of the Lord's great comfort for the Church: 'Can a woman forget her sucking child, that she should not have compassion on the son of her womb? Yea, they may forget, yet will I not forget thee,' and so on.

## 1. The sorrow of the Church

When we think of the sorrowing of the Church, we realise that in our own day and generation we have a measure of that sorrow among ourselves. We see many turning away from the Lord and from his cause. The Church of Christ seems to become weaker and weaker, smaller and smaller. But she will always be there—perhaps not in any particular place, but she will always be there. God says that he will not forsake her. The sun and moon may depart, but his kindness will not depart. The Church will be there as long as sun and moon are there.

Here we have the sorrowing Church that came out of captivity. We also see that since then, in various parts of the world, in various times. 'Zion' is one of the names given to the Church of Christ. It means 'a high place'. There's no place so high, spiritually, as the Church of Christ. And yet Zion said, 'The LORD hath forsaken me, and my Lord hath forgotten me.' She calls him 'the LORD' and she calls him 'my Lord'. He is so precious to her. Although men should forsake her, although kings should forsake her and governments and friends forsake her, when the Lord forsakes her and forgets her, that is different. These are the two terms she uses. She says, 'He has forsaken me, and forgotten me.' What a terrible feeling to have in one's heart, when one feels that the Lord has turned his back upon him and upon the cause! That drives God's people to prayer, to agony of heart, but the affection of the Church for the Lord remains: 'My Lord.'

You can see the same thing in the experience of Mary Magdalene. She thought she had lost her Lord. He died, he was crucified, he was buried, and she thought that at least the body would be there and she could, perhaps, anoint Christ in some way. He was already anointed, and a winding sheet was around him, but perhaps she could anoint the head, or the hands or whatever. Then when she came to the grave, the body was not there. But she still called him 'my Lord'. 'They have taken away my Lord, and I know not where they have laid him.' When she met Christ, she did not recognise him. Initially she did not recognise his appearance, she did not recognise his voice, and she said, 'If thou hast taken him, tell me where thou hast put him, and I will carry him away.' Christ was anointed with a hundred pounds weight of aloes and myrrh, and the winding sheet was around him. The weight of his body, the weight of the winding sheet, the weight of the hundred pounds of ointment put on him, all of that would make him a fearful burden for her to carry. But love is like that. 'Tell me where thou hast put him, and I will take him away.' She was not asking if she had any right to take him away. Did he belong to her so that she might take him away? But her love meant that she desired to find him and desired to keep as much of him as she could to the very end. She also had living faith, although she felt that she could understand nothing of what had taken place. She couldn't put it all together at that time; it didn't fall into place. But her faith could not die. He was her Lord. She called him 'my Lord'.

That's how the Church thinks of Christ in every generation: he is 'my Lord'. He is the husband of the Church, he is the Beloved of the Church, he is the chief corner stone, he is the true vine, he is the foundation of the temple, he is the Lord and Saviour of his own people, the One whom they desire above all. So she feels it greatly when it appears he has forgotten her and gone.

If we look at the beginning of the next chapter, the Church seems to be saying that the Lord had divorced her and sent her away (Isaiah 50:1). A Jewish husband could divorce his wife and send her away if there was a sufficient reason for it. However, in chapter 50 the Lord is asking, 'Where is the bill of your divorcement to prove that I put you away?' 'Where is the bill? Where is the writing?' In other words, 'There's no such writing. There is no such bill. There is no such divorce. It doesn't exist!' The devil may say it exists, the world may say it, and unbelief in the heart may say it. But no, the Lord will not put away his own. The mountains may depart, the hills may be removed, but his kindness cannot depart from his own.

This is what we have in Psalm 42, which we were singing earlier. It has words which seem to resonate with the thoughts of the Church:

> And I will say to God my rock,
>   why me forgett'st thou so?
> Why, for my foes' oppression,
>   thus mourning do I go?
>
> 'Tis as a sword within my bones,
>   when my foes me upbraid;
> ev'n when by them, Where is thy God?
>   'tis daily to me said.

It is not easy for the child of God when he's afflicted by unbelief, when he comes into a very low state of heart and mind before God, feeling the Lord has turned his back on him and is forgetting him and forsaking him. But yet, he never comes to despair: faith is there, it's always there. If the Lord began a good work, he will carry on that work. He will put his people through trials and through troubles, but it's because he's out to bless the faith they have—it's a trial of their faith, which is much more precious than the trial of gold that perishes. The trial is precious in the eyes of the Lord, and we have to look to him in everything that we go through. 'Still trust in God; for him to praise / good cause I yet shall have,' he says, looking forward in faith to the time when his soul would yet have opportunity to praise God anew.

## 2. The Lord's comfort for the Church

We see the Lord's great comforts in verse 15. God says, 'Can a woman forget her sucking child, that she should not have compassion on the son of her womb?' A mother loves her child. There is no one who loves the child like the mother of the child. She carried her child in her body many months, and she brought the child to birth, and she suffered in doing so, and she rejoiced in the child who came into the world. She loves that child, she would do anything for the child, and she would always want to care for the child.

Even the very animals and birds have it in their nature to fight for their offspring. Some birds will stand up on their nests to fight an animal that approaches the nest, even when that animal could easily destroy the bird. Animals will fight to the very end to protect their young. It's an instinct that is in them. God put it in them, until the time comes when the animal or the bird will send its offspring away when it is old enough.

But mother love in humans goes beyond the care that birds and animals have for their young. When the human mother is old and grey-headed, she still loves her young. When she reaches old age and the son of her womb reaches middle age or comparative old age, she still loves that son just as she loved him from the beginning—it's mother love, and people correctly speak of that. The mother thinks so often of her son. He may be abroad, at the other side of the world, but wherever he is, her heart and mind go out to that son. And the Lord is referring to this mother love. 'Can a woman forget her sucking child, that she should not have compassion on the son of her womb?'

I remember reading in a tract about one woman in the Highlands. She was carrying her son in a plaid on her back. She had travelled a good many miles, but it began to snow. She was caught up in the snowstorm, with a long way to go, and she was afraid that she'd never make it. On the way, she came across a rock with a cleft in it. She wrapped her child in the plaid and put it into that cleft. She couldn't do any more for it. She died in the storm, and people found her body in the morning. When they traced her route back, they found the child alive in the rock. That woman died. When she couldn't do any more for the child, she showed love for the child.

The Lord is saying that it is possible for a mother to lose her love for her child. You never know what may happen. He may become an evil person, he may turn against his parents, he may carry out fearful deeds, he may become a monster of iniquity. The Lord says it is possible. God said, 'Yea, they may forget.' That did happen in Israel. The Word of God tells us that some of them actually sacrificed their children to Moloch. And to punish Israel, God said that the day would come when even some of the women, who were so refined that they hesitated to put their very feet on the ground, would finish up eating their own children in the famine.

These things can happen. Yes, these things are possible. But here is something that is totally impossible. What is totally impossible is that the Lord will forget his own. He says, 'Yea, they may forget, yet will I not forget thee.' The Lord will never, never, forget his own people. How can he? Christ cannot forget those God gave him from all eternity, those who are to be his Bride, those whom he himself loved from eternity. How can he forget them? He doesn't have to remember them because he never forgets them. That's the teaching we have here, that he never forgets them. 'I will not forget thee.'

The Lord says, 'Behold, I have graven thee upon the palms of my hands.' We know what engravings are. Job says of his own words: 'Oh that my words were written! Oh that they were printed in a book! That they were graven with an iron pen and lead in the rock for ever.' He wanted the rock to be cut with some kind of iron implement, so that the words would be cut into the rock itself—not mere writing on the surface, but engravings going into the rock itself—carving, embedding, entering into the rock. That was writing that could not be rubbed out, writing not easily effaced. Job wanted an iron pen and lead in the rock for ever. 'I know that my redeemer liveth.' That's what he wanted to be engraved into the rock.

Here the Lord says that he has engraving upon the palms of his hands. What does that mean? Well, there is activity within the Godhead—Father, Son and Holy Spirit. Some people think of the Triune God as being inactive within himself, but there is nothing but activity within the Godhead. God is love. Love needs fellowship and the highest fellowship is the fellowship within God—three persons, who are one God. It's higher than husband and wife, two who are one in marriage. There is total activity within the Godhead throughout all eternity. But also the Lord works outside himself. He didn't need to work outside himself, he didn't need to have activity outside himself, but he does it and he begins to create.

It is through the second person of the Godhead that he's going to show his glory. Scripture tells us that 'by him', that is, by Christ, 'all things were made, and without him was nothing made that was made'. Through Christ as Creator and through Christ as Saviour—especially through Christ as Saviour—God is going to show a portion of his glory to created creatures. When he made, as it were, the first building block of creation, if we can put it like that, his mind and heart were really upon the Church, not just upon the sea and the earth and the trees and the rocks. Yes, his mind was on those things, but remember that Christ loved his own with an eternal love. That love doesn't embrace the rocks and the trees and the sea and the fishes and the animals: it is his own saving, eternal love for his own people. He was raised up as a Saviour from eternity for sinners. He loved them, and so when he began to create, it was only a first step towards salvation. Evolutionists want to leave things like that. They don't know these things, they don't understand these things.

That's why God speaks of these people being engraved upon the palms of his hands. The palms are the working parts of the hands, and they are the parts which come into contact with things when you're working. 'Well,' he says, 'the contacting parts have the Church engraved upon them. All my work, all my creation, all my upholding of creation, all that I do to sustain it all, has to do with the Church.' It is the Church, it is Zion, that is engraved 'upon the palms of my hands'. And who can take the engraving away? It's not mere paint or mere ink. It's not even a tattoo: it's deeper than that. The whole reason for God beginning to operate outside himself at all was so that Christ would have the Church as his Bride. Don't ask me to explain the whys and the wherefores. I do not know why he should love sinners. I do not know why he should desire sinners to be his Bride. I only know that it is so, that the One who cannot lie says so. The One who is faithful and true, he says so—the Lord, the One who came as Saviour, the One who's speaking at the beginning of the chapter about Judah rejecting him. The Lord has his own people engraved upon his palms—note the plural, the two palms, which is as much as to say that all his working is aimed at the Church. What a wonderful thing that is, that every child of grace is a product of his hands, that he brings them alive through the Holy Spirit, that he gives them the Holy Spirit! He gives them faith through the Spirit, he gives them grace, he gives them strength, he gives then renewing, he gives them promises, he gives them his own love and sheds it abroad in their own hearts. What wonderful hands to which we can turn!

He says elsewhere that he plucked his own 'out of the burning'. His hand could go into the fire, but the fire could do nothing to his hand. He 'plucked them out as brands out of the burning', branches that were alight. He made them into living branches in the vine Christ Jesus. Now instead of being burning brands, they are living branches, and they bear fruit. That is the work of his hands, that is how he works.

The angels sang when the universe, including the world, was created. That was wonderful. But it's even more wonderful when you go to Zechariah, you read of Christ singing. But it's not over the created world he's singing. He's singing over his Bride, when he cast his garment over her shoulders. He's singing over his Bride. He loved her and he's going to complete the work. Everyone given to him by the Father will come to him. Yes, he plucked them as brands out of the fire, but none can pluck them out of his hands, out of these hands where they are engraved. He will work in their souls and make their souls like unto the soul of Christ. He will work in their bodies—he will raise the bodies up out of the dust, out of the sea, out of the air—and make them like unto the body of Christ. He will glorify them along with himself. They will be joined to him as his Bride: they are called 'one spirit'. The hands of Zerubbabel laid the foundation of the temple, and he finished it. So it is with the Lord. The Church is called the work of God's hands, and he will finish the work. That's how the Lord is: he will finish it, the work of his hands.

### 3. The walls of Jerusalem

The Lord goes on and he says, 'Thy walls are continually before me.' Now, the walls in Jerusalem were the walls of the city and the walls of the temple. The Edomites (who represent and epitomise the enemies of the Church) hated the people of God. They used to say of the walls of Jerusalem, 'Raze, raze it quite.' 'Raze' means 'to bring down', 'to destroy'. 'Raze it quite!' That's what the Edomites wanted, to see the walls completely destroyed.

Then when the inhabitants of Jerusalem were carried off into captivity, a great part of the walls were destroyed and turned into rubbish. Their enemies used fire to break up the stone and make them rubbish. When Nehemiah came to look at the walls for rebuilding them, he couldn't go very far, and the builders who tried to build the walls complained, 'There's so much rubbish, we cannot build.'

But when the Lord builds he says, 'Thy walls are continually before me.' Human builders may fail. They'll say, 'We cannot do it. There's too much rubbish. We cannot do it because Sanballat and Tobias and these other enemies come after us, threatening us. And because we are very tired of the work and we don't have the ability or the materials or the skill.' But God says, 'Thy walls are continually before me.' That is, 'I see the finished walls from all eternity. Not a broken wall, but, thy walls are continually before me. I see them complete and entire. That's what I'm gazing upon in the eternal covenant. I see a perfect Zion with perfect walls. The walls are Zion itself, the Church of Christ, and the walls are intact; they are complete. I have done that with my own hands, hands upon which you are engraved. Thy walls are continually before me.'

In your eyes the walls of Zion may seem broken at times. You may see the cause of the Lord being destroyed here and there. You may fear and you may mourn, but for the Lord it is different. 'Thy walls before me are there, whole and finished. I see the beginning from the end, and the end from the beginning. A thousand years in my sight are as a day, and one day as a thousand years.' That's indeed how it is. That's the comfort. That's what he says to Zion. Isn't that comfort enough for Zion? Isn't that good enough when the Lord says that to the soul?

Ah, friends, to be among these people is everything! You see, Scripture says that we are 'complete in Christ'. For this speaks of what the Lord is speaking of here: the walls complete, continually. All is well. It doesn't matter what happens to the child of God, he's engraved in the Lord's hands, and all is well. The world is hastening on to its end when every child of God will be gathered to be with him. That day will come. It won't be very long in coming. And in that day those who love his appearing will receive 'a crown of righteousness', as Paul says. They will receive that, along with Paul himself, and they will throw all the crowns at the feet of Christ, to whom pertains all glory and honour.

May the Lord be pleased to add his blessing. Let us pray.

## Concluding prayer

O gracious Lord, we pray thee to bless us and to help us. Give us to praise thy name and to remember thee at every time. And when our hearts fail us, give us to turn to the Lord who will never fail his own people. Thy promises can never be broken. Thy promises can never fail. The world will lie, the devil will lie. They will go around thy walls seeking to find fault with thy work and thy cause, but it can never be. Thou sayest, 'I am the Lord: that is my name: and my glory will I not give to another, neither my praise to graven images.' Bless us then, O Lord, in parting. Give us journeying mercies, give us the Sabbath spirit to be within our souls, and take away our sins. For Jesus' sake. Amen.

# 15

# The glory of the city of God

9th September 2018, Lord's Day morning, Leverburgh

*Glorious things are spoken of thee, O city of God. Selah.*
Psalm 87:3

THE word '*selah*' appears twice in this psalm. It's a Hebrew word. It's not translated. Nobody is quite sure what it means. We think it is a musical stop, used when they sang the psalms. Some kind of change would come in at every *selah*. We think *selah* was used for some way of directing the Levites to make some sort of change when they worshipped in the temple by singing and playing instruments. But no one is certain, so the word is left as it is. It may be that one day the Jews will be able to tell us with certainty what it's really there for, but the translators left it as it was. They found it in the Word of God when they were translating it, and they left it as it was, out of their respect to the Word of God. They weren't going to leave it out. It was there. It was written. So they left it as it was.

We should like to look at the verse we have here: 'Glorious things are spoken of thee, O city of God.' What do we understand by the city of God? When Moses was leading the children of Israel out of Egypt, through the desert for forty years, God said to them in the wilderness that he would give them a land—the land of Canaan—and he said, 'In that land will be a city, and I will place my name there.' Just one city in the whole world where the name of God was to be placed! The name of God, of course, means God revealing himself in a special way. His glory, his truth, his power, his wisdom, his mercy—he was going to reveal himself in a special way in that city. That city was Jerusalem. There was no other city under the sun where the name of God was to be set upon it, but that city. That's the city where the temple of God was to be built: there was to be no other temple but that one temple in Jerusalem. And Jerusalem is the city where the palace of the king was.

But when the psalmist speaks here of the city of God, he's not speaking of that material Jerusalem. That was made up of stones and mortar and wood. Instead he's speaking of the spiritual Jerusalem. When you go through Scripture the terms 'Jerusalem' and 'the city of God' denote the collective people of Christ. The people of God are the people who have been converted, who have been changed, wherever they are. They are scattered one from one another but in God's eyes they are still one city. They belong to each other. They are fellow citizens in that city. They have the same language, the language of Canaan. They worship God, they love God. Their God is their Saviour. So the city of God we're speaking of is God's people. It's his city and it's their city, and his name is there. It's the only city in this world that has his name.

The question for us is, 'Am I in that city?' If I am not in that city, I'm a wanderer in this world—without Christ, without God, without hope. O yes, I can be in a place of worship but, good as that is in the eyes of men—and we praise that, we are thankful for that—still we need to be inside the city or else we will never go to heaven when we leave this world. Part of the city is in heaven. Part of the city is here. It's the city of God.

# 15   The glory of the city of God

'Glorious things are spoken of thee, O city of God.' Glorious things! People can speak of cities. They tell us of cities they have seen. They go on cruises. We've heard of various lovely cities throughout the world, and we see these wonderful cities in brochures and newspapers and magazines. But whatever their glory may be, it fades into nothingness compared to this city. This city will endure for ever. All these other cities will go, and all their glory will go. It's only like the glory of the grass, the flower of the grass. The grass withers, the flower thereof falleth away.

## Verse 1: The holy mountains

What glorious things are spoken of the city of God in this psalm? First of all, and at the very beginning, it says this city's foundation is in the holy mountains. Jerusalem is built on a mountain, but the spiritual Jerusalem has its foundation in the holy mountains.

The holy mountains speak to us of holiness. What is holiness? Everybody thinks that he knows what holiness is, but friends, nobody knows what holiness is until a holy experience has come into his life. You ask people who sit under the gospel what it is to be holy and how to become holy, and if they don't know Christ, the only way they can think of it is by making themselves better. But that doesn't make you holy. Because you can't make yourself better. Oh, you can stop telling lies, you can stop being immoral, you can stop slandering. Yes, but holiness is in the heart. Can you make your heart better? Can you make yourself love God? Can you make yourself into a saint of God? No, nobody knows holiness except those into whom the Holy Spirit has come. It is the Holy Spirit who teaches us holiness. He blesses the Word to us, and we are converted, brought alive, and we come to trust in Jesus as our Saviour. That's the first class where you begin to learn about that holiness, without which no man can see the Lord in heaven.

The other meaning of holiness is separation. They used to speak of things being 'sanctified' or made holy. Sheep that they took out of the flock to sacrifice were 'sanctified' in the sense of being separated to a holy use. Men were sanctifying them. That didn't mean anything for the heart of a sheep. It was the same with the vessels they made for the temple. The vessels were sanctified, meaning they were set apart.

When a man is born again, the Holy Spirit sets him apart from the world. Holiness has entered his heart, and he has been set apart. He's set apart unto God, unto Christ. He now sees that sin is a bitterness. He has lost his taste for many of the things in which he indulged. For example, the kind of worldly language he used to have—the cursing and the swearing. Away with it all! The immoral talk and the things that drew his heart. Sheer worldliness! Now the Word of God draws him, prayer draws him, God's people draw him. The fellowship of Christ draws him. He's been set apart, you see. Not only that: the work of holiness involves growing in holiness. It goes on in his heart. He progresses. It may be gradual, but he's progressing in his heart in holiness.

Now let us consider the mountains. You've got to think of God's holiness. God is apart. He is the totally holy one. He is the well of holiness. He is the spring from which all holiness has come. There is no holiness that was not derived from him. And he is so greatly 'set apart' that he's separate from all his creatures. The distance is infinite. He is the all-holy One. He is holiness—utter, utter holiness. Eternal holiness. Immeasurable holiness. Unchangeable holiness. That is God.

The Scripture says that the heavens are not clean in his sight. But, you may say, the heavens are holy, with the angels and

## 15  The glory of the city of God

those that have gone to be with Christ. It's a holy place, nothing in it but holiness. But Scripture says the heavens are not clean in his sight: not meaning that the heavens are filthy, but meaning that God is so holy. He has uncreated holiness. What you have in heaven is only created holiness: men who became holy, angels who were created holy. But holiness is the great, great attribute of God. We speak of his love, of his power, of his grace, of his truth, of his mercy, of his long-suffering. All his attributes are holy attributes. Holiness sums them all up. Holiness sums up God. He is the all-holy God.

Why do we speak of God here, then? Because we are speaking of the foundation of the Church. The psalmist speaks here of the foundation as being holy mountains. The mountains are created by God. Mountains are powerful. Mountains are high. Mountains are strong. What kind of foundation do we have for the Church? Well, Christ, the second person of the Godhead. He is God. He has all the holiness of God. He came into this world. He took your nature and my nature, and in that nature he suffered and died, taking the room and stead of all his covenant people. He knew no sin. How could the all-holy one know sin? He knew no sin! In his experience he became sin, he became the one who was the sin-bearer, the one upon whom the guilt was laid. He was made sin for us, that we might be made the righteousness of God in him.

The mountains were made. Christ had to be the foundation of the Church of Christ. No other foundation would suffice. Sin was so terrible. Sin was so fearful against the all-holiness of God. This was the only way in which sin could be dealt with. It was the sin of men, so Christ took the nature of men. And in that nature he satisfied the justice of God. He died and he rose again to show that he had given total satisfaction to the justice of God. That is the foundation.

Christ is the foundation of the Church. It rests upon him, like the foundation of a temple. Solomon's temple was built upon bedrock, a rock that was in the mountain.

Is Christ your foundation? Do you rest upon Christ? Do you look to him to take away your sin? To sanctify you? To glorify you? To keep you?

## Verse 2: The gates of Zion

We read in verse 2: 'The LORD loveth the gates of Zion more than all the dwellings of Jacob.'

'The dwellings of Jacob' just means all the cities and all the villages of Jacob, or Israel, the nation. God loves the gates of Zion. Zion is just another name for Jerusalem. Sometimes it is spelt with a Z, sometimes with an S: Zion or Sion. In Gaelic there are no Z's, so it's always spelled 'Sion'.

God loves the gates of Zion, the gates of the city of God. That is a figure of speech: the gate stands for the city. In every one of the walled cities there would be a place at the gate where the elders of the city would meet, and the councils would meet there. A place would be walled in, like a room or a hollow, at the gate. For example, Christ says in Psalm 69 that those that sat in the gate spoke against him. When Boaz wanted Ruth for a bride, he went up to the gate where the elders were, and there spoke to them, so that he might have Ruth as his bride. And in various other places in Scripture, you'll read about the gate of the city and the elders in the gate, where they had their council meetings. The gate was used as a figure of speech for the city. You would expect the wisest and holiest men to be in the gate, in the council. So 'the gates of Jerusalem' just means Jerusalem.

It says here, 'The LORD loveth the gates of Zion more than all the dwellings of Jacob.' He loves the gates of Zion. He loves Jerusalem. He loves his people. The Lord loves them. Yes, he shows kindness to other places. We are all under God's hands, we've seen his benefits in this world. God is kind to us all. He gave us our lives. He could have left us without the life we have. We came into the world as sinners. He could have extinguished our lives at the very beginning. But he didn't: he gave us our life. He gives many of us marriage and children and work. He gave us the various benefits and blessings we have in the world. But that's not salvation! That's not saving love. He loves the gates of Zion above all the dwelling-places of Jerusalem. He loves his own.

Ah, how his own people mourn at how small their own love is for him! The only way in which we come to love him is because he put his own love into our heart. You'll never love him as he loves you. Never! Even in heaven itself you will never love him as he loves you. O soul, what it is to be loved by Christ! But how can we come to that? We must come by faith. Faith is the only way. We must come as beggars to his feet—as sinful beggars putting our trust in him, and in faith that everything else is included. Inside faith is the beginning of love for God.

## Verse 3: Glorious things are spoken of Zion

'Glorious things are spoken of thee, O city of God.' Inside that city you'll find faith. True saving faith in Christ. Outside of it you'll find faith as well, but it's not true saving faith. All of us believe that the Bible is God's Word. That is good as far as it goes. That is faith in a sense, but it won't save your soul. You may say, 'We believe in a judgment, we believe in a resurrection, we believe the things that the Bible says that Christ was in the world and he's now in heaven.' But that's not going to save your soul. Saving faith is a trust in Christ as your Saviour. Inside this city is that saving faith. And inside that city is love for Christ. They all love him. Yes, they know him—everyone, from the smallest of the flock. They all have a true hope. They all desire his fellowship. They all love the Scriptures. They are all praying from the heart. They all love holiness. That's the great mark of God's people, that they love holiness. Yes, glorious things are said of thee, O city of the Lord.

All of these things are glorious. But the world that passes by knows nothing about all that. As it is said in Psalm 48, they wonder at the people of God. But though they were wondering, they would not stay: they passed on. They just wonder to see God's people, how they live. They may see godly parents, and they wonder, but they still pass by. They may see godly elders, godly visitors, but they still pass by.

But glorious things are spoken of the city. The inhabitants of it have fellowship in Christ that the world knows nothing of, and it's an eternal fellowship. It will never be broken. Yes, good men and good women will leave this world, and congregations will miss them. They will lose them, but their fellowship is with Christ. It is a fellowship that goes on and on and on.

## Verse 4: People are born in the city

Then the Psalmist continues, and he says in verse 4, 'I will make mention of Rahab and Babylon to them that know me: behold Philistia, and Tyre, with Ethiopia; this man was born there.'

He's speaking now of people being born in this city. Other nations seek to know nothing about the city, but he will make mention of people born in this city. He's going to speak about them and to them. About what? About being born in the city. About the new birth. As Christ said, 'Ye must be born again.'

# 15  The glory of the city of God

Not the natural birth but the spiritual birth. You've got to be born in this city. But how can that be? Look at what he says here: 'I will make mention of Rahab.' Now Rahab here is not the Rahab who was in Jericho. Rahab is used as another name for Egypt. It's a name that seems to speak of ferocity and opposition, and we know how Egypt was against the Israelites. 'I will make mention of Egypt and Babylon.' The Israelites came out of Egypt. They came out of Babylon as well, after their captivity. These nations were oppressors.

'Behold Philistia,' the great enemy, which had five cities. David often fought them. The Philistines were haters of Israel, 'and Tyre, with Ethiopia', countries that were further off. God says, 'I will make mention of them.' Something will take place within them all. God says, 'I will have children in Babylon. I will have children in Egypt, in Ethiopia. I will mention that this man was born there.' There is a register of births in the city of God, and men and women are born there—they are born again.

Nicodemus came to Christ. He was a master in Israel. He was a rabbi. 'Art thou a master of Israel? Art thou a rabbi? Art not thou the teacher in Israel?' Christ was a teacher—the word 'rabbi' means 'teacher' or 'master'. 'Art thou not the teacher in Israel?' He was a teacher of the Bible in Israel. That was the title that Nicodemus had. And yet when Nicodemus, the great rabbi, the great teacher came to Christ, he called Christ 'Rabbi'. Although Nicodemus had been through the schools of learning, still he said to Christ, 'No man can work the work that thou doest unless God has sent him.' Unless Christ had come from God. Nicodemus gave Christ the title of teacher, even though Nicodemus was the high teacher in the land.

Christ said to him as a teacher that he must be born again. That's where the teaching begins. 'Ye must be born again.' That is the first lesson in the school of learning: 'Ye must be born again.' Nicodemus asked, 'How can a man be born when he is old?' Well, except a man be born again he cannot *see* the kingdom of heaven. And except a man be born again he cannot *enter* the kingdom of heaven. Without the new birth he cannot enter it and he cannot see it—that is, he cannot see it from the inside. He'll have no experience of the kingdom of heaven. The kingdom of heaven is this glorious city. It's in the world as well as in glory. 'Ye must be born again.'

Think of those who are born again. Think of Saul of Tarsus, who hated the name of Christ above all names. He was the biggest enemy of the Church in the world. Yet he was born again. Yes, 'I am the servant of Christ,' or 'the slave of Christ,' he said. 'For me to live is Christ.'

Think of Manasseh, who made the streets of Jerusalem to run with the blood of the saints. When he was caught fleeing, hiding himself among the thorns, among the briars, they hauled him out. At that moment, he turned to the Saviour and was heard. He was born again.

Think of other people in Scripture who were born again. Zaccheus up upon on the branch of the tree gazing down at Christ, heard Christ utter his name, 'Zaccheus.' They'd never met but, of course, Christ knew him. He knew it all. 'Zaccheus, come down.' And the heart of Zaccheus was opened. He was born again. He entered into a new kingdom. He entered into the city. He became a child in the city.

### Verse 5: Zion is established by the Lord

We go on to read, 'And of Zion it shall be said, This and that man was born in her: and the highest himself shall establish her.' Yes, the highest—the Lord—establishes her. He causes men and women to be born again.

## 15    The glory of the city of God

This city can never die out. It will be persecuted in the world. It will be desecrated in many ways, but once in Christ, always in Christ. Enemies can kill God's people, but still the Church will be there in the world as long as sun and moon do last, through ages all, to the very end. The Church—God's people—will be there at the very end, the survivors of this world. When Christ returns, the only ones who will survive will be God's people. The rest will be destroyed by his return. He will establish this city. Until then, the world will be the world. The world will pass by. But those who were cursing and swearing will go to hell. That's where they'll dwell with their cursing and their swearing. And they will curse God forever. In hell they will curse the Church of God and they will hate the Church of God. They may have come out of godly homes, but they will hate the Church of God in hell. They will hate God. They will also hate those who are with them in hell. They will know no love. There is no love in hell for anyone or anything.

O friends, if we are not born again, where are we headed? Where are we going?

### Verse 6: The Lord records his people

It says in verse 6, 'The LORD shall count, when he writeth up the people, that this man was born there.' The Lord has the writing: he writes them up.

We read about the book of life. All those who are in the eternal covenant, they are written there. They are written upon Christ. They are engraved upon him. Deeper than any engraving, for they are in his heart. He loved them with an eternal love. That's their book of life. But they have to be born again. And no man will know that he's in the book of life until he is born again. Make your calling and your election sure. Your calling: what is that? It is Christ as the Good Shepherd calling, and the sheep listening and following the Good Shepherd. Make your calling sure. The sheep know him. The sheep believe in him. They trust in him alone.

'This man receiveth sinners and he eateth with them.' He doesn't just receive them and leave it at that. No, he wants them to sit down with him, to eat and drink with him, to have fellowship with him.

When God writes, his writing is sure. 'This man was born there.' The devil can come to God's people with doubts and fears. The devil can say to God's people, 'It's all a farce. You were never converted. You don't have true faith at all.' And he would almost convince them. The devil is so convincing. He would convince them, but for the Holy Spirit who maintains them. And the devil will come and say the Word of God is not true. 'Hath God said? He says a lot, but what has he done?' And the devil will convince them, but for work of the Holy Spirit. He cannot do it, for their names are written. God has written them in the book of life. They are not going to be lost. None can pluck them out of the Lord's hands. None!

## Verse 7: Music in heaven

So then he goes on, in verse 7: 'As well the singers as the players on instruments shall be there: all my springs are in thee.'

Singers and players on instruments will be there. That's what they had in the temple. Only the Levites had instruments of music. The priests used trumpets that made only one sound. That one sound could be loud or low. But the Levites' instruments made many sounds, much music. And the temple singers sang too.

The psalmist is telling us that in the city of God will be singing. All the songs in this world will die out, all the love songs, all the worldly songs that people have made up. When the islanders went to Canada, they made songs to stir themselves, speaking about the island they had left behind. They were in a strange land in Canada, and they still loved where they were brought up. Yet these songs will all go too. But the songs of heaven will not go, and Christ is in them all, God is in them all. The Saviour is the supreme subject sung of in glory.

And the instruments, along with the singing, just illustrate the beauty of the music of heaven. It's a figure of speech to illustrate the beauty of the music—music that this world can never know. The world can have their orchestras. They can use various instruments as they like. They can put them all together in any order and have singers among them, and they might draw thousands, and indeed they do that. Yet that music will die out. But the music of heaven is the music in the souls of all of God's people. It is the praise of the Lord. The praise of the Lord will last for ever and for ever. And when death comes, death cannot mute it. Death cannot smother the mouth of God's people when they go into eternity. They will go and sing when they leave the world. They leave, singing in their souls.

**Verse 8: Wells of water**

Then there's one thing left: 'All my springs are in thee.' These are wells of water. Some of us knew what it was to have wells before we had piped water. Some had to walk—maybe a quarter of a mile at times—with pails to the well. Now just think of dry and arid countries, like in the Middle East where the Psalmist was. Wells were so precious! The people of God have found wells and they're all in the Lord. And they're drawing water out of these wells.

David at one time said, 'Oh that one would give me drink of the water of the well that is beside the gate at Bethlehem!' He couldn't get near it because of the Philistines. But three of his mighty men broke through the Philistines and came back with water from that well. When he looked at that water, he said, 'Look at the price of that water. Three men going to the danger of their lives to bring back that little water to me. It is too precious for me to drink.' And so he poured it out as a drink offering unto the Lord. They always remembered the taste of that water beside the well, beside the gate in the well of Bethlehem.

God's people have wells of salvation. They drank and they were saved. They have been drinking since then at the wells. They come to gather together, and sometimes they are unable to drink great, copious draughts from the well. Sometimes the Lord Jesus fills them so much. But sometimes it's a little they have, just enough to keep going, as it were. They find it in the book, this wonderful book they call the Bible. They find it in their meditations. They find it on their knees in prayer.

Yes, all these wells are in him. They are living wells in a living Saviour. Living water, it's called. Christ said to the woman of Samaria whom he had asked for a drink, that if she had asked him for a drink, he would have given her living water. Living water! And it would be in her like a well of water springing up unto everlasting life. 'All my well-springs in thee are.' And we can draw out of these springs. They're all in the Lord, in the Saviour.

## Application

So, these are some descriptions of the city of God. Look how well-off the city of God is! Are we of the city of God, then? Or where are we, if we are not in the city of God? Which city are we in? Where are we going? What will the end be, if we are not in the city of God?

# 15 The glory of the city of God

Let us pray to the Lord to bless precious souls among us in our families, and around us in our congregations, in our villages, in our area, in our island. Let us call to the Lord. Who knows but that the Lord may visit us with great blessing. The people in the city of God unite in prayer in these things. Ah, friends, may we know the city of God and the God of the city!

Let us pray.

## Concluding prayer

Gracious and glorious Lord, we beseech thee to bless us. Give us to value what we have. Give us to value salvation in Christ Jesus, and grant to be with us this Sabbath Day in our meditations, in our homes. Give us not to cast aside all that we hear, but give us to bring it up as the sheep will bring up the food to its mouth again. Give us to meditate. Oh, give us to think of these things. Bless us in parting. Be with us in the evening exercise of worship. Be with the worship of thine own people throughout the whole earth. Take away our sins. For Jesus' sake. Amen.

# 16

# Scoffers in the last day

9th September 2018, Lord's Day evening, Leverburgh

*Knowing this first, that there shall come in the last days scoffers, walking after their own lusts, and saying, Where is the promise of his coming? for since the fathers fell asleep, all things continue as they were from the beginning of the creation. For this they willingly are ignorant of, that by the word of God the heavens were of old, and the earth standing out of the water and in the water: whereby the world that then was, being overflowed with water, perished: but the heavens and the earth, which are now, by the same word are kept in store, reserved unto fire against the day of judgment and perdition of ungodly men.*
2 Peter 3:3–7

PETER was one of the apostles, and yet he showed a great deal of ignorance during the days of Christ in the world. Later though, Peter was taught by Christ and by the Holy Spirit. Along with the rest of the apostles, Peter was told by Christ before he left them that they would be given the Holy Spirit to bring to their remembrance all things that ever he taught them. That meant that the apostles were able to teach the gospel infallibly before it was put into writing. The Holy Spirit brought perfectly to their remembrance the teaching that Christ gave them, and also the history of Christ. The

# 16  Scoffers in the last day

letters at the end of the Word of God—the epistles—were almost all written before any of the four Gospels were written. So when anyone wanted to be sure of the gospel, they had to listen to the apostles. The apostles had that authority until the Scriptures were complete, but they made sure that during their lifetimes it was written, and we have it written four times as the four Gospels.

Peter wrote his general epistles, and they were not to any specific congregation in the first instance. He's writing to the Church at large, everywhere—and not only everywhere, but also in every generation, to the end of the world. His two letters were meant for all believers, everywhere and to the end of the world. And indeed his prayer is that these letters would be blessed, not only to believers but also to non-believers, so that they might become believers in Christ.

Peter's name was Simon, and Christ turned his name to Peter, which means a stone. Peter was to suffer many blows; he was to go through a lot of suffering, but Christ made him a stone.

Now we can look at what he wrote here. He's speaking first of all about scoffers in the last days: 'Knowing this first, that there shall come in the last days scoffers, walking after their own lusts.' We can say a little about these scoffers. Then secondly, he speaks of the ignorance of these scoffers. In verse 5 he says, 'For this they willingly are ignorant of.' So they are willingly ignorant. And then thirdly, he speaks of the end of the world in verse 7. 'But the heavens and the earth, which are now, by the same word are kept in store, reserved unto fire against the day of judgment and perdition of ungodly men.'

## 1. Scoffers

First of all, we will say a little about the scoffers who will come in the last days. 'Knowing this first, that there shall come in the last days scoffers walking after their own lusts.' The Word of God speaks of scoffers in all times. You had them in every generation, and you had them at the cross of Christ—wicked, malign men, witnessing but not understanding the greatest agony that ever was: Christ suffering in the stead and room of sinners. The drunkards made their songs about Christ, and they sang. And others sat down and mocked him, saying that if he came down from the cross they would believe in him. They called him the king and they mocked him as king, and they put a crown of thorns on his head and smote him. They treated him in a manner that showed that they were indeed scoffers.

But what we have here is a bit different. Peter is speaking about the visible Church of Christ, the professing Church of Christ in the world. Now, you wouldn't expect scoffers to arise in the professing Church of Christ. You wouldn't expect to find people in the visible Church who are really against Christ. But Peter says that in the last days that will happen. So, what he does he mean by 'the last days'? Here and there we find the term 'the last days', or sometimes 'the latter days'. When we hear of the last days in the New Testament it means the time between the first coming of Christ and the second coming of Christ. So far the 'last days' have lasted for two thousand years. We are living in these last days.

There will come scoffers in the visible Church in the world in the last days. These scoffers reject things that are said in the Word of God, even though the Church was formed through the preaching of the Word of God. Now, you see what has happened. Worldly men and worldly women have come into the professing Church of Christ everywhere. They bring their worldly ideas, and foolish people in the churches are willing to let them in to swell the numbers. In this way they destroy themselves, although they don't realise it. Their churches cease to be churches.

# 16 Scoffers in the last day

Lots of the people begin to take the Word of God and to say, 'Well, we'd better make a new version. We don't understand the Bible too well, we don't follow these things too well. Let somebody write it in plain English in new versions.' When you read the new versions like the NIV you see how they changed words, and they have robbed Christ of his divinity in various places. The damage appears in a subtle way in these translations. The translators miss out little things here and there, and change little things here and there. Friends, the Word of God was given by the Holy Spirit. It was given in Hebrew and Greek: Hebrew in the Old Testament, Greek in the New. What a terrible thing it is to tamper with the Word of God, to change anything in it!

The Authorised Version we use was translated in such a manner that the translators sought to bring in every word from the original language into English, as far as possible. That's the same for the Gaelic version. Sometimes they had to slightly change some idioms to allow the meaning to be understood. Where they needed to do that they put in a few words to make the meaning clear in our language. The translators wrote these extra words in italics. By doing that they were saying, 'We put in these words. They weren't in the original: we put them in to make sure that you would understand what was meant.' So they were totally honest. They trembled before the work they had to do. They prayed over it. They wrestled over it. They sought to be faithful to God. But in the latter days scoffers have come in, and they don't hesitate to take away bits of God's Word.

The Readers' Digest brought out a translation which is only a third of the Word of God. They have cut it down, making things easier for people. But no one has any right to tamper with the Word of God. All parts of it—yes, *all* parts of it!— have been used by God for the good of men and women in this world. Who am I, who are you, who is anybody, to dare tamper with the Word of God? Christ uses it to bring in his own people.

In any case, scoffers don't believe in lost sinners. They don't believe in things like heaven and hell. They don't believe in judgment. They laugh at that, in the same way as they laughed at Christ when he was on the cross, saying, 'Come down from the cross if you are the Christ, the Son of God, the King of Israel.' But we see that when he died there was an earthquake and he cried with a loud voice, and many were afraid then. They began to beat their breasts in fear, and the centurion in charge came to believe. This was the Son of God, he realised, and many along with him believed that this was the Son of God. The very soldiers who nailed him to the cross said, 'This was the Son of God.'

Scoffers in the last days come into the churches. They are perhaps fine people in some ways, although not always. They bring in their own practices. They want to change the churches, they want to change the way of worship. They say, 'We don't need the Psalms of David. These are old-fashioned things. We'll bring in our own hymns.' Although the apostles, who were used by Christ to show us how to worship, didn't use any such hymns and didn't use instruments of music, the scoffers want to change that. 'It's not what Peter or Paul did, but they don't control us. We'll bring in our hymns and instruments of music.'

Other people come along with sinful practices in their lives. They say, 'We too want to join this club,' and people in the churches say, 'Yes, you come in.' But what about the sins that the Bible condemns? 'Oh, it doesn't matter. These stuffy people speak about these great sins in your life, but never mind about them.' The Bible condemns them, but still the churches say, 'It doesn't matter. We can miss out that part of the Bible. Come into the professing Church, sit at the Lord's Table. It's alright, it doesn't matter what lifestyle you have in private—or indeed what lifestyle you have in public. Just join us. We don't believe in disapproving what you do. We're a modern church. This is a modern era. This is the time of sending rockets to the moon. This is the time when we have so many inventions. We don't go back to those old-fashioned things.'

Some churches have no gospel left. I sometimes listen to the radio in the morning, about quarter to eight, and I hear 'Word for the Day' before the news. Sometimes the speaker is a minister, a bishop, a rabbi, a priest, or whatever. But when I listen to hear what the message is, I never ever hear the word 'sin'. Never! It may be that I may have missed it, but over the course of a few years I have never heard the word 'sin' mentioned by any of these people in the morning. And I have never heard any of them say that we need the blood of Christ to cleanse us. I have never heard any of them say that Christ suffered to satisfy the justice of God in the place of sinners. No! It's all been, 'Let's be good in the world, let's be kind in the world, let's treat others with respect—other people, other countries.' That's it! They're not guided any longer by the Word of God. It's laid aside. They're guided by their own judgments.

Timothy mentions these scoffers inside the Church, just as Paul did (2 Timothy 3:1–5): 'This know also, that in the last days perilous times shall come. For men shall be lovers of their own selves, covetous, boasters, proud, blasphemers, disobedient to parents, unthankful, unholy, without natural affection, trucebreakers, false accusers, incontinent, fierce, despisers of those that are good, traitors, heady, highminded, lovers of pleasures more than lovers of God; having a form of godliness, but denying the power thereof: from such turn away.' They are scoffers. They hate the true things of the gospel. They have no time for it. They are destroyers of the cause of the Lord. But these things were foretold in the prophets; these things were foretold by the apostles. So we should not be dismayed or surprised. We see that Scotland has gone that way. More scoffers will come in, and these so-called churches will change even more.

The Church of Scotland at the time of the Reformation was the jewel among the Reformed churches. It was a precious jewel. John Knox led this church in 1560, but nowadays people want to airbrush John Knox out of history. They don't want to mention him. They don't want to have any memorial to him. They don't want to teach the Reformation in school. These things they want to put away. They scoff at them. The devil, you see, has come into the Church. But there's still a true Church, nevertheless. There's a body of true believers inside the professing Church. And oh, to belong to them, to know Christ, to believe in the gospel and to walk in the fear of the Lord!

The scoffers come saying, 'Where is the promise of his coming? For since the fathers fell asleep, all things continue as they were from the beginning of the creation.' People in the church say to them, 'But Christ is coming again and there will be a judgment.' The scoffers mock that. 'Where is the promise of his coming? How and when? Two thousand years have passed. We don't see it happen.'

But, you know, even your own common sense will tell you that the end will come. Think of the various ways in which people themselves can destroy the world. Think of the various atomic weapons that many nations have, that could obliterate all life in this world. Think of the nerve agents that they have produced, which could wipe out all of mankind. Various poisons can spread so easily and in various ways. People are gaining weapons and power to wipe out mankind in various ways. Even common sense says an end must be coming. But these scoffers say, 'When is the end coming?' Scripture tells us that it is coming. Christ will return. People can mock, but they will live their short lives and go into eternity. They will meet Christ at the point of death, and their souls will go to their own place. But nobody in hell mocks God. In hell they hate God, in hell they curse God, but they cannot mock God. They know in that lost eternity that God has spoken the truth. Everybody in hell tonight knows that Christ is coming and knows that the Word of God is true. They know that God is the God of truth. Yes, they know it.

## 2. The ignorance of scoffers

The second point is the ignorance of these scoffing people. Listen to what the Scripture says. 'For this they are willingly ignorant of.' That's a strange thing to say. We know what ignorant people are—they don't have knowledge, so they don't know. But God is telling us that scoffers, both in the Church and out of the Church, are *willingly* ignorant. They *want* to be ignorant. That's what Peter is telling us: they don't want to know. They don't want evidence. They don't want to listen to what God says. That's what Peter says. 'For this they willingly are ignorant of, that by the word of God the heavens were of old, and the earth standing out of the water and in the water: whereby the world that then was, being overflowed with water, perished.' They don't want to know that God made the world.

But just imagine if you went out to the hills and mountains of Harris and you came upon, say, an aeroplane lying there. If somebody said to you, 'All these parts of the aeroplane came together by chance,' you would say they were fools to talk like that. If they came upon a machine that was many times more intricate than an aeroplane and they said it all came together by chance, you'd call them fools. These things do not come by chance. If I found even a chair out on the hills I would know that somebody made it. Nobody could tell me that even a simple chair came about by chance.

Now, the most intricate machine that we know is the universe in which we live. It's so minutely made. Think of the human body, which is so minutely made, with miles of blood vessels and miles of nerves. Think of the intricacy of the heart, of the lungs, of the eyes. Think of man's mind, which can think of eternity, and about God. Man is such a complicated machine and yet the scoffers say it all takes place by evolution—that it all came by chance, by lots of different coincidences. All of these things are so full of lies.

Think of the whole created universe. The first chapter in Romans tell us quite plainly that mankind is inexcusable. God has given everyone enough evidence in creation. You don't need the Bible to have this evidence: it's there for all to see. Look up into the heavens, look around nature, look at your own self, and you realise everything was made. There's an intelligent mind behind it all. That intelligence is not only behind the creation of the great creatures but also the tiny creatures in the dust, or in the water—things that we cannot see with the naked eye. If you put a drop of water under a microscope and look at it, then you will see tiny creatures in every drop of water. It's all so minute, and God made it all. Scientists in the world—evolutionist scientists, not Christians—examining all the heavenly bodies, everything out there, all the stars, all the galaxies, came to the amazing conclusion that there are more bodies out there in space than there are grains of sand on every seashore in the world. You say, 'That's impossible.' But I'm not saying it: *they're* saying it! Non-believers are saying it. And if that doesn't bring them to their senses, what will? But it doesn't because they are scoffers when it comes to the Word of God. There is no excuse for anyone not to say—not to admit, not to proclaim—that there is a Creator. That's the great condemnation for scoffing people that are inside the Church. They have the Bible, but they have thrown it away.

# 16 Scoffers in the last day

The ignorance of the scoffers is not only to do with the creation but also the Flood. Peter says they're willingly ignorant of this too, that 'the world that then was, being overflowed with water, perished'. How can they be ignorant of that? Wherever you go—in Britain, Russia, America, China—all over the world you will find great cliffs, full of bones of creatures that perished. It is evident, and it can't be denied, that these cliffs are made up of mud that once existed, and these creatures perished in the mud. But now because of great changes in the world, from earthquakes and other events, we see cliffs, a hundred yards high, full of millions of bones, telling of a flood, a fearful flood. Scientists examine them, but they won't face up to the evidence. You see, they're scoffers. They want to believe the lie. But the evidence is there. There's no way of avoiding the evidence of a world-wide flood when they see the depth of the mud, how the soil and vegetation were destroyed, and great basins were formed, in which vegetation was trapped under the mud. That vegetation became oil. Where does the oil come from that they pump out of the ground? Where does the gas come from that they pump out of the ground? They know that it comes from vegetation that has been trapped under great masses of mud, and changed into the oil which we use. There's no other explanation, but they are willingly ignorant of it.

Think too of those first men who went to the moon. Evolutionists spoke of a great danger in going to the moon. They said that the moon is so many millions of years old—the smallest estimate would be about 28 billion years—and they estimated the rate at which cosmic dust would gather on the moon. They said, 'There must be at least a hundred and fifty feet of dust on the moon, and if a man goes to the moon he'll sink down in that dust.' It was a great problem for them, but still they sent men to the moon. The dust they found was only one eighth of an inch deep, and following their own measurements, that shows that the moon is only a matter of thousands of years old. But they are willingly ignorant of this: they don't want to know. They don't want to search Scripture. They don't want to be humbled. They don't want to get on their knees before Christ and to ask for mercy. They don't want to believe they are sinners on a way to a lost eternity. They want to block it all out, to mock God, to curse God with their foul language, to have foul practices, to live foul lives. They are willingly ignorant.

Ah friends, you and I have a short life. We are on the way to eternity. Never mind what you read in papers and magazines, or what the so-called experts say on the television. If a million years doesn't suit them, they will make it twenty million or a hundred million. They change their theories all the time, but the Bible cannot change. We cannot change the truth of God.

### 3. The end of all things

Well then, what about the end of all things? Listen to what the Bible says about the end, in verse 7. 'The heavens and the earth, which are now, by the same word are kept in store, reserved unto fire against the day of judgment and perdition of ungodly men.' Everything is kept by the word of God. Now God doesn't speak words as we speak words. When God created, it says he spoke. But who was he to speak to? What it means is that he spoke in his own heart. That is, he willed creation into being. By the same will, by the same power of his will, he brings about the end. The whole of time is short compared to eternity. It is a mere pinpoint compared to eternity.

What is my life and your life compared to eternity? We are on the way to eternity. We're going to lift up our eyes, either in heaven or in hell, forever and forever. If we go wrong, we go wrong. If we listen to these scoffers we are lost forever. There is only one way of escape, and that is by believing the Word of God and trusting in Christ for salvation.

# 16 Scoffers in the last day

The world at the end will be destroyed by fire. It is reserved unto fire. We read elsewhere that people will be getting married and being given in marriage. Normal life will be going on, social events will be going on. Everyone will think everything's going to continue, but Christ will come at a time when the world itself does not expect it. We read here that the day of the Lord will come as a thief in the night. Now, when Christ comes to the judge the world there will be a resurrection. All will rise out of the graves. God's people will rise with bodies like the body of Christ. They will be holy creatures when they go to be with him. Those who loved Christ will rise, and their bodies will be like Christ's body.

When we have children we pray for them. I pray for my children and my grandchildren, that they might know Christ. I know that if they do not know Christ they will be lost forever, therefore I pray for them. Others among us here pray for their own dear ones, that they might believe in the Lord Jesus and be saved. There is no other way to stand in the day of judgment.

We read here about the day of judgment. All will appear before the judgment throne of Christ. He knows all about us. He knows who believe in him savingly and who do not. He will divide all mankind. That will be the very last division of mankind, and these two parties will never meet again. Never! Yet if the believer's children are lost, the believer in heaven will not mourn, because the Holy Spirit will make him holy and will make him to understand these things as God understands these things, and he will wipe all tears from their eyes. We can weep here for our loved ones, and we can wrestle in prayer for them, but when eternity comes, that weeping will be over.

We read about the perdition of ungodly men. These scoffers will perish, and others who did not scoff as much as they scoffed, will perish too. They did not go as far in scoffing, but they still had no Saviour, and so they will perish. It will be an eternal perishing, an eternal destruction, a continual destruction right through eternity. All the restraints of the Holy Spirit which were laid upon us in this world will be taken away. We could be kind to our fellow men. We could be kind to our children. We could love and cherish. But if we're lost, all that goes, and goes forever. We have the same nature as the devils.

Now, friends, listen to what the Word of God says. 'The Lord is not slack concerning his promise, as some men count slackness.' He's coming but he's long-suffering. That's why he leaves the world as it is. He's long-suffering, he's patient. He's 'long-suffering to us-ward, not willing that any should perish, but that all should come to repentance'. But the day of the Lord will come as a thief in the night. He will come when it's night-time somewhere, and it's daytime somewhere else, but he will come. It will interrupt the marriage ceremony, interrupt the clubs, interrupt the gatherings, interrupt the watching of television—if they will still have television in those days, or something more sophisticated. It will interrupt all that we have in this world forever; it will all be over forever.

When the Lord comes, the heavens shall pass away—the heavens we see, the planets, the stars. 'The heavens shall pass away with a great noise, and the elements shall melt with fervent heat'—the smallest elements, the building blocks of creation, whatever these are. Whether they are atoms or something smaller, it doesn't matter: they will all be destroyed with fervent heat, a heat that will dissolve them and destroy them. The heat will destroy the very elements, everything. The earth also and the works that are therein shall be burned up. All the cities will go, the oceans will be burned up. Everything will melt and be dissolved with fervent heat. We remember doing experiments in school as boys. You put something into water, and it dissolves. It disappears in the water. It disappears, it's gone. So the earth and the heavens will dissolve with a great noise of burning—a roaring noise before, and then they go. Then everyone will be gone, and will have gone to their own place.

'Seeing then that all these things shall be dissolved, what manner of persons ought ye to be in all holy conversation and godliness?' What ought we to be? Ah, dear friends, seek Christ. That's all I can say, that's all I can preach. That's the sum of all that I ever preach. That's why I preach, so that men and women and children would seek Christ. He knows what you think. He knows what is in your heart. He knows if you think you're the greatest sinner ever and cannot be forgiven. But you *can* be forgiven. 'The blood of Jesus Christ, God's Son, cleanseth from all sin.' There is no sin that cannot be forgiven. There is no sin too black to be forgiven. Even if you resembled a devil standing on mercy's ground, if you're still on mercy's ground the blood of Jesus can cleanse you, and he says, 'Come unto me, all ye that labour.' If you worry in your mind, in your soul, about salvation, and where you're going to spend eternity, and what will happen if you die tonight, know that Christ says to come to him—not physically, but in our souls. Pray to him, call upon him in our minds and souls. 'Look unto me, and be ye saved, all the ends of the earth'—no matter how far off—'for I am God, and there is none else.'

May God bless his Word. Let us pray.

## Concluding prayer

Bless us, we pray thee, O Lord. Go before us and teach us. Give us to seek thee early, whilst thou are to be found, and to call upon thee whilst thou art near. Give us to turn to the Lord who will graciously receive us, and to our God who will abundantly pardon. Have mercy upon this congregation, we pray thee. Bless the minister who will come here. May his ministry be a great blessing among them. Help us all on the way to eternity, and cleanse us. For Jesus' sake. Amen.

# 17

# God's poor and contrite people

3rd February 2019, Lord's Day morning, North Tolsta

*Thus saith the Lord, the heaven is my throne, and the earth is my footstool: where is the house that ye build unto me? and where is the place of my rest? For all those things hath mine hand made, and all those things have been, saith the Lord: but to this man will I look, even to him that is poor and of a contrite spirit, and trembleth at my word.*
Isaiah 66:1–2

WE come here to the end of the prophecy of Isaiah. Isaiah preached Christ in the Old Testament. His prophecy is full of Christ. This last chapter, when it is examined, is seen to speak of the time when the old dispensation was passing away and the gospel was taking its place, the time when the temple worship was passing away. God says, 'Where is the house that ye build unto me? and where is the place of my rest?' And he says, 'But to this man will I look, even to him that is poor and of a contrite spirit, and trembleth at my word.' Instead of looking at the temple, he says, 'I look at people who are poor in spirit, who are contrite and who tremble at my word.' That is what Isaiah brings us to when he is speaking of the Spirit of God. As Christ said to the Samaritan woman, the time now was when they would no longer wor-

## 17  God's poor and contrite people

ship God in the temple in Samaria, Gerizim, and no longer worship God in the temple at Jerusalem, but those who worshipped God would worship him in spirit and in truth. Why was that? Because the gospel was in the whole world. It wasn't just a teaching and worship confined to a small nation, it belonged to the whole world.

When we look at the meaning of the chapter, we see in verse 3 how things had deteriorated in the temple worship. You remember that when Christ came to the temple at the beginning of his ministry, and again at the end, he had to cleanse the temple. He had to drive out those who were selling sheep and oxen, and the money-changers. You could see that the spirit of worship had been taken away, as it were, and another kind of spirit had taken over. The world had come into the things of the temple. So in verse 3 he says of the temple worship, 'He that killeth an ox is as if he slew a man; he that sacrificeth a lamb, as if he cut off a dog's neck;'—and dogs were unclean—'he that offereth an oblation, as if he offered swine's blood;'—and swine were unclean—'he that burneth incense, as if he blessed an idol. Yea, they have chosen their own ways, and their soul delighteth in their abominations.' And that is how things were when Christ came.

Also, when the Lord was in the world, he condemned the Pharisees and the priests. He condemned the teaching class and the preaching class, because of what things had come to. In verse 5 we see how the people of God were treated: 'Your brethren that hated you, that cast you out for my name's sake, said, Let the Lord be glorified.' The people of God were being cast out of the temple, they were forbidden temple worship because they had turned to Christ, as if they had no business to be in the temple at all.

When you come to verse 7, you read of a travail—a mother bringing forth a child. 'Before she travailed, she brought forth;

before her pain came, she was delivered of a man child. Who hath heard such a thing? who hath seen such things? Shall the earth be made to bring forth in one day? or shall a nation be born at once? for as soon as Zion travailed, she brought forth her children. Shall I bring to the birth, and not cause to bring forth? saith the Lord: shall I cause to bring forth, and shut the womb? saith thy God.'

What you have here is the Old Testament Church, as it were, in travail. The child of the Old Testament Church is the New Testament Church. The child of the ceremonial law was the gospel. Things were changing: a people were to be born in one day, and that's what the Lord was doing. When the Lord Jesus died and rose again, and sent the apostles out to preach, they were persecuted and driven out of the temple, but they spread rapidly and the gospel spread north, south, east and west. And a nation was born, as it were, in one day.

There are various things in the chapter that could be brought up but it would take up too much time at present. Verse 22 says, 'For as the new heavens and the new earth, which I will make, shall remain before me, saith the Lord, so shall your seed and your name remain.' It says there's a new heaven and a new earth now. He's speaking of the Church. He's speaking of how things have changed. The ceremonial law has passed and, in a sense, there's a new heaven. Christ has gone there in our nature. And there's also a new earth—that is, there's a new form of worship; they are now worshipping in the light of the gospel. He says that that will remain. There's to be no more change. The gospel is the last dispensation, so there will be no more change. The ceremonial law could change and become the gospel, but that will not change.

The new heaven and the new earth will remain, he says. They will not change. And he speaks of those who will come to the new heavens and the new earth, that is the Church of Christ,

## 17  God's poor and contrite people

coming and looking forth at 'the carcases of the men that have transgressed against me: for their worm shall not die, neither shall their fire be quenched; and they shall be an abhorring unto all flesh' (verse 24). That is, those that the gospel dispensation, the believing Church of Christ, will see, will believe that those without Christ are under the wrath of God in the fire where the worm will not die, the conscience will not die. These are God's people who will see that, and they preach that and they believe that. That's how Isaiah finishes his prophecy. He has come in this last chapter to the gospel dispensation—the new birth of a new nation, which he calls a 'new heaven and a new earth'.

### God's real dwelling place

But then, where does God dwell? 'Thus saith the Lord, The heaven is my throne, and the earth is my footstool: where is the house that ye build unto me? and where is the place of my rest?' Where does God dwell? Where is God? Well, we often speak of that. God, of course, is everywhere. It's not really a matter of where is God, but where is he not? He's in heaven, he's in hell, he's in the world, he's in every blade of grass, he's in the stones, he's inside the devil himself. He's upholding all his creatures, wherever they are. He's giving them their existence, wherever they are. God is everywhere, he's upholding his whole creation that he made. But where does he really dwell? Where does God really dwell as God?

Well, we speak of his immensity. He's greater, he's more immense, than all the universe. God cannot be put into a container, as it were. You cannot say the universe contains God. He's greater than the universe. Our logic quails at that. We are not able to understand that, but we must believe it. He dwells too in his own holiness, his own uncreated holiness—not in mere created holiness, but in his own holiness. He dwells in his own infinite power, which has no limits. He dwells in all his attributes. They're all eternal attributes, they're all without limit. He dwells in himself. There is no ultimate dwelling-place for the Lord of glory but in his own glory, in himself.

That is all true, but that is not quite what he speaks of here. He says, 'The heaven is my throne, and the earth is my footstool.' He's telling us that he has a throne and a footstool, and he says the heaven is his throne and the earth is his footstool. Now, that's a picture that is brought up right through Scripture—that the Lord sits on a throne in heaven, and his footstool is on earth. What does he mean by that? Well, when he speaks of his throne being in heaven, he dwells among his own people in heaven, in a gracious manner. Christ is there. He's been there since his ascension, exalted there, in a gracious manner, as if he's on a throne. He's with his own people there. They can see his glory, in a way that those upon the earth cannot see his glory. Where the throne is, you can see the glory of that throne. We on earth can only see these things in a measure, but those who are with Christ in heaven have no sin. They are totally sanctified. They are waiting until their bodies are taken to be with them, and they are gazing, as it were, upon the King of glory. They are gazing upon the enthroned Lord and they worship him. They are in his glory, and they see his glory, and they have fellowship with him in his glory. Those who have gone to be with Christ have gone home. It's a wonderful thing to be in heaven, to be with Christ, and to see his glory, and to have his fellowship there in heaven. 'Heaven', he says, 'is my throne,' and that throne will never be overthrown. Never! It cannot be usurped, no one else can take over. The God-man is there with his people for ever and for ever.

He has more than a throne: he has a footstool too. The king would sit on the throne and his feet would be on the footstool. 'The earth', he says, is his 'footstool.' When you examine the history of Solomon, you will see that Solomon had the most glorious throne that ever was in Israel. It was made of ivory

## 17 God's poor and contrite people

and pure gold. There was no throne like it. The footstool was covered with gold, and tied to the throne. The throne and the footstool were tied together. So, you have the Church in heaven and the Church on the earth tied together. Christ is on the throne; his feet are on the footstool. The footstool is precious, as if it was made of gold, because it is his own people in this world.

In 1 Chronicles 28, long before Isaiah's time, God speaks of his people who worshipped in the temple as being his footstool. In 2 Chronicles 9 we read about Solomon's throne and the footstool, two precious things joined together, and Solomon occupied both. In Lamentations, Jeremiah speaks to the Lord to 'remember the place of his footstool'—that is, to remember his cause on the earth, for Jeremiah saw how the Lord's people were afflicted in his day, and he prayed to the Lord to remember his footstool.

Here in Isaiah chapter 60, the Lord says, 'I will make the place of my feet glorious.' The gospel was to be preached in the world and the gospel was to be blessed, and where it was blessed, it was the place of his people and his glorious footstool. The footstool is glorious—not as glorious as the throne, but it's tied to the throne and it's glorious. It's glorious when you know Christ, even when you're still a sinner. It's glorious even when you're falling and sinning. In the midst of a world where the devil is rampant, and where the world seeks to draw you away from the things of the Lord, it's still glorious.

If you have faith in the heart, if you know Christ as your Saviour, you belong to this footstool, and it's glorious. It's the place for his feet, it belongs to him, he regards it. And we should point out a little about what Isaiah says at the end of verse 2: 'But to this man will I look, even to him that is poor and of a contrite spirit, and trembleth at my word.' Isaiah couldn't build a house for God, he couldn't build a temple for him, no matter how glorious: these things had no value in God's eyes. But this is what *does* have value in his eyes. 'To this man will I look.' I won't look at the temple. The stone temple was destroyed. The Babylonians destroyed the temple of Solomon. Then it became later on the temple of Zerubbabel or Herod. That temple was destroyed too and there is no temple now. There is no stone of the temple left. God couldn't look at that in favour—that's not what he desires.

The poor Jews are deluded. Many of them think of building a temple, but God tells us in Scripture that there is a band over their eyes, and they are blind. And that band over their eyes is over their hearts as well. They cannot understand. They are still caught up in the old ceremonial law, but they can't even sacrifice: there's no altar, there's no priesthood, there's no priest functioning as a priest, there is no temple. Nothing! They are worshipping in a vacuum. God has destroyed the temple and they cannot understand it, so they go around like blind men until the Lord will give them light again. He will open the eyes of the Jews again and they will see that Christ was the Messiah after all, and then 'they will mourn for him as for an only son'. Then many of them will turn to him and believe in him, and that will be a great blessing to the whole world, and to God's people everywhere.

## The Lord's regard for his people

Now meanwhile, and when the Jews come in, this is how it is: 'To this man will I look,' that is, with a look of favour, a look of love, a look of regard, a look of care. It's wonderful for a child to be under the eyes of a mother who cares for their child and is watching its every movement. Will it do something wrong? Will it hurt itself? Will it fall? Will it put something in its mouth that might harm it? Will it swallow something that might kill it? Any noise that the child makes during the night will wake the mother up, because of the love, the care, the

## 17  God's poor and contrite people

regard. The Lord has regard for people in this world—sinners, poor sinners who have come to Christ and trust in him as their Saviour. We do not realise how great that regard is, because God's people look at themselves and they feel ashamed of themselves. They see their own sin and say, 'My sin I ever see.' At times they find it almost difficult to believe that the Lord would look upon them with a look of love. Yes, a look of love! The same way in which he looks upon Christ in our nature. That's the kind of look that he gives to his own people: as he loves his Son, so does he love them. And with that is his care and regard for them.

God's people go through difficult things in this world, and they wonder how the Lord has regard for them. Now death comes, sickness comes, various trials and troubles come, but the Lord is out to teach his people. He will chastise them because he loves them, and he's out to sanctify them—to make them like himself, to prepare them for heaven. They are all individuals, and he treats them as individuals, and their circumstances are individual circumstances. The Lord is there all the time, leading and guiding his own people, blessing them and upholding them because he looks after them. He regards them. He cares for them. Oh, to be among his people!

See what God says. 'To this man will I look, even to him that is poor.' It seems to be unexpected that anyone would have a special regard for the one who has nothing, who's poor. But that's how it is. God's poor ones are special to him. 'Blessed are the poor in spirit,' said Christ, 'for theirs is the kingdom of heaven.' He calls them 'the poor', and he says they are rich. They 'are poor in spirit' but 'theirs is the kingdom of heaven'. Yes, they will move from being on the footstool to being where the throne is.

Has the Lord ever made yourself poor? You know how it is when you seek salvation, you begin to wonder how to do it, how to seek to be saved. You begin to make yourself better, or so you imagine. If you were swearing, you say, 'Well, I'll stop swearing.' If you were immoral, 'I'll stop being immoral.' If you were a thief, 'I'll stop thieving,' and so on. You try improving yourself. But it doesn't work that way. Many have tried that. Millions have tried that, and they're still trying it. And those who are seeking salvation, who are trying to improve themselves, stop here and there in anguish because they say, 'I'm not any better; if anything, I'm worse. I may have stopped doing this. I may have stopped doing that. But what about my heart? I didn't make my heart any better. What about my heart?' And they're in anguish over it. But you see, the Lord works in a mysterious way. He leads many in these things, so that they would try them, and so that they would realise the utter futility of a person thinking he can save himself. You cannot make yourself holy. You cannot take away your past sins. You cannot take away one sin. And after all you have done, after all the times you read the Bible, and all the prayers you offer up, and all the listening you do and all the DIY self-help—it all comes to nothing, except that you feel worse than you felt before. Yes, you feel worse, not any better. Worse! If the Lord is working, he's out to make a person poorer.

So, you come to the end of it all. You might even say, 'It were better for me to be dead than to be alive. I am so miserable. So miserable, I wish I had never been born. I fear I'm not in God's election. I fear my place is in a lost eternity, and I envy the cats and the dogs and the sheep and the cattle which have no soul, which have no eternity.' When the Lord is working in people's souls, he brings them down and down and down until they say before God, 'I have nothing. I don't know how to pray properly. I don't even know where to begin. I don't know how to believe. I don't know how to entertain a saving hope. I'm just empty. I have nothing.'

## 17 God's poor and contrite people

No one has come to that state, of being totally empty before God in that manner, but by the power of the Holy Spirit bringing him or her to that state. There are some who think, to the end of their days, that doing their best is the way of getting to heaven and they'll stay like that. They'll stay like that, and die like that. But others have come to a state where they saw that they had nothing. No strength, no fitness, nothing. Just a mass of iniquity before God, resembling hell on two feet. 'In me there dwelleth no good thing. How can I plead? What can I say before God?' Well, that is how it is. The Holy Spirit brings home to the person that he is a sinner. It brings home to the person that he must look away from himself for salvation.

And then the person begins to look, and begins to see something in Christ. 'Can it be that there is something there for me?' The Word of God tells us that there is! Christ came into the world to save sinners from their sin. He's a Saviour of sinners. He's a Saviour of the poor, and until we are poor we don't need any help. It's 'the poor man and the indigent', the one who has no help of man at all: that's the one that the Lord helps. The one who can do it himself, he doesn't get the help—he doesn't need it. He doesn't think he needs it, but when he's convinced that he can do nothing of himself, then he begins to cry in a different manner. He begins to cry to God to have mercy. And mercy is something you are given, that you do not pay for. Mercy cannot be paid for. It's a gift, without being paid for. It's something for nothing!

It's good to be in that state. It's not a comfortable state, it's not an easy state, at least to begin with. It's not easy when you cannot see properly where you are. When, out of your total poverty, you call upon the Lord, 'I've no food, I've no drink, I've no clothing, I've no shelter, I have nothing.' Then you will listen to what the Lord is saying. And you will listen to Christ speaking to sinners, 'Come unto me, all ye that labour and are heavy laden, and I will give you rest. Look unto me, and be ye saved, all the ends of the earth.' Yes, it's the Lord's own right hand that brought him salvation: the Lord has it all. The poor man and the indigent—the man who has nothing—only has to receive. 'Blessed are those', said Christ, 'who are poor in spirit.' The Pharisees listening to that must have been amazed to hear him say, 'Blessed are the poor in spirit.' The Pharisees were so full of pride! Pride is in the human nature. Myself—pride. 'For theirs', he said, 'is the kingdom of heaven.' It seemed like a contradiction in terms, but that's the truth of the matter. That's just the way it is with the footstool, those on the earth with whom he deals.

### A contrite spirit

Then Isaiah goes on and he speaks of 'him that is poor and of a contrite spirit'. Contrition: that is the exercise of one who has real sorrow for sin, one who repents. God looks at the one who repents, who looks into the mirror of God and sees himself, and abhors himself in dust and ashes. 'Oh, what a fearful sight I am in the mirror! What a fearful sight I am!' He turns from sin with abhorrence and with grief. He sorrows for his sins, and he hates his sin. That's God's work in the soul—when you hate your sin, and you sorrow for it.

But it doesn't stop there: you turn from sin to the Lord and to a new obedience. The first act of new obedience is believing in the Lord Jesus Christ. The Holy Spirit makes them turn from sin, and the turning brings them to Christ. And there they stop. They don't go beyond him when they're turning. They don't look to somebody else: they look to Christ. They see how the Word of God tells them how he can save them to the very uttermost. It tells them how he can cleanse them, how the blood cleanses them, how Christ suffered and died in the room and stead of sinners, how he loved his own with an eternal love and came to save them.

# 17 God's poor and contrite people

Along with that faith there's repentance. Repentance is called a saving grace. Someone who repents is a saved person. He may not know that, to start with. That knowledge may come into the consciousness gradually. It may come rapidly, it may come right away, but it may just come gradually. He might come to say, 'Well, could it be that Christ is my Saviour? Could it be that I am saved? Could it be?' Then in a moment he says, 'No, it's not. Surely I'm not saved.' And then after a while he may begin to say, 'Well, I think I *may* be saved. I think so.' Then that gets stronger and stronger, and gradually as he reads and as he's taught in Scripture, he begins to say, 'Well, I think I *am* saved.' There may be doubts and fears, and these might follow him to the end of his life, but still he says, 'I think I am saved.' The assurance of faith might not be so strong that he will say, 'I am saved. I don't doubt it. I *am* saved.' But at least he will know that something took place in his soul. Now he can say, 'God's people are the ones I desire to be with. I love the things that they love, and I hate the things that they hate. I desire the fellowship of the Lord Jesus. Whatever I am, I desire to worship God with God's people. The Word of God draws me. I get my food and drink there. I cannot live without prayer. I want to be holy. I want to grow in love to the Lord.'

These marks follow these poor people who repent. There's the contrite and the broken heart that the Lord will not despise. And here's what Scripture tells us: he will never, never, despise that kind of heart. Oh, friends, would it not be good if you and I had that kind of heart—a broken heart, a contrite heart, a repenting heart? The Lord regards a repenting heart, he looks at it.

Oh, how the angels must wonder when they look at God's people! No angel has ever repented. The holy angels don't have to repent, and the angels that fell are left in their fallen state. No angel can understand repentance. The angels gaze with wonder at sinners hating their sin, and repenting and turning from sin in all its power and action to Christ. They wonder at that. It's something totally outside the experience of angels. They are not in God's family. They are servants, but still they wonder, and they gaze into these things.

## A trembling people

Isaiah goes on and speaks of the one who trembles at God's word. There might have been a day when they trembled in a different way. They trembled because they heard about the judgment, they heard about the great white throne, they heard that those without Christ would perish for ever and for ever. Maybe they lost their sleep—maybe they couldn't sleep at all—afraid that they would wake up in hell, as the rich man in the parable did when he opened his eyes in hell.

But the trembling we have here is not that trembling. It's God's people trembling at God's Word. They desire to honour it; they don't wish to dishonour it. The desire is to obey it and to be taught by it. It is God's Word—it's from his mouth, and they want to obey him. They want to honour him, so that's why it speaks of them trembling at his Word.

They tremble because they love him. It's not easy for them to speak of loving God. You see, it's a spiritual love. If it was a natural love, it would be easier for them to understand—natural love relates to flesh and blood. When we come to speak of spiritual love it is more difficult. But then, as we go on, we begin to understand it, when grace is in the heart. Spiritual love shows itself when we begin to respect God's Word and honour his Word, and seek to live by his Word, and live by feeding upon his Word, and by feeding upon himself in his Word. This love shows itself when we cannot live without his Word. And spiritual love also shows itself in this way: when his Word is opposed, we feel it. When there are preachers who say that parts of the Bible are wrong, and reject parts of his Word, then we feel it. It hurts us because we tremble at his Word. They are sitting above the Word and judging it, whereas the Word should be above us and should be judging us. Those who tremble at God's Word desire to respect the Lord's Word. They believe that the Holy Spirit has given us the Word, and has looked after the Word in every generation.

There are people who try to change the Word, to change it into a different form. But we look at the original Greek and Hebrew. We don't trust the mere translations: we must go back to what we have in the beginning and how the Lord has kept copies of that for every generation. The Lord verifies and preserves his own Word because he regards his own, he loves his own, he wants them to be brought alive, he doesn't want any falsehood to come into the truth of the Word. It's called the Truth. Christ believed the Word entirely. He believed the Old Testament entirely and he looked after the New Testament as well as the Old one. That is because he's looking after his footstool, his people who are in the world.

Ah soul, where are you then, today? Where are you? You're on the way to eternity, the same as I am, soon to give an account. I must give my own account as to how I spoke to my fellow creatures about their souls, and that worries me. But it should worry us all. 'Did I really make use of the Word I heard? Did I make use of the many sermons I heard during this lifetime? The many people who spoke to me about my soul, the many prayers I heard? The many family worships we had? The godly conduct I saw here and there? Did it not impress me at all? Did it leave me just without God, without hope in the world?' Oh friends, we need the Holy Spirit to bless the Word to us. That is our prayer, that he would work among us. That he would bless this village, a village which is precious in my eyes for various reasons.

May the Lord then bless his Word. Let us pray.

## Concluding prayer

Gracious and glorious One, we pray thee to draw nigh to us in saving power. Leave us not in a state of nature, O Lord. Leave us not as proud creatures, who feel that they can do sufficiently well by themselves, who think that they are wiser than the Word of God. Make us poor, we pray thee. Make us contrite. Make us to tremble at thy Word. Bless us, each and all of us, this Sabbath Day. Oh, that it might be, for us, one of the days of the Son of man! Cleanse us. For Jesus' sake. Amen.

# 18

# Delighting in public worship

14th April 2019, Lord's Day evening, North Tolsta

*How amiable are thy tabernacles, O LORD of hosts! My soul longeth, yea, even fainteth for the courts of the LORD: my heart and my flesh crieth out for the living God. Yea, the sparrow hath found an house, and the swallow a nest for herself, where she may lay her young, even thine altars, O LORD of hosts, my King, and my God. Blessed are they that dwell in thy house: they will be still praising thee. Selah. Blessed is the man whose strength is in thee; in whose heart are the ways of them.*
Psalm 84:1–5

THE Psalmist begins by saying, 'How amiable are thy tabernacles, O LORD of hosts!' 'How amiable' means 'how pleasant', and 'tabernacle' is just the word 'tent'. So he's saying, 'How pleasant are thy tents, O LORD of hosts!' He's speaking to the Lord, and he's telling the Lord how pleasant his house is.

### Verse 1: God's tabernacle

When Moses was in the wilderness he was commanded by God to build him a tabernacle. He built two rooms—the holy place and the most holy place. Sometimes it wasn't just called '*a* tabernacle'; sometimes it was the plural, 'tabernacles'. That was because the holy place was one tabernacle and the holy of holies was another: they were joined together. Together they were the tabernacles—everything that belonged to the house of the Lord. As time had passed, that house was now becoming decrepit, worn out. It had been made mainly of wood and material—cloth and linen—rams' skins dyed red, goat hair, along with some brass and gold and silver. It had been erected in Shiloh when they came into Canaan but now it was coming to an end. But it was the house of God, and no matter how it seems to be coming to an end, it doesn't come to an end, it cannot come to an end. The cause of the Lord cannot come to an end.

Later on, David wanted to build a stone temple in its place. God did not allow him: he left that for David's son Solomon. But listen to what David the man of God is saying. 'How pleasant are thy tabernacles!' How pleasant! He had a joy in these tabernacles. You didn't have temples all over, they just had one tabernacle that God allowed. They may have had little local gatherings, but this one tabernacle was the centre of gathering, the centre of worship, the centre of sacrifice, the centre where the priesthood was: this was the house of God, the tabernacle of the Most High. That is why David was driven so strongly to say that the tabernacles were so pleasant and so amiable.

David names the Lord the 'LORD of hosts'. Some people say these hosts are the hosts of angels, which are beyond number. That is true, but when it comes to the things of the Lord and the things of the Church of Christ, surely the hosts that really matter are the hosts that will be with Christ in heaven. Most of God's people did not yet exist when David called Christ the Lord of hosts. But they had been given to Christ in the eternal covenant, and they will come to the Lord. Wherever they are, they will come. It is good to be among the hosts who will come from north, south, east and west. It is good to come to know the Lord as the Lord of hosts, our own God and Saviour. What a worship there will be when they are all gathered together! 'In the midst of my brethren,' says Christ, 'I will sing praise unto thee.'

## Verse 2: The courts of God's house

Listen to what David says next. In verse 2 he says, 'My soul longeth, yea, even fainteth for the courts of the LORD.' David was out in the desert. King Saul was seeking to slay him. David was being hunted. He sought to shake Saul off, and so he came down as far as the Dead Sea, into an area without water, where a man could not live more than a day or two. Afterwards, of course, some of David's own sons sought his life and again he had to flee for his life. So here you have David in the desert, and he's not thinking of his throne. There is not one single word about the throne that God had promised him. What is David thinking of? What is he longing for? 'My soul longeth, yea, even fainteth for the courts of the LORD.'

He longs, and the longing is so great that he calls it fainting. He desires to come to the house of the Lord but he cannot get there. He's kept back. He cannot reach it, but the longing is there.

Ah, just think of our day, friends. The worship of the Lord is accessible to all, but how many long for it? When the gospel was first preached in our island, people couldn't hear the gospel preached so very often. If a preacher was there—itinerant preachers like Finlay Munro or one of the early ministers—if the people knew he'd be there, they would crowd to hear him. They didn't have churches, so they crowded outside, and they crowded in their thousands, so eager to hear the word of life. When the sermon was over, very often the hearers refused to go: they wanted something else. They wanted another exposition, something else about the Word of God. They were reluctant to go home. One minister said that it was snowing as he was preaching, and everyone was covered with white snow so that he could only make out their faces, and nobody wanted to go home. These were days when the Holy Spirit was blessing the Word of God.

Nowadays we can hear sermons any time. It's so easy to hear a sermon, but where is the thirst, where is the desire? But when the Holy Spirit begins to work in your heart and you know that you are a sinner, a perishing sinner on the way to a lost eternity, without Christ and without hope, then you desire to hear the Word of life. 'Oh, let me hear something that will save my soul, that will save me from going down into the pit, something that will save me from being lost eternally, in hell fire.'

Once, a young Christian in the island, just a young girl, was standing at the fire, and she stumbled and fell part-way into the fire. Her father took hold of her and lifted her, and she was all right. But what she said was, 'Father, I only fell into a fire that would burn me and these small burns will get better again. But just imagine if I fell into the fire out of which I could never come again.' Ah, think of these things, friends. You, who have a precious soul, think of that. Don't let it go.

David longed for the courts of God's house. We spoke of the two parts of the tabernacle—the holy place and the holy of holies. Outside there was also an area called the courts. The people would gather there to worship. They didn't have chairs or anything to sit on: they would stand there. And what did David desire? He desired just to be among them, to stand there. He didn't desire to have a throne in the court of God's house. He just desired to be in the court, in the place of worship, among other worshippers, among God's people, worshipping the Lord.

## 18  Delighting in public worship

You know, it's a precious thing when you come to know Christ as your personal Saviour. It's a precious thing to come to a prayer meeting where God's people gather, and to think, 'I'm now among God's people. Everyone, as far as I can see, belongs to the Lord, and it's good to be among them. They have the same desires as I have.' Now, the world and the devil would seek to do away with these desires. The devil says, 'Will you not spend more time looking at your television and then you'll be more broad-minded as a Christian?' The world with its blandishments says, 'You've got to mix with people. You can't just be reading your Bible and speaking about the Lord and things like that.' The devil is so insidious, and the devil is no lover of mankind. The devil hates every soul of us. The devil hates you, and would destroy you if he could. He uses whatever he can to attack you. But our only hope is in the Lord. The Holy Spirit makes the means of grace precious, he makes salvation precious, he makes Christ precious, he makes the Word of God precious and the secret place of prayer precious.

That was David's longing, then. He says, 'My heart and my flesh crieth out for the living God.' Why does he want to come to the courts of God's house? Is it just to stand there along with God's people? No, there's more than that to it. He says, 'My soul, my heart and my flesh—that is, my whole being—cry out for the living God.' And when the Holy Spirit works efficaciously within us, that is how it will be. We will desire the living God. Nothing else will satisfy us but the living God. 'I desire to belong to him. I desire him to be my living God.' He's the living God—not just One who lives, but the living God. He is the One who is life—life eternal, with no beginning, no end. He gives life to creatures, he gives plant life to plants, animal life to animals, and spiritual life to souls. He is the living God, who gives life to souls. He is the living God, who can give us salvation. Christ Jesus is the living God. He says, 'I am the resurrection and the life.' He says that if we believe in him, though we die, yet we shall live. It's a wonderful thing to know Christ as your Saviour, and then to come face to face with death. Death can do nothing against this life that God puts into the soul. Christ is in the soul. The Holy Spirit is in the soul. Grace is in the soul. Death can do nothing against a living soul that trusts in a living God. The soul enters into death with joy—yes, with joy!—and enters into heaven, into the joy of the Lord. That's how David was.

## Verse 3: The sparrow and the swallow

But listen to what else he says. He begins to think of the sparrows and the swallows, 'Yea, the sparrow hath found an house, and the swallow a nest for herself, where she may lay her young, even thine altars, O LORD of hosts, my King, and my God.' Small birds, like sparrows and swallows, actually come into the court of God's house and actually make nests there, not far from the altar, and raise their young there, and nobody touches them. The Jews used nets to catch small birds like these, so that they could eat them. Christ said, 'Are not five sparrows sold for two farthings?' You might say, 'That doesn't seem even. Surely it's four sparrows for two farthings?' No, it's four sparrows and an extra one if you buy the four, that is how cheap they were. So Christ said, 'Are not five sparrows sold' in the market place 'for two farthings?'

Then Christ tells us about the sparrow falling to the ground—that is, dying. He says, it does not die 'without my heavenly Father'. God the Father of the Church has respect even to that tiny life, the sparrow that lived two to three years, as well as the sparrow that was thrown in for nothing, along with the four sparrows—a sparrow that cost nothing, that seemed worthless. God had respect for it. 'How much more valuable are ye than many sparrows?' Ah, what precious teaching of the Lord Jesus!

## 18  Delighting in public worship

If the sparrows and the swallows came to the court of the Lord's house, they were safe. Nobody was going to lay a hand on them. There were no nets there, nothing to catch them: they were safe. That's how the soul is. Outside Christ, they're in danger. The devil is there with his snares and his nets, and he's out to catch your soul and destroy it. He wants to destroy the young. He wants to bring in drink and drugs and immorality, He wants to bring in all sorts of things that we really hate to talk about, but they are there. There's only one safe place for us, and that is in the court of God's own house.

I once knew a man from this village, and he used to be among people who spoke about the things of the Lord. He felt that it was affecting him, and he began to be afraid that he might be converted later. So he went over to Canada and took a contract for six months there, cutting cordwood. He went into a forest, and his work was cutting wood and making it into small bundles. He did that for six months, and he barely saw anybody in those six months. He said, 'The very thoughts that disturbed me when I was at home in Lewis and on the mainland, they followed me into the forest. I couldn't shake them off. It wasn't the people who gave me these thoughts. It wasn't the company that was to blame: it was something else. It was the Lord working in my soul.' So as soon as the six months were over he came back over here again, seeking the company he had fled from.

The sparrow and the swallow go to the court of God's house. The Psalmist speaks there of the swallow building a nest and bringing up its young. There's something beautiful in that: a family being brought up in the ways of the Lord. How fortunate any family is that has the teaching of the Word of God in it, where the children hear prayer, they hear the Word read, they know their father and mother love their souls and desire them to know Christ as their Saviour. What a wonderful way to be brought up! The Royal Family were brought up with silver spoons in their mouths, but that was nothing. Never envy that. The poor crofters we had here in Lewis, who had godliness, who had the Word of God among them, and taught their children—these are the ones to be envied for what they had.

'Yea, the sparrow hath found an house, even thine own altars, O LORD of hosts, my King, and my God.' The sparrows couldn't build their nest on the altar, or immediately by the altar, because of the fire and the sacrifices, but they could be quite close, and the priest would never harm them.

The Psalmist addresses God again, and says, 'O LORD of hosts', using the same term again. It may be in the days of Christ that true believers in heaven and on earth were very few, comparatively, but Christ was still the Lord of hosts. The ones given to him by the Father were going to come to him. And later on, the gospel would be preached among our own people, among the darkness of our own island. Just think of your great-grandfathers or great-great-grandfathers, and how they were in darkness. They had no gospel: they perished. Is that in your thoughts, that those from whom we came, in this village, perished? But then the gospel came around 1800. That's not so very long ago: just over two hundred years. Oh, the goodness of the Lord, that he gave us the gospel, and that the gospel came at that time! Are we then going to despise the gospel and pass it by? Are we not rather going to make use of the gospel, that our souls might sing the praises of Christ forever? The Lord of hosts is the One who made provision for poor sinners, that they might be saved.

David goes on to say, 'O LORD of hosts, my King, and my God.' He calls the Lord 'my King'. Now the strange thing is that the Lord Jesus was going to be descended from David. And here David calls him 'the Lord, my King'. David was a king, and the Lord is his king. The kingships of this world are nothing. All of God's people will be made kings and princes in glory. They will have such honour in Christ. But he is the King of glory. He is the King of kings and the Lord of lords. And when you have a king, the real King, you want to kneel at his feet, you want to praise him and adore him, the One who did all for you and who loves you, who cares for you, who will destroy your enemies, who will take away your sin and take you to be with himself forever. 'My King,' he says, and 'my God.'

Can you say that to the Lord, 'My King, and my God'? Think now of Thomas, doubting Thomas, who said, 'If I cannot see the marks of the nails and the wound in his side, I am not going to believe.' But when Christ met him and said, 'Stretch out your hand, put your hand into my side, into the wound,' he didn't do that. He just said, 'My Lord and my God.' Doubting Thomas had faith. He didn't have to touch Christ. Faith was enough to recognise him, and he confessed him as 'My Lord and my God'.

Do we have faith in Christ? If we do not have faith in Christ, we have nothing. Nothing at all! We might come to worship a thousand times, from the time we were small to the time we become old and grey-headed, but if we don't have faith in Christ, it's only counted against us, because the gospel was there, and the hands of the Lord were stretched out all the day long. 'I would have gathered thy children,' he says, 'and ye would not.'

### Verse 4: Dwelling in God's house

The Psalmist goes on and says, 'Blessed are they that dwell in thy house: they will be still praising thee.' Who would dwell in the Lord's house, in the tabernacle? Well, the priests ministered in the tabernacle, so they'd be there for a while. The high priest would enter the holy of holies, but just one day a year. The priests and the high priest were there, but they weren't really dwelling as such. David was thinking of something deeper. Just imagine being able to dwell in the house of the Lord! Just imagine heaven, the real house of the Lord, the real holy of holies! Just imagine dwelling there! Blessed are they that dwell in his house. David could say, 'They dwell there in the house of the Lord. And here am I, and I cannot even get to the tabernacle. I long and I thirst. I faint. My heart and soul cry out. My flesh cries out for the living God. But blessed are they who will dwell in the house of the Lord forever.'

Ask, 'Am I going to dwell in the house of the Lord forever? Am I going to dwell in the house of the Lord at all? I've got to come to know him, the Lord of the house. I have to believe in him as my Saviour, my Saviour-God. I have to speak to him.'

'Oh,' you say, 'I read the Word of God, but I haven't found Christ yet.' Did you speak to Christ? Did you come to Christ and say to him, 'I have looked for you in the Word, I don't seem to be able to find you. Help me!' Will you not call upon him to help you, to open your eyes, to lead and guide you? You've got to deal with the Lord. You see, at the very end, everyone deals with the Lord. At the throne of judgment, we will all deal with the Lord. But would it not be wonderful if we could deal with the Lord on mercy's ground? A poor broken sinner, unworthy, covered with his sin and guilt, coming to Christ and saying, 'Have mercy upon me, a sinner,' speaking to him as well as listening to him—that's how it begins. There has to be a dialogue.

'Blessed are they that dwell in thy house.' When Christ was forty days old, he was taken to the temple to be presented to the Lord. There in the temple was Simeon, who took him up, and also Anna, an old woman. It's said that Anna never departed from the house of the Lord. Oh, she had to depart for food and drink and various things, but all the time she had to give, she would give it to attending at the house of the Lord.

And there she met Christ in the flesh. In the house of God, in glory, Simeon and Anna would meet Christ in the flesh. They would see Christ, with the wounds that he suffered in the house of his friends, and which he suffered because he loved every one of his own personally, not just as a group. 'Who loved me,' said Paul, 'and gave himself for me.' It's a personal thing. It's a whole Christ for every sinner.

### Verse 5: The strength of the believer

The Psalmist then says, 'In whose heart are the ways of them.' There are ways in their heart, and the Lord has put these ways in their heart. He puts the way of faith in your heart—a heart that never had faith before—and faith comes alive. The Holy Spirit does that. There's a heart that has no love for God, and God says, 'I will open a way in that heart.' It's a road called love, in a heart that had no hope in God before, a heart that didn't desire the fellowship of Christ. God says, 'I will open a way,' and the result is a heart that loves Scripture, a heart that loves the Bible. 'I will open a way.' And now there is a heart that needs to pray. And new ways have been put into the heart—before then, it was a wilderness. There was no way, there were no roads in it, just a wilderness leading to a lost eternity. But now God has put ways in the heart. What a fortunate heart that is! And the Lord himself walks in these ways and has fellowship with the believer's heart.

Let's just look at one little bit more, 'Blessed is the man whose strength is in thee.' Where is the strength of the Christian? 'Oh,' you say, 'he gets grace and that makes him strong.' No: grace makes him weak. When you are weak you have to lean upon somebody else. That's how God's people are. They are made weak in themselves, and they lean upon Christ. 'Who is this that cometh up from the wilderness, leaning upon her beloved?' Who is this? She loves him. That's obvious in the way in which she is leaning upon him. Her weight is on him, he is upholding her, and she's coming up from the wilderness.

Ah, the strength is in him! He gives 'strength in every time of need'. He gives grace according to need. We cannot put it into the bank. You cannot build up your grace in a bank so that you're going to be a prominent Christian. So don't think of such things. Just think of being a poor broken sinner, clinging to the Lord, because 'the last shall be first, and the first shall be last'. You must beware of ambition; you must beware of trying to be better than others. The devil will bring in those sorts of suggestions, but Paul could say, 'When I am weak, then I am strong.' Paul lived by the strength of the Lord and no other way. 'I am what I am.' Yes, he lived by the strength of God, by the grace of God. There was no other way.

Friends, can you or I follow anything of that? When the Holy Spirit works, even the children will follow it. The strange thing is that you can have old people who just shake their heads and say, 'I cannot understand it.' Oh friends, may we not come to the end of our lives, saying, 'I cannot understand it.'

I have spoken before about a man from this village who used to go around with a group of others, revelling and drinking, as the young folk used to do, and still do in many places. That was the pastime they very often had in those days. But when he was converted, he would speak to those who had belonged to that group, and to one young man in particular, the youngest of them. He felt that he had corrupted that young man, that he had led him in the ways of folly. Over the years he spoke to him often, and at last that young man was in hospital, dying. The older man went to see him for the last time, to speak to him about Christ for his soul. The young man turned his head away from him, and what he said was, '*Tha e ro fhad' a-nis.*' In English: 'It's too late now.' And then he died. Friends, may we never say, '*Tha e ro fhad' a-nis.*'

God has a delight in mercy. He is a father of mercies, he's a God of mercies. He has a delight in mercies—far more delight and pleasure in saving you, than you can ever have in being saved and coming to know his love. Yes, *far* more pleasure! May he be your God and Saviour.

Let us pray.

## Concluding prayer

O gracious Lord, we pray thee to bless us. We are on the way to eternity. The day now is far spent. This Sabbath Day is far spent, and we will go to our homes. And we ask thee, O Lord, what will we do when we go back to our homes? Will we forget it all? Will we call upon thee? Will we be on our knees? Will we think earnestly? Will we deal with thyself, O Lord? Or will the devil take the seed out of our hearts? Because thou, O Lord, hast said that he can do that, taking out of our hearts the seed that had left an impression. We pray thee, gracious Lord, to bless thy Word to us. Bless the young children, put thine own arms around them, and give them to turn to thee, that they might be a chosen generation in this village. And bless each one of us, we pray thee, for each one of us has a precious soul, and a whole eternity attached to it. Give us to be solemnized by these things. Bless the preaching of thy Word worldwide, nation-wide, and island-wide. Grant, O Lord, to glorify thy great name. May many crowns be thrown at the feet of Christ. May thy glory be far advanced above the starry frame. Take away our sins. For Christ's sake. Amen.

www.ingramcontent.com/pod-product-compliance
Lightning Source LLC
Chambersburg PA
CBHW070721160426
43192CB00009B/1266